THE³ READING PROCESS

AN INTRODUCTION TO COLLEGE READING

Diane M. Bosco
Suffolk County Community College

Janice L. Buchner
Wayne Community College

McGraw Hill **Learning Solutions**

Boston   Burr Ridge, IL   Dubuque, IA   New York   San Francisco   St. Louis
Bangkok   Bogotá   Caracas   Lisbon   London   Madrid
Mexico City   Milan   New Delhi   Seoul   Singapore   Sydney   Taipei   Toronto

The McGraw·Hill Companies

The Reading Process: An Introduction to College Reading, Third Edition

8 9 0 QVS QVS 14 13

ISBN-13: 978-0-07-811979-8
ISBN-10: 0-07-811979-0

Learning Solutions Consultant: Philip Rudder
Production Editor: Nina Meyer
Printer/Binder: Quad/Graphics

Contents

UNIT I: THE READING PROCESS

Chapter 1: Before Reading

Chapter 2: During Reading

Chapter 3: After Reading

UNIT I REVIEW: THE READING PROCESS

UNIT II: VOCABULARY

Chapter 4: Vocabulary Strategies

UNIT II REVIEW: VOCABULARY STRATEGIES

Unit III: Main Ideas

Chapter 5: Topics and Main Ideas

Chapter 6: Unstated Main Ideas

Chapter 7: Supporting Details

UNIT III REVIEW: MAIN IDEAS

UNIT IV: PATTERNS OF ORGANIZATION

Chapter 8: Chronological Order and Listing Patterns

Chapter 9: Definition and Illustration/Example Patterns

Chapter 10: Comparison and Contrast Patterns

Chapter 11: Cause and Effect Pattern

Unit IV Review: Patterns of Organization

Chapter 12: Introduction to Inference

Preface

The Reading Process: Introduction to College Reading was written to address the needs of the first level college reading student. Central to the approach of this text is the belief that meaning is constructed by the reader and that literacy instruction should exist within meaningful context. To this end *The Reading Process* places concise reading instruction within the context of interesting and timely thematic units. The exercises and reading selections within each chapter explore a real life issue of interest to students. The chapters on unstated main ideas and chronological pattern of organization, for example, focus upon risk-taking and career choices, respectively.

In addition, *The Reading Process* offers a variety of activities that encourage students to extend their writing and critical thinking skills—that is, to see meaning as something which they actively construct. Throughout the text, portfolio activities in particular allow students to show their effort, progress, and achievement and to make connections as they learn. All the activities of *The Reading Process* may be assessed by either traditional means, by the use of a portfolio approach, or by a combination of these methods.

While its primary focus is reading, this text recognizes, through its range of activities, the interrelation of reading, writing, speaking, and listening skills. By developing these interrelated skills, students can truly enhance their literacy skills and become lifelong readers.

Text Features

- **Thematic organization and holistic approach to reading.** Each unit explores a theme throughout its chapters' exercises and readings. The unit themes of relationships, heroism, fear and social issues make skills-building activities and reading selections coherent and relevant for the student and help to expand students knowledge of concepts basic to that theme.

- **High interest readings.** Chosen from a wide variety of interesting, readable contemporary sources, the readings expose students to selections from magazines, journals, newspapers, novels, and the Internet. Chapter readings address a topic related to the unit themes. Love, phobias, health, censorship and violence are some of the chapter topics.

- **Focus on the reading process.** Reading is presented as a process in which the student actively participates. *Before, during,* and *after* reading strategies encourage students to activate their background knowledge, create a purpose for reading, and monitor their understanding of a selection, both during and after reading.

- **Application of strategies.** Reading skills such as finding the main idea, identifying supporting details, understanding text patterns, and defining vocabulary in context are developed through the use of reading strategies throughout the text.

- **Vocabulary concepts**. Vocabulary is presented before reading with words to preview and after reading through word connections. Students are asked to go beyond a word's definition to complete word maps, concept of definition maps, use word parts, or explain a concept.

- **Critical thinking connections.** In each chapter, integrating ideas in writing and class discussion, as well as portfolio activities guide students in applying critical thinking skills.
- **Collaborative work.** Each chapter contains a collaborative activity that allows students to explore the theme of the chapter and develop their skills with their peers.
- **Graphic organizers.** Each chapter and unit is summarized through the use of a graphic organizer, giving students a visual representation of the strategy presented.
- **Appendix.** Forms or charts used by the student are provided in the appendix to minimize duplication needs.

Organization

All units and chapters of *The Reading Process: Introduction to College Reading* are organized using a clear, easy to follow pattern.

Unit structure: The five units are organized as follows. Units begin with

1. **Unit Introduction:** A quotation and several paragraphs that establish the unit's theme.

2. **Unit Overview:** A brief description of the reading skills and strategies to be covered.

3. **Unit Objectives:** A list of the strategies that students will learn by the completion of the unit.

Units end with

4. **Unit Review:** A summary of the reading strategies that have been presented within a unit.

5. **Unit Summary Graphic Organizer:** A visual representation of how the reading strategies covered in the unit relate to one another to be completed by the student.

6. **Unit Portfolio Suggestion:** A new additional activity for the student to complete.

7. **Portfolio Vocabulary Suggestion:** A vocabulary exercise dealing with the unit theme.

8. **Want to Know More?** A list that allows students to further investigate the theme through books and web sites.

Chapter structure

The chapters of *The Reading Process* are organized to model the reading process using the *before, during,* and *after* reading strategies. Each chapter is organized as follows:

1. **Chapter Introduction:** A quotation and several paragraphs introduce the chapter's theme. The chapter theme is related to the unit theme. Students are encouraged to activate their background knowledge about the theme.

2. **Chapter objectives and a "Focus On" section:** Chapter objectives state the particular strategies that students will learn by the completion of each chapter. "Focus On" sections provide a clear and concise explanation of each reading strategy and skill, modeled for better understanding.

3. **Short exercises**: These activities provide students with an opportunity to practice and evaluate their understanding of the strategy.

4. **Reading selections:** This section gives students the opportunity to apply reading strategies they have learned to authentic, thematically linked selections. These readings may be in the form of a short essay, an article, a poem, or an excerpt from a book. Related exercises and support apparatus include:

   - *Before reading* (strengthens the practice of previewing a selection);
   - *Words to preview* (provides the definition and part of speech of unfamiliar words);
   - *During reading* (Comments, questions, and descriptions are a consistent reminder to the reader to predict, visualize, and monitor comprehension as he or she reads);
   - *After reading* (provides the reader with an opportunity to evaluate and recall and review the selection);
   - *Word Connections* (vocabulary questions pertaining to words found in the selection; students may be required to complete a word map, fill in a concept of definition map, and/or explain the concept of a word); and
   - *Connecting meaning* (asks questions to help the student evaluate his/her understanding of the selection; the questions also help to review and recall important information).

5. **Portfolio activities:** a variety of engaging activities promote critical thinking skills:

   - *Integrating ideas* (allows students to connect new concepts to those they already know);
   - *Extending concepts* (provides an opportunity to integrate reading and writing);
   - *Collaborative activity* (affords an opportunity for students to work with peers); and
   - *Additional portfolio suggestion* (furnishes a chance for students to be creative in their class work).

6. **Chapter summary graphic organizer:** This feature gives students an opportunity to complete a visual representation of the strategies covered and establishes a model for a student's own use of graphic organizers.

Acknowledgements

We wish to thank our students—they are at the heart of this book and a constant source of inspiration.

We are grateful for our colleagues for all of their ideas, comments and suggestions.

As always, we are most grateful for the unending encouragement and support of our wonderful families.

Diane M. Bosco
Janice L. Buchner

To The Student

What is a Portfolio?

A portfolio is a collection of pieces that showcases your work. Many instructors will ask you to collect your course work into a portfolio that will show your effort, progress, and achievement. Throughout this text, you will find suggestions of items that you may include in your portfolio. These recommendations will relate the theme and strategies presented in each unit.

In most cases, choosing what goes into your portfolio is an individual decision. One student may place reading journal entries, a reading log, a literacy autobiography, and a special report in his portfolio. Another student may choose to include test scores, comprehension strategies, self-assessment notes, and a tape of her oral reading. Though some items may be included at the request of the instructor, most will reflect your choices.

Choosing what to include gives you an opportunity to evaluate your growth as a reader and writer. You create a window onto your learning and make connections across reading, writing and thinking. The ongoing process of assembling your portfolio is at least as important as the finished product.

The Reading Process

Theme of Readings: Relationships

"No man is an island."

JOHN DONNE

Relationships

In *Reaching Out*, David Johnson states, "From the moment we are born to the moment we die, relationships are the core of our existence. We are conceived with relationships, are born into relationships, and live our lives within relationships." We have no choice: we depend upon others for food, shelter, education, love, fun, and identity. Life becomes a series of interactions that begin with the first people we know, our families. With growth, relationships change and evolve. We become acquaintances, friends, coworkers, lovers, and spouses. These and other relationships affect our everyday lives.

The readings in this unit explore relationships on a variety of levels. Family, friends, and lovers form the most basic relationships. Some relationships may be simple, stable, and easy to maintain. Others may be complicated, short-lived, or filled with ups and downs. Each of you has, by now, experienced many relationships. As you read, compare your own experiences with those presented in the readings. An author is trying to establish a relationship with you, the reader, in order to share thoughts and experiences. By connecting your experiences with those the author writes about, you will construct meaning and understanding. This relationship forms the basis of the reading process.

The Reading Process

What is reading? People often think of it as an important part of life, an enjoyable activity, an essential skill. These points are all true, but there is another valuable way to consider reading–the process by which the reader constructs meaning from text. Constructing meaning is making sense of what you read. Meaning does not come from the author alone. You, the reader, must be an active participant in the process. You bring your language, thoughts, experiences, and knowledge to the text as you build meaning. Because each of us is different, no two readers will ever produce the exact same meaning from a given text. No reader's meaning will ever be exactly the same as the author's meaning.

When does the process of reading begin? Most students think that reading starts as their eyes hit the first word of the first paragraph. In fact, the reading process begins before this point. An effective reader uses strategies before actually reading the body of the text. These strategies help make sense of the text. They include

- previewing the text,
- thinking about what you know about the topic,
- establishing a purpose for reading.

The process continues while you are reading. As an active, involved reader, you are

- making predictions about the text,
- confirming these predictions,
- visualizing the material,
- monitoring your comprehension.

After you read the text, the reading process still goes on. You take additional steps to evaluate your understanding of the reading by:

- deciding if you have met your purpose for reading,
- questioning your understanding of the text,
- recalling important information,
- relating information you have read to your own knowledge or experience with the subject.

What you, the reader, do *after* reading is just as important as what you do *before* and *during* reading.

To be an effective reader, you must incorporate *before, during, and after* reading strategies into the reading process. Unit I addresses each of these areas.

Unit Objectives

After completing the unit, you will be able to:

1. Understand reading as a process involving both the author and the reader.

2. Construct meaning by applying *before, during,* and *after* reading strategies.

Chapter 1

Before Reading

Theme of Readings: Families

"While we try to teach our children all about life, our children teach us what life is all about."

ANGELA SCHWINDT

Families

Father, mother, sister, brother, grandmother, grandfather, uncle, aunt, niece, nephew, cousin are all terms for people who make up our family. Families are groups related by blood, by marriage or adoption, or by some other long term relationship or living arrangements. The underlying purpose of a family is often the raising and nurturing of children. Children represent renewal and the cycle of life beginning again. They bring love, laughter, tears, and stress in the best and worst of families. But other factors form strong bonds too: shared enterprises, stories, histories, the intertwining of relationships, and commitments to common needs and goals.

These days, the traditional structure of a mother, a father, two children, and a dog no longer is the typical American family. Single parent families, same sex couples, unmarried couples who live together, and blended groups from divorced parents are also families. However "family" is defined, it remains a fundamental element in society, important to each of us individually, and as part of a larger, social whole.

Chapter Objectives

After completing this chapter, you will be able to:

1. Preview the reading.

2. Connect your knowledge to the author's ideas.

3. Establish a purpose for reading.

Focus on *Before Reading* Strategies

A good athlete knows that before you begin a workout you must warm-up. Your muscles need to stretch and your mind needs to focus on whatever sport you are about to play. These activities will maximize your performance. Before you start to read, you also need to "warm-up" your brain. You have to focus your attention on the task at hand and start thinking about what you are going to read. Focus your attention before reading by:

- previewing the material,
- thinking about what you know about the topic,
- establishing a purpose for reading.

These strategies will maximize your reading performance.

Before you start to read, you need to become familiar with the ideas presented by the author or authors. You can get a sense of what the reading is about by previewing it. First, read the title. Does the title tell you what the topic is? If not, does the title give you any clues or hints? From the clues given, can you make a prediction about the topic? For example, looking at a book by Rudolf Dreikers, Pearl Cassel, and David Kehoe entitled, *Discipline Without Tears,* you may predict it to be about how to deal with children who misbehave. Another person may predict that it is about the personal discipline necessary for success.

After you have thought about the title, skim the chapter titles and read the information given on the book jacket. For a shorter reading such as an article, essay, or short story, skim the reading. Are there any headings that can give information about the topic? If there are no headings to preview, look at the first and last paragraphs and glance at the first sentences of the other paragraphs. Was your prediction about the topic correct?

After skimming *Discipline Without Tears,* you would find the book to be about strategies for dealing with a wide range of childhood misbehaviors. Think about what you know about the topic. What experiences have you had with this topic in your reading, in the media, or in your life? By starting to think about what you know, you start to connect with the author.

Once you have finished skimming and predicting, establish a purpose for reading. Ask yourself, "Why am I reading this particular chapter, article, or essay?" Are you looking for an understanding of information? For example, you may read the daily newspaper to better understand a local community issue. If you are assigned a reading for a college course, your purpose may be to understand the information being taught in that course.

You may read for other purposes beyond the gaining of knowledge. You may read for entertainment or to explore an argument and perhaps have your opinion changed. An article about your favorite hobby would be entertaining. You might read an article discussing two opposing views of gun control to explore the argument and change or strengthen your opinion. Your purpose depends on what you are reading and why you are reading it.

By previewing, connecting your knowledge, and setting a purpose for reading, you will be a more effective reader. All three *before reading* strategies work together so that you may construct the most understanding of your reading.

Short Exercises: *Before Reading* Strategies

Predicting the Topic

Directions: *Read the following titles and write your prediction about the topic.*

1. *Adoption Without Fear* by James L. Gritter

_____

2. *Dr. Tightwad's Money-Smart Kids* by Janet Bodnar

_____

3. "Rethinking the American Family" by Lauren Tarshis

_____

4. *Three Steps to a Strong Family* by Linda Eyre, Richard, Eyre, and Stephen Covey

_____

5. "Dining Together Strengthens Ties" *USA Today (Magazine)*

_____

6. "All In The Family" by John Bingham *Runner's World*

_____

7. *The Shelter of Each Other: Rebuilding Our Families* by Mary Bray Pipher

_____

8. "Today's Stepmother: Myths and Realities" *Ebony (Magazine)*

_____

9. *Family Abuse: A National Epidemic* by Marie Hong

_____

10. *The ABC's of Parenting* by Anthony P. Witham, Debbie Hansen, and Jeff Maniglia

_____

Thinking About the Topic

Directions: *List what comes to mind when you think about these topics.*

Example: *If the topic is* discipline, *the following thoughts may come to mind: My mother sent me to my room when I misbehaved. Children need some kind of discipline. Spanking is a controversial issue.*

1. Curfews

   _____

   _____

2. Sibling Rivalry

   _____

   _____

3. Effects of Divorce

   _____

   _____

4. Aging Parents

   _____

   _____

5. Family Vacations

   _____

   _____

6. Adult Children Returning Home

   _____

   _____

7. Changing Family Structure

   _____

   _____

8. The Right to Privacy

_____

_____

9. Family Values

_____

_____

10. Managing Family Money

_____

_____

Reading Selections

Selection One: **Get a Closer Look**

Ira Wolfman

Before Reading

Before you read the story, "Get a Closer Look," complete the following:

Predict what the topic may be.

Skim the reading to see if you have correctly predicted the topic. Look at the first and last paragraphs and glance at the first sentences of the other paragraphs.

Think about this topic. Relate what you know to "Get a Closer Look."

Set a purpose for reading this story. Do you expect to be entertained, gain knowledge, or explore an argument?

Word to Preview

attributes *(n.)* quality or characteristic of a person *(par. 1)*
genealogical *(adj.)* about the family tree or history *(par. 6)*
emigrate *(v.)* to leave one country to settle in another *(par. 11)*

Get a Closer Look

12 Tips for Successful Family Interviews

Ira Wolfman

How do you get relatives talking? A good family history interview isn't easy to conduct. You need to combine the best attributes of caring friend, hard-nosed reporter, and sensitive psychologist. But do it well and you may be rewarded with wonderful stories.

Interviews are different from normal conversations. One person has a goal: to get information from another person (let's call him or her the "talker"). You want the talker to feel comfortable, but you also need to direct the conversation to the points you are interested in.

You also have to be flexible. Sometimes an unexpected topic can turn out to be wonderful. Other times you'll need to lead your talker back to the main point—without hurting his or her feelings. This can be difficult, but you will become better at it as you go along—practice will make you skilled. Be patient with yourself and expect some mistakes. To make things easier, keep these tips in mind:

1. **Before any interview, give advance warning.** Explain what you want to do, why you want to do it, and why the talker is important to you and your research. You can call or write a letter or e-mail. Here's an example of the kinds of things you should say:

   > *Dear Aunt Gus:*
   > *I'm working on a history of our family, and it would be very helpful if I could sit down and talk with you. I'm particularly interested in your memories of my great-grandparents (your mother and father) and the family's early years in Minnesota. I'd also love to look at any old photographs or documents you have.*
   > *I won't need much more than an hour of your time and would like to hold our talk at your home. Any weekend day would be fine. Can you let me know a date that is convenient for you?*
   > *Thanks so much for your help.*

   By writing this letter, you've given your relative a chance to start thinking about the topics you're interested in, and you may have even jogged her memory. Of course, not

---

Get a Closer Look, Ira Wolfman Annual Editions.

all your relatives will be close by, and your arrangements may be more difficult than "any weekend day." That just makes your writing–and planning–even more important.

2. **Prepare before your interview.** Find out whatever you can about the talker *before* the interview. Where does she fit in the family? What documents might she have? What other genealogical jewels might she have?

Gather as much information as you can ahead of time about her relationship to everyone in your family. Your parents can probably help you with this.

3. **Think out all your questions beforehand.** Interviewing requires structure. Write your questions on a sheet of paper, organized by subject. One easy way to organize what you want to ask is by year: Start with your relative's earliest years and then move on from there.

"So, Aunt Gus, you lived in the house in a town outside Minneapolis till you were 10–about 1922, right? Then where did you move?" Or "You say Great-grandpa worked as a tailor in St. Paul. Did you ever visit his shop? Where was it? What years did he have the business there?" As this interviewer did, it's a good idea to summarize what you already know so that your subject can verify your facts. Then move on to a request for more detail.

Sometimes the simplest questions can hit the jackpot. I asked my great-uncle Max, "How old were you when you went from Poland to America?" I didn't get an answer; I got a story:

I must have been about 15 when I went to Warsaw to get a visa to emigrate. I got the visa, but then the counselor at the examination said, "Listen, boy, you are underage. You can't go without your father." He crossed out my stamp.

I went back to our town and told my father. He said, "Don't worry, we'll take care of that."

Ready, Set, Research . . . Your Family Tree

- Interview your parents about their family history. Practice interviewing with them.
- Make appointments to interview other family members.
- Prepare your questions. (For a list of good questions for family interviews, see www. workmen.com/familytree.)
- Type up your notes from interviews. Ask the relatives you interviewed to review them and correct or add to them.
- Write a thank-you note to every family member you interviewed.

Get a Closer Look, Ira Wolfman Annual Editions.

My father was a religious man, but he also knew how to get things done. He called a policeman from our town and asked him to make me older.

I got new papers. Now I turned from 15 to 18 or 19. I went back to Warsaw, and I was able to leave. And on February 20, 1920, I took the boat Susquehanna from Danzig to New York.

Remember to also ask open-ended questions. "What do you remember most about the apartment on Division Street?" or "Tell me about your relationship with your brothers" may yield something unexpected and wonderful.

4. **Bring a video or tape recorder if possible.** A small tape recorder usually doesn't disturb anyone, and it catches every bit of information, including the way your talkers sound and exactly how they answer questions. If you plan to videotape, be sure someone comes with you to run the camera. You need to focus on your talker.

5. **In any case, bring a notebook and a pen.** Even if you have [an audio tape or video] recorder, always take handwritten notes. Recorders can break down.

During the interview, write down names and dates and double-check them with your subject. Facts are important, but the most important information your talkers offer are their stories. Try to capture the way they talk and their colorful expressions: "That ship was rolling on the ocean like a marble in your hand."

There's another good reason to bring pen and paper with you. You won't have to interrupt when you think of a question; just write a note to yourself so you'll remember to ask it at an appropriate time.

6. **Start with easy, friendly questions.** Leave the more difficult or emotional material for later in the interview, after you've had time to gain your talker's trust. If things aren't going well, you may want to save those questions for another time.

It's also a good idea to begin with questions about the person you're interviewing. You may be more interested in a great-grandfather if he is the missing link in your family chart. But first get some background information about your talker—your aunt, for example. This serves two purposes. First, it lets her know she's important to you, that you care about her, and that her life is interesting, too. Second, as she talks, she may reveal some other information that you would never have known about otherwise.

7. **Bring family photographs with you.** Look for photos, artwork, or documents that will help jog your subject's memory. Bring the pictures out and ask your talker to describe what's going on. "Do you remember when this was taken? Who are the people? What was the occasion? Who do you think took the picture?" You may be amazed at how much detail your relative will see in a photograph and also at the memories that come spilling forth.

8. **Don't be afraid of silence.** You might feel uneasy and want to rush in with another question when your talker stops speaking. *Don't.* Silence is an important

Get a Closer Look, Ira Wolfman Annual Editions.

part of interviewing and can sometimes yield to interesting results. Because people often find silence uncomfortable, they often try to fill it if you don't—and in doing so, they may say something you might not have heard otherwise.

Sometimes silence is also necessary for gathering thoughts. Don't forget—you are asking your subjects to think back on things they may not have considered for years. Calling up these memories may spark other thoughts, too. Allow your subject time to ponder. You may be thrilled by what he or she remembers.

9. **Ask the same question in different ways.** People don't know how much they know, and rephrasing a question can give you more information. This happens all the time. "I don't know," a relative will tell you, sometimes impatiently. They do know—they just don't know that they know. The most common version of this occurs when an interviewer asks, "What was your father's mother's name?" The relative answers, "I never knew her. I don't know." Then a few minutes later, in response to "Whom were you named after?" this answer comes; "My father's mother."

Try to find a couple of ways to ask important questions. You may feel like you're being repetitive, but you never can be sure what you will learn.

10. **Be sensitive to what you discover.** Sometimes people become emotional talking about the past. They may remember long-dead relatives or once-forgotten tragedies. If your talker is upset by a memory, either remain silent or quietly ask, "Is it all right if we talk some more about this? Or would you rather not?" People frequently feel better when they talk about sad things; you should gently give your relative the *choice* of whether or not to go on.

11. **Try not to interrupt.** If your talker strays from the subject, let him or her finish the story and then say, "Let's get back to Uncle Moe" or "You said something earlier about … " By not interrupting, you make the conversation friendlier, and the story may lead you to something you didn't expect.

Of course, there is always the exception to the rule. If a story goes on forever and seems useless, the best way to handle it may be to say, "Gee, Aunt Gus, could you hold the rest of that story for later? I'd like to get the facts out of the way and then come back to that."

12. **Ask for songs, poems, unusual memories.** You may discover something wonderful when you ask your subject if she recalls the rhymes she used to recite while jumping rope as a little girl or the hymns she sang in church. Probe a little here—ask about childhood games and memories, smells and tastes and sounds.

Get a Closer Look, Ira Wolfman Annual Editions.

Selection Two: **Two Positives**

From *Gifted Hands* by Ben Carson with Cecil Murphy

Before Reading

Before you read the story "Two Positives," complete the following:

Predict what the topic may be.

Skim the reading to see if you have correctly predicted the topic.

Look at the first and last paragraphs, and glance at the first sentences of the other paragraphs.

Think about the topic and relate what you know to "Two Positives."

Set a purpose for reading this story. Do you expect to be entertained, to gain knowledge, or to explore an argument?

Words to Preview

compulsory *(adj.)* required *(par.)*
unflagging *(adj.)* not declining or weakening *(par.)*

Two Positives by Ben Carson

Halfway through my fifth grade the school gave us a *compulsory* eye examination.

I squinted, tried to focus, and read the first line–barely.

The school provided glasses for me, free. When I went to get fitted, the doctor said, "Son, your vision is so bad you almost qualify to be labeled handicapped."

Apparently my eyes had worsened gradually, and I had no idea they were so bad. I wore my new glasses to school the next day. And I was amazed. For the first time I could actually see the writing on the chalkboard from the back of the classroom. Getting glasses was the first positive thing to start me on my climb upward from the bottom of the class. Immediately after getting my vision corrected my grades improved–not greatly, but at least I was moving in the right direction.

When the mid-term report cards came out, Mrs. Williamson called me aside. "Benjamin," she said, "on the whole you're doing so much better." Her smile of approval made me feel like I could do better yet. I knew she wanted to encourage me to improve.

I had a *D* in math—but that did indicate improvement. At least I hadn't failed.

Seeing that passing grade made me feel good. I thought, *I made a D in math. I'm improving. There's hope for me. I'm not the dumbest kid in the school.* When a kid like me who had been at the bottom of the class for the first half of the year suddenly zoomed upward—even if only from F to D—that experience gave birth to hope. For the first time since entering Higgins School I knew I could do better than some of the students in my class.

Mother wasn't willing to let me settle for such a lowly goal as that! "Oh, it's an improvement all right," she said. "And Bennie, I'm proud of you for getting a better grade. And why shouldn't you? You're smart, Bennie."

Despite my excitement and sense of hope, my mother wasn't happy. Seeing my improved math grade and hearing what Mrs. Williamson had said to me, she started emphasizing, "But you can't settle for just barely passing. You're too smart for that. You can make the top math grade in the class."

"But, Mother, I didn't fail," I moaned, thinking she hadn't appreciated how much my work had improved.

"All right, Bennie, you've started improving," Mother said, "and you're going to keep on improving."

"I'm trying," I said. "I'm doing the best I can."

"But you can do still better, and I'm going to help you." Her eyes sparkled. I should have known that she had already started formulating a plan. With Mother, it wasn't enough to say, "Do better." She would find a way to show me how. Her scheme, worked out as we went along, turned out to be the second positive factor.

My mother hadn't said much about my grades until the report cards came out at mid-year. She had believed the grades from the Boston school reflected progress. But once she realized how badly I was doing at Higgins Elementary, she started in on me every day.

However, Mother never asked, "Why can't you be like those smart boys?" Mother had too much sense for that. Besides, I never felt she wanted me to compete with my classmates as much as she wanted me to do my best.

"I've got two smart boys," she'd say. "Two mighty smart boys."

"I'm doing my best," I'd insist. "I've improved in math."

"But you're going to do better, Bennie," she told me one evening. "Now, since you've started getting better in math, you're going to go on, and here's how you'll do it. First thing you're going to do is to memorize your times tables."

"My times tables?" I cried. I couldn't imagine learning so much. "Do you know how many there are? Why that could take a year!"

She stood up a little taller. "I only went through third grade, and I know them all the way through my twelves."

"But, Mother, I can't–"

"You can do it, Bennie. You just have to set your mind to concentrating. You work on them, and tomorrow when I get home from work we'll review them. We'll keep on reviewing the times tables until you know them better than anyone else in your class!"

I argued a little more, but I should have known better.

"Besides"–here came her final shot–"you're not to go outside and play after school tomorrow until you've learned those tables."

I was almost in tears. "Look at all these things!" I cried, pointing to the columns in the back of my math book. "How can anyone learn all of them?"

Sometimes talking to Mother was like talking to a stone. Her jaw was set, her voice hard. "You can't go outside and play until you learn your times tables."

Mother wasn't home, of course, when school let out, but it didn't occur to me to disobey. She had taught Curtis and me properly, and we did what she told us.

I learned the times tables. I just kept repeating them until they fixed themselves in my brain. Like she promised, that night Mother went over them with me. Her constant interest and *unflagging* encouragement kept me motivated.

Within days after learning my times tables, math became so much easier that my scores soared. Most of the time my grades reached as high as the other kids' in my class. I'll never forget how I felt after another math quiz when I answered Mrs. Williamson with "Twenty-four!"

I practically shouted as I repeated, "I got twenty-four right."

She smiled back at me in a way that made me know how pleased she was to see my improvement. I didn't tell the other kids what was going on at home or how much the glasses helped. I didn't think most of them cared.

Things changed immediately and made going to school more enjoyable. Nobody laughed or called me the dummy in math anymore! But Mother didn't let me stop with memorizing the times tables. She had proven to me that I could succeed in one thing. So she started the next phase of my self-improvement program to make me come out with the top grades in every class.

Portfolio Activities

Integrating Ideas

Think about one of your own family experiences. What were your reactions? How did your parents' or guardians' reactions differ from your own? If and when you are a parent, what would you do differently in these or other situations? Reflect on these ideas in writing or in class discussion.

Extending Concepts

Your own family history may surprise you. Whom in your family are you particularly close to? Who in your family is much older than you or your parents? Is there someone you would like to know more about? Choose someone in your family to interview. Follow the guidelines given in "Get a Closer Look." Write about one of the stories they shared with you in the interview.

Collaborative Activity

In groups, first define the concept of family including the members and their roles. Next choose a television program that portrays a family and describe the TV family and their members and roles. Then compare the groups' definition of family to the TV family. Report back to the class as a whole on your findings.

Additional Portfolio Suggestion

A literacy autobiography tells the story of your development as a reader and writer. This process began when you were very young and continues throughout your life. Explore your growth as a literate person to better understand your current abilities. A series of questions to guide you are provided in Appendix B of this text.

Chapter Summary Graphic Organizer

Complete the steps that explain the Before reading process.

Before Reading

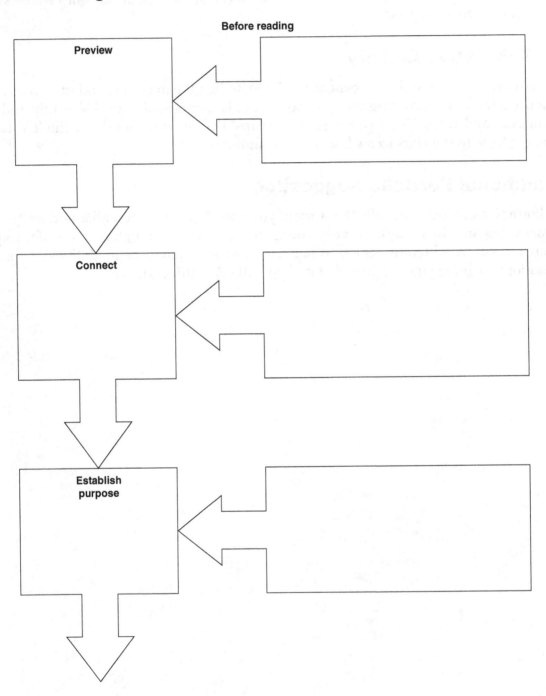

Chapter 2

During Reading

Theme of Readings: Friendship

"A real friend is one who walks in when the rest of the world walks out."

Walter Winchell

Friendship

Friendship is a special bond that you have with certain people. It keeps your life from being lonely and makes life more fun and meaningful. You can sit in a room full of people but without a friend you are still alone. Whom will you talk to? Who knows how you feel? Who will share this time? Friends help make the good times better and the hard times more bearable.

It is the freedom to choose your friends that makes friendship special. Friends share interests, attitudes, problems and experiences. If you share an interest in music, you may listen to music, play instruments, or write lyrics to a song together. Hours may be spent talking about the perfect sound system for a car. Common computer knowledge may lead to developing a web site or new software. Friends provide companionship, the sharing of information, and insights. Similar interests enhance a friendship.

Friends also depend on each other and trust each other. They give advice and emotional support when it is needed most. Friends listen. Maintaining a friendship is not automatic, however. Ralph Waldo Emerson said, "The only way to have a friend is to be one." You have to work at being a good friend. It takes time, energy, and commitment, but friendship is its own reward.

Chapter Objectives

At the end of this chapter, you will be able to:

1. Predict as you read.

2. Visualize the reading.

3. Monitor your comprehension.

Focus on *During Reading* Strategies

As a passenger in a car, you don't usually pay attention to the roads and turns the driver takes. You do not take an active part in getting to the destination. When you change from the passenger to the driver, you may not remember the exact route even though you have been there many times—sometimes you get lost. Many students read as if they are the passenger in a car; they do not become involved in what they are reading and often find themselves lost.

How many times have you finished reading something and were unable to remember what it was about? It doesn't matter whether you read a newspaper, magazine, novel, or textbook. You went through the "motions" of reading but didn't retain the information because you were not involved with what you were reading.

You begin your involvement using the *before reading* strategies. To continue the process you need to focus on the reading and work at constructing meaning. To accomplish this, you will predict, visualize, and monitor your comprehension while you read.

Prediction

As you read, words, phrases, and sentences trigger thoughts about what may happen in the reading. Your mind is always ahead of where your eyes are on the page. It continuously predicts what the next word or idea will be. As you read, you confirm those predictions that are correct or those which are not. At the same time, you continue to make new predictions.

For example, a student reads the first sentence of a story, "I was sure he was coming to get me." The student makes several predictions about the story: someone is afraid of an attack, someone is waiting for a ride, or someone is looking forward to an excursion. As you read, you confirm those predictions that are correct or those that are not. The reader realizes that a little boy was having a nightmare—no one was going to be attacked, and no one was waiting for a ride. The student adjusts her predictions and continues to make new ones as she reads the story.

Whether your predictions are correct or not, is not important. It is the process of making those predictions that connects you to the author and actively involves you in the reading.

Visualization

The strategy of taking words and ideas from a reading and forming a mental picture is visualization. Effective readers create images as they read. Readers' images are unique because their visualizations depend upon their own experiences. For instance, if a story describes a castle in Germany, a reader who has visited the country will picture one image. Someone who has never traveled to Europe may picture a castle they saw on television or Cinderella's castle at Disneyworld. Your mental image will depend on your background and experiences. As you read, your mental pictures are modified. The process of visualization further strengthens your connection to the author.

Monitoring Comprehension

Every day you drive your car to work, school, or home without ever thinking about what is happening in the car's engine. If you never check the oil of your car, it may run well for a while, but eventually it will break down. In the same way, if you were to withdraw money from your bank account without keeping track of the balance, your checks would eventually bounce. You need to check, or monitor, these and other daily activities to prevent problems.

If you read an entire chapter but remembered little or nothing of what you read, you have not checked your understanding while you were reading. Just as you need to monitor activities in your life, you must monitor your comprehension. You must realize that you are in charge of constructing meaning from what you read.

Be actively involved in monitoring your comprehension as you read. Use the following techniques:

• Continually ask yourself, "Does this make sense?"
• Carry on a conversation in your head about the reading.
• Mentally state in your own words what the author is saying.

For example, while reading a magazine article about unsafe foods, you may start to think of what the author is saying about beef and deadly bacteria. Could you explain the reading to another person? If the reading does not make sense, or you are unable to explain it, your comprehension has broken down.

Effective readers recognize or monitor these breakdowns in comprehension and take actions to repair them. If you realize you do not understand, stop reading and attempt to figure out where the problem began. Was it with a word, phrase, or sentence? Reread the section and look for a clearer understanding. You may have thought that stopping and rereading are actions to be avoided. On the contrary, they are a crucial part of effective reading. Monitoring your comprehension allows you to understand if you are connecting to the author.

Short Exercise: *During Reading* Strategies

The following exercise demonstrates *during reading* strategies. After reading the suggested predictions, visualizations, and monitoring statements, which are in italics, try it on your own. Talk about your responses with your classmates.

"The Dinner Party"

excerpted from *Among Friends* by Letty Cottin Pogrebin

Five years ago at my house a well-known actor-screenwriter asked the others gathered around the dinner table to give him some ideas for a script in progress.
I see a fancy table with candles and special dishes and lots of crystal and silver with eight or ten people nicely dressed sitting and chatting. [Visualizing]

The Dinner Party from Among Friends by Letty Cottin Pogrebin.

The movie is about friendship, he explained.

I wonder what movie this is going to be. I bet it will be like that old movie, "The Big Chill."
[Predicting]

I need to know what role friendship plays in the average person's life.

By role, I think he means what part of life is friendship. [Monitoring]

   I think the people at this dinner party will say friendship is very important in their lives.
[Predicting]

What do you look for in a friend?

I look for someone who will support me and be there when I need them. [Monitoring]

How many really good friends do you have and how often do you see them?

What does he mean by "really good friends"? I don't think you have to see someone often to consider them a really good friend. [Monitoring]

   I picture my friend Debbie, she is a really good friend. We do lots of things together.
[Visualizing]

What did you do together?

1. _____

   _____

   _____

Could you stay friends after a serious fight?

2. _____

   _____

   _____

Did you ever lose a meaningful friend?

3. _____

   _____

   _____

Do you keep making new ones?

4. _____

   _____

   _____

The Dinner Party from Among Friends by Letty Cottin Pogrebin.

Is there such a thing as having too many friends?

5. _____

   _____

   _____

Reading Selections

Selection One: **"Real Friends"**

Catherine Weiskopf

Before Reading

Before you read the story, "Real Friends," complete the following:

Predict what the topic may be.

Skim the reading to see if you have correctly predicted the topic.
Look at the first and last paragraphs, and glance at the first sentences of the other paragraphs.

Think about the topic and relate what you know to "Real Friends."

Set a purpose for reading this story. Do you expect to be entertained, to gain knowledge, or to explore an argument?

Words to Preview

catalyst *(n.)* substance that increases rate of chemical reaction *(par.2)*
reciprocal *(adj.)* experienced by both sides *(par.3)*
reappraise *(v.)* to evaluate again *(par.9)*
exalt *(v.)* to glorify; praise *(par.11)*

During Reading

As you read "Real Friends," continue to predict what will happen next in the article, visualize the story, and monitor your understanding. Use the guide questions that are printed in the margins of the reading to help you with this process.

Real Friends

1 Friends: They can make a boring class bearable; a *blustery* day warm; a teeth-grinding worry disappear. Friends are an important part of your life. The 1996 Mood of American Youth Survey found friends were the number-one reason why teens liked school, and being with friends was the number-two nonschool activity. You will have many different friends over the course of your life, but what draws you to certain people? What qualities do you look for in friends? For that matter, why do you even need friends?

> Can you picture your friends?

> What qualities do you look for in a friend?

What Makes You Friends

2 Are you and your friend major basketball fans? Do you both have the same strong views about recycling? Maybe you've both survived a common tragedy. At all ages, common interest is the *catalyst* for friendship. This doesn't mean friends are similar in every way, but you are similar in the ways that are important to you. Adam Bonjour, age 15, says his friendships developed "because we have a lot of things in common. We like to do the same stuff together." Similarities with friends tend to change as you get older, but they are always there. Faye Steuer noted in her book, *The Psychological Development of Children*, that friendships involving younger children have more behavioral similarities while adolescent friendships tend more toward similarities in attitude.

> What's a catalyst?

> Do you share the same attitudes as your friends?

3 When Helen Swanson is looking for a friend, she looks for someone who is "funny, not too serious, and nice." Adam Bonjour wants friends who are "thoughtful, kind, honest, and fun." Marcus Schneider wants his friends to have "intelligence, kindness, and be nonconforming." Everyone wants friends who are nice, kind, and supportive. Beyond these traits, you want friends who are similar to you. If you are artistic, you want friends who are the same. If you value honesty and thoughtfulness, you look for friends who have the same values. What do the experts say people look for in friends? One recent study found certain aspects of friendship appear to be present at all ages: "similarity, emotional supportiveness, shared activities, confiding, and *reciprocal* liking, trust, and acceptance."

> I predict people look for _____ and _____ in friends.

> Was my prediction confirmed?

Friendship—Not All Peaches and Cream

4 Sometimes people get messed up about what friendship means. You may expect a friend to never be late. You may

> Do you have a mental image of a time when a friend hurt you?

expect a friend to never disagree. But friends aren't copies of yourself, and friendships aren't perfect. Anytime people are close, they're bound to hurt one another's feelings. But you need to balance what they've done wrong with what they've done right.

5   It is also important to remember being a real friend isn't always easy. Sometimes, to be a real friend, you have to be brutally honest and tough. Real friends may take keys away from a drunk friend even if it might mean the loss of his or her friendship. Real friendship isn't all peaches and cream.

Making and Keeping Friends

6 Every friendship starts with a smile, a hello, and a simple icebreaker, writes psychologist Dr. Lillian Glass in an article about attracting terrific people. The icebreaker can be homework or the news or the weather.

7   When you're interested in becoming friends with an acquaintance, first think about what you look for in a friend. There's an old saying, "To have a friend is to be a friend." It's true. Are you a good friend? Lesson one on developing friendship is to show interest in the other person. Be a good listener, show your interest, and treat the person as if he or she is special.

> How do you develop friendships?

8   Once you've spent time and energy developing friends, you need to put that same energy into keeping them. So how do you keep friends? "I keep friends by staying loyal. I always keep appointments, and I'm always honest," says Marcus Schneider. It all boils down to showing your friends the respect and appreciation that you want from them.

Better Than an Apple a Day?

9 You know friends make your life better, but did you know studies show they also improve both your psychological and physical health? A study done by D. Buhrmester in 1990 found, "Those who had closer friendships saw themselves as more competent and sociable and having higher selfesteem than youngsters without close friends." Friendships may be beneficial in part because they allow you to talk about your problems. According to Brant R. Burleson, professor of communications at Purdue University, talking about your troubles helps you clarify them. "Discussing a traumatic event helps the distressed person get some distance on it—*reappraise* it—and integrate new perspectives on it within a broader view of life."

> Do you share respect and appreciation with your friends?

10   Good friends are also good for your physical health. In a study done at the University of Texas, researchers found, "Social support boosts the immune system, improves the quality—and possibly the length—of life, and helps reduce heart disease." In other words, a good friendship can be just as good as an apple a day at keeping the doctor away.

> How do friends make your life better?

11   Friends–they increase your health and your happiness and possibly even lengthen your life. The glories of friendship have been *exalted* in poetry and vocalized in songs. Perhaps one of the best songs about the nature of friendship is "Lean on Me," written by Bill Withers. "Lean on me when you're not strong and I'll be your friend–I'll help you carry on. For I know that it won't be long 'til I'm gonna need somebody to lean on."

Selection Two: The Introduction from ***The Pact***

Drs. S. Davis, G. Jenkins, and R. Hunt

Before Reading

Before you read the story "The Pact," complete the following:

Predict what the topic may be.

Skim the reading to see if you have correctly predicted the topic.
Look at the first and last paragraphs, and glance at the first sentences of the other paragraphs.

Think about the topic and relate what you know to "The Pact."

Set a purpose for reading this story. Do you expect to be entertained, to gain knowledge, or to explore an argument?

Words to Preview

perpetuating *(v.)* prolonging the existence of something *(par.2)*
riddled *(v.)* spread throughout *(par.3)*
ravaged *(v.)* brought heavy destruction on *(par.3)*
reigned *(v.)* had a widespread influence *(par.3)*
pact *(n.)* a formal agreement *(par.3)*
vulnerable *(adj.)* liable to give in to temptation or persuasion *(par.6)*

During Reading

As you read the Introduction from *The Pact*, continue to predict where the author is headed, visualize the story, and monitor your understanding. Use the limited guide

"Real Friends" by Catherine Weiskopf. From *Current Health* 2, February 1998, v24, n6, p. 16(2). Special permission granted, *Current Health* 2®, copyright © 1999, published by Weekly Reader Corporation. All rights reserved.

questions in the margin of the reading to help you with this process. Add your own comments, questions, or descriptions as you read.

Introduction to The Pact

1 We treat them in our hospitals every day.

2   They are young brothers, often drug dealers, gang members, or smalltime criminals, who show up shot, stabbed, or beaten after a hustle gone bad. To some of our medical colleagues, they are just nameless thugs, *perpetuating* crime and death in neighborhoods that have seen far too much of those things. But when we look into their faces, we see ourselves as teenagers, we see our friends, we see what we easily could have become as young adults. And we're reminded of the thin line that separates us—three twenty-nine-year-old doctors (an emergency-room physician, an internist, and a dentist)—from these patients whose lives are filled with danger and desperation.

> Can you picture your scene?

3   We grew up in poor, broken homes in New Jersey neighborhoods *riddled* with crime, drugs, and death, and came of age in the 1980s at the height of a crack epidemic that *ravaged* communities like ours throughout the nation. There were no doctors or lawyers walking the streets of our communities. Where we lived, hustlers *reigned*, and it was easy to follow their example. Two of us landed in juvenile-detention centers before our eighteenth birthdays. But inspired early by caring and imaginative role models, one of us in childhood latched on to a dream of becoming a dentist, steered clear of trouble, and in his senior year of high school persuaded his two best friends to apply to a college program for minority students interested in becoming doctors. We knew we'd never survive if we went after it alone. And so we made a *pact*: we'd help one another through, no matter what.

> My role model is my uncle who is a successful business owner.

> What is a pact?

4   In college, the three of us stuck together to survive and thrive in a world that was different from anything we had ever known. We provided one another with a kind of positive peer pressure. From the moment we made our pact, the competition was on. When one of us finished his college application, the other two rushed to send theirs out. When we participated in a six-week remedial program at Seton Hall University the summer before our freshman year, each of us felt pressured to perform well because we knew our friends would excel and we didn't want to embarrass ourselves or lag behind. When one of us made an A on a test, the others strived to make A's, too.

5   We studied together. We worked summer jobs together. We partied together. And we learned to solve our problems together. We are doctors today because of the positive influences that we had on one another.

"Introduction," from *The Pact* by Sampson Davis, George Jenkins, and Rameck Hunt, with Liza Frazier Page. Copyright © 2002 by Three Doctors LLC. Reprinted by permission of Riverhead Books, and imprint on Penguin Putnam Inc.

6   The lives of most impressionable young people are defined by their friends, whether they are black, white, Hispanic, or Asian; whether they are rich, poor, or middle-class; whether they live in the city, the suburbs, or the country. Among boys, particularly, there seems to be some macho code that says to gain respect, you have to prove that you're bad. We know firsthand that the wrong friends can lead you to trouble. But even more, they can tear down hopes, dreams, and possibilities. We know, too, that the right friends inspire you, pull you through, rise with you.

7   Each of us experienced friendships that could have destroyed our lives. We suspect that many of the young brothers we treat every day in our hospitals are entangled in such friendships–friendships that require them to prove their toughness and manhood daily, even at the risk of losing their own lives. The three of us were blessed. We found in one another a friendship that works in a powerful way; a friendship that helped three *vulnerable* boys grow into successful men; a friendship that ultimately helped save our lives.

> Have you ever had a destructive friendship?

8   But it wasn't always easy. There were times when one of us was ready to give up, and times when we made bad decisions. Some of that is ugly and difficult to admit, and we suffered pain and other consequences. But we have laid it all out here nonetheless.

9   We did this because we hope that our story will inspire others so that even those young people who feel trapped by their circumstances, or pulled by peer pressure in the wrong direction, might look for a way out not through drugs, alcohol, crime, or dares but through the power of friendship. And within our story are many others, of mentors, friends, relatives, and even strangers we met along the way, whose goodwill and good deeds made a difference in our lives. We hope our story will also demonstrate that.

Selection Three: "The Electronic Friend? Video Games and Children's Friendships"

Cheryl K. Olson

Before Reading

Before you read the story "The Electronic Friend? Video Games and Children's Friendships" complete the following:

Predict what the topic may be.

Skim the reading to see if you have correctly predicted the topic. Look at the first and last paragraphs, and glance at the first sentences of the other paragraphs.

Think about the topic and relate what you know to "The Electronic Friend? Video Games and Children's Friendships?"

Set a purpose for reading this story. Do you expect to be entertained, to gain knowledge, or to explore an argument?

Words to Preview

detriment *(n.)* damage, harm, or loss *(par. 1)*
scant *(adj.)* being just short of a specific amount; inadequate amount *(par. 2)*
qualitative *(adj.)* pertaining to or concerning quality *(par. 3)*
quantitative *(adj.)* expressed as a quantity *(par. 3)*
epidemiology *(n.)* the study of an outbreak of contagious diseases *(par. 3)*
ubiquity *(n.)* existence everywhere at the same time *(par. 4)*
speculation *(n.)* the act of reflecting or meditating on a subject *(par. 14)*

During Reading

As you read "The Electronic Friend? Video Games and Children's Friendships," continue to predict where the author headed, visualize the story, and monitor your understanding. There are no guide questions given. As you read, write your own comments, questions, or descriptions in the margins.

The Electronic Friend? Video Games and Children's Friendships

Cheryl Olsen

1 A 2007 survey of teachers by the British charity Save the Children, widely reported by newspapers, concluded that children were spending more time on solitary pursuits such as computer games to the detriment of their social skills. This assumption that video games undermine friendships is widespread. When we talked to parents of teen boys in focus groups, one of the first concerns they raised—ahead of violent video game content—was that game play might be isolating or interfere with social functioning. As one mother said, "Five, six years from now, will they be able to socialize in a group amongst people who don't necessarily play these games?".

2 Based on surveys of arcade-gaming preteens, Selnow concluded that videogames were primarily a solitary activity, and that this "electronic friend" might substitute for human companionship. However, there is scant evidence that modern video and computer games promote social isolation.

3 In a set of qualitative and quantitative studies at Massachusetts General Hospital, we looked at the "epidemiology" of adolescent video game play: the who, what, where,

The Electronic Friend? Video Games and Children's Friendships.

when and how, as well as the why. We found that video and computer games are central to the social lives of many young teens, especially boys, and serve a number of social functions.

4   In this article, I'll draw on our school-based survey of 1,254 middle-school youth in South Carolina and Pennsylvania, as well as data from focus groups with 42 boys in the greater Boston area. We were struck by the ubiquity of electronic games in children's lives. Just 17 of our survey subjects had never played electronic games; 63 others had not played in the previous six months. (Their responses were excluded from our analyses.)

5   We asked children whether they agreed or disagreed (on a 4-point scale) with a series of possible reasons for electronic game play. Many agreed that social factors motivated their play, … including competition, joining friends in play, teaching others how to play, and (least frequently) making new friends. Boys were significantly more likely than girls to agree with the first two of these motivations.

6   "To compete and win" was particularly popular among boys; 57% "strongly agreed" that this motivated their video game play (second only to "it's just fun"). Focus group comments supported this finding. A typical example: "Usually me and my friends, when we're over at each others' houses, and they have a good game, [we'll play it]. They're like, 'Oh, I'll kill you in Madden 2005.' It's fun to beat them."

7   These results are in line with a recent large study by the British Board of Film Classification (which rates video games in the U.K.). Their report noted that "the social rewards of gaming–talking about how you are doing, playing together, helping or beating each other–are less a part of the attraction for females than males." It's important to note, however, that the urge to compete is not limited to boys. In our survey, 61% of girls who played games were motivated in part by the chance to compete and win.

8   We speculate that for boys, video games may serve some of the same purposes as "rough and tumble" play, in terms of jockeying for social status. Boys can gain status among peers by owning or mastering a popular game. In fact, a study of adolescent male social identity by Tarrant et al. found that "good at computer/video games" was one of the most desirable traits, ranking second only to being "fun" among one's "ingroup" members.

9   Along with friendly competition, boys and girls gain satisfaction from teaching others how to play. In focus groups, boys described sharing advice and tips: "'Oh, this guy is the best.' 'Where are you in this game?' 'Oh, I'm having a hard time in the queen's castle' or whatever." They direct each other to web sites for the latest "cheat" codes. In surveys of (mostly adult) online game players, Yee found that helping other players and being part of a group effort were important motivators for play.

10 Boys told us that games are a frequent focus for conversation among their peers. When I asked one boy what the kids at school would talk about if they weren't talking about games, he replied: "I don't know. Probably like girls, or something like that, … I don't even know, 'cause the most they talk about is girls and games–the two Gs."

The Electronic Friend? Video Games and Children's Friendships.

11 Although making new friends was not among the top motivations for video gaming in our survey, video games clearly create common ground that young people can use to make friends. As one boy explained in a focus group, start by asking "'Do you own a system, a game system?' If he says 'yes,' then, 'What kind?'"

12 Making friends was a higher-ranked motivator, however, for the 78 children we surveyed who were classified as mildly learning disabled. Children in this group were more likely to be victims of bullying, and to report being left out or excluded by their peers. Their overall top reasons for playing games reflect their needs to connect with friends: playing because their friends did, to make new friends, or to teach others. They were also significantly more likely to play to cope with feelings of loneliness.

13 Most children who play video games play alone at times, whether for fun, out of boredom, or to help them deal with stress. Boys are more likely than girls to report playing by themselves; 62.8% play "often" or "always" alone, compared to 45.6% of girls. However, boys are also more likely than girls to play often/always with multiple friends in the same room (33.4% vs. 12.5%). Children who are heavy game players (the 12.6% of boys and 1.5% of girls who report playing more than 15 hours in a typical week) are more likely to play in groups, whether in person or over the Internet … . Playing video games alone almost all of the time is not typical, and may be a marker for social or emotional problems. More research is needed on healthy and unhealthy patterns of video game play, especially among children with emotional problems or develop mental delays.

14 Much of the debate about video games, among both academics and the public, has focused on the potential influence of violent content. Despite the frequent media speculation, no link has been found between school shootings and violent video games. (It's important to note that it's the media coverage of school shootings, rather than the rate of violence, that has increased). Nevertheless, we dread the thought of a socially outcast child holed up in his bedroom, engrossed in practicing various methods of murder. Fortunately, this is by no means typical. Our survey found that children who play Mature-rated, violent games are not more likely than other children their age to play games alone. In fact, … compared to children who don't play M-rated games regularly, M-game players were significantly *more* likely to play games in social settings. The majority of boys in our sample (including the 12-year-olds) routinely played at least one M-rated title, along with 29% of female game players. Though the thought may be discomforting, violent video game play has become a normal part of male childhood.

15 And it may not be all bad. Some researchers have questioned whether we worry too much about teens who play violent games in groups, and speculate on possible benefits. Jansz notes that "the gamer wants to experience particular emotions with his friends to intensify their mutual bonds." Goldstein takes a cultural/historical perspective, noting that "Violent entertainment appeals primarily to males, and it appeals to them mostly in groups. People rarely attend horror films or boxing matches alone, and boys do not often play war games by themselves. These are social occasions, particularly suitable for … communicating a masculine identity to your mates."

The Electronic Friend? Video Games and Children's Friendships.

Portfolio Activities

Integrating Ideas

Now that you have read three selections about friendship, define and describe your concept of friendship. Think about the friends that you have or had. What was it about these relationships that made them good or bad friendships? Reflect on these ideas in writing or in class discussion.

Extending Concepts

Opinions vary on whether video games are good for children or not. Do you play video games? Do you think it is a way to make friends? Do you think video games make children (especially boys) more solitary? Write your opinion about whether video games help to create friendships or not. Support your view by describing your experiences or those of others.

Collaborative Activity

In a group, compose a list of questions to use for an interview about friendship. Then, using these questions, interview someone in the class to learn about their concept of friendship. After the interview, share your findings with the group.

Additional Portfolio Suggestion

Look back at the model of *during reading* activities on pages 19 and 20. Using a reading of your choice, create a similar model with your comments, questions, and descriptions. Use at least ten consecutive sentences from the story.

Chapter Summary Graphic Organizer

Complete the steps that explain the During Reading Process.

During Reading

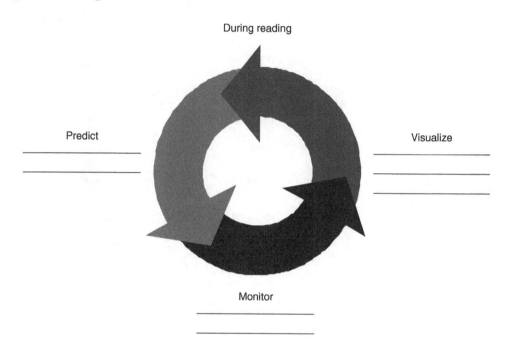

During reading

Predict
_____
_____

Visualize
_____
_____
_____

Monitor
_____
_____

Chapter 3

After Reading

Theme of Readings: Love

"A heart that loves is always young."

GREEK PROVERB

Love

Pick up a magazine. Listen to the radio. Watch a television show. View a movie. Read a novel. Share a conversation. One theme is easy to find in all of these activities—love. Since ancient times, love has been an enduring and inspiring topic in literature and the arts. To love and be loved is a life-long goal, sought after by young and old. You can find recipes for love, descriptions of lost love, and poems, cartoons and greeting cards about love. Some cultures even dedicate a day to love—St. Valentine's Day.

Preoccupation with love begins when you are very young. Small children pretend to be married and play house. Ten year olds claim boyfriends and girlfriends, even though they barely speak to each other. Teenagers struggle with the insecurity of dating as they approach adulthood. All have one goal in mind—receiving and giving love.

As preoccupied as each of us may be with the pursuit of love, love is not always easy to find or to keep. Maintaining a long term love relationship in today's society may be one of the most difficult things you do. Like friendship, it takes time, energy, and commitment; it also takes communication skills, the ability to compromise, and a touch of luck, and long term love may be yours. Whether it lasts a month or a life time, a loving relationship is one of life's greatest experiences.

Chapter Objectives

After completing this chapter, you will be able to:

1. Evaluate your understanding of the reading.

2. Review and recall the ideas presented in the selection.

Focus on *After Reading* Strategies

An article catches your eye in your favorite magazine. You skim it, find it interesting, and read the entire article. When finished, you toss the magazine aside without a second thought. Even though you became actively involved in reading by using *before* and *during reading* strategies, your reading remains unfinished. If you neglect to do anything after you read, the reading process is incomplete. An effective reader evaluates their understanding of the reading to complete the process.

To evaluate your understanding, you must review the reading and recall information. Ask yourself: *Did I meet my purpose for reading? Did I understand what I just read? Were there any confusing parts that I need to reread? What is important to remember? Can I relate the information to my knowledge or experience?* These questions will guide you in evaluating your understanding. You increase your memory of what you read by reviewing and recalling the information.

To understand *after reading* strategies, read the excerpt from Leo Buscaglia's *Living, Loving & Learning* and the model questions and responses that follow.

Don't miss love. It's an incredible gift. I love to think that the day you are born, you're given the world as your birthday present. It frightens me that so few people even bother to open up the ribbon! *Rip it open! Tear off the top!* It's just *full* of love and magic and life and joy and wonder and pain and tears. All of the things that are your gifts for being human. Not only the really happy things–"I want to be happy all the time"–no, there's a lot of pain in there, a lot of tears. A lot of magic, a lot of wonder, a lot of confusion. But that's what it means. That's what life *is*. And all *so exciting.* Get into that box and you'll never be bored.

I see people who are always saying, "I'm a lover, I'm a lover, I'm a lover. I really believe in love. I act the part." And then they shout at the waitress, *"Where's the water?!"* I will believe your love when you show it to me in action. When you can understand that everybody is teaching everybody to love at every moment. And when you ask yourself, "Am I the best teacher," and if your answer is "Yes"–great. Go around–listen to how many times a day you say, "I love," instead of, "I hate." Isn't it interesting that children, as they learn the process of language, always learn the word "no" years before they learn the word "yes"? Ask linguists where they hear it. Maybe if they heard more of "I love, I love, I love," they'd say it sooner and more often.

Review the Excerpt. What is Important to Remember?

The author feels love and life are gifts for being human. Life is exciting and if you see it that way you'll never be bored. The author feels that we are teaching each other about love. We need to hear the word love more often.

From *Living, Loving, & Learning* by Leo F. Buscaglia, Ph.D., edited by Steven Short. Published by Ballantine Books. Copyright © 1982 by Leo F. Buscaglia, Inc.

What is the Author's Definition of Love?

Love is a gift to be opened and experienced.

How do people's actions differ from their beliefs about love?

People say one thing but do another. For example, they will say they believe in love but yell at the waitress over getting a glass of water.

Short Exercises: *After Reading* Strategies

The following selections are excerpts from *Don't Sweat the Small Stuff . . . and It's All Small Stuff* by Richard Carlson. After you read, use the questions to help you to evaluate your understanding and review and recall the selection.

Tell Three People (Today) How Much You Love Them

Richard Carlson

Author Stephen Levine asks the question, "If you had an hour to live and could make only one phone call—who would you call, what would you say, and why are you waiting?" What a powerful message!

Who knows what we are waiting for? Perhaps we want to believe we will live forever, or that "someday" we will get around to telling the people we love how much we love them. Whatever the reasons, most of us simply wait too long.

As fate would have it, I'm writing this strategy on my grandmother's birthday. Later today, my father and I are driving out to visit her grave site. She died about two years ago. Before she passed away, it became obvious how important it was to her to let her family know how much she loved us all. It was a good reminder that there is no good reason to wait. Now is the time to let people know how much you care.

Ideally, you can tell someone in person or over the phone. I wonder how many people have been on the receiving end of a phone call where the caller says, "I just called to tell you how much I love you!" You may be surprised that almost nothing in the world means so much to a person. How would you like to receive the same message?

If you're too shy to make such a phone call, write a heartfelt letter instead. Either way, you may find that as you get used to it, letting people know how much you love them will become a regular part of your life. It probably won't shock you to know that, if it does, you'll probably begin receiving more love as a result.

1. Review "Tell Three People (Today) How Much You Love Them."

_____

_____

_____

2. Why is it important to tell people that you love them?

_____

_____

_____

Spend a Moment, Every Day Thinking of Someone to Love

Earlier in this book I introduced the idea of spending a moment, each day, thinking of someone to thank. Another excellent source of gratitude and inner peace is to spend a moment, every day, thinking of someone to love. Remember the old saying, "An apple a day keeps the doctor away"? The love equivalent might read, "Thinking of someone to love each day keeps your resentment away!"

I started consciously choosing to think of people to love when I realized how often I could get caught up in thinking about the opposite–people who irritate me. My mind would focus on negative or strange behavior, and within seconds I was filled with negativity. Once I made the conscious decision, however, to spend a moment each morning thinking of someone to love, my attention was redirected toward the positive, not only toward that one person, but in general throughout the day. I don't mean to suggest that I never get irritated anymore, but without question it happens much less frequently than it used to. I credit this exercise with much of my improvement.

Every morning when I wake up, I close my eyes and take a few deep breaths. Then I ask myself the question, "Who shall I send love to today?" Instantly, a picture of someone will pop into my mind–a family member, a friend, someone I work with, a neighbor, someone from my past, even a stranger I may have seen on the street. To me, it doesn't really matter who it is because the idea is to gear my mind toward love. Once the person to whom I'm directing the love is clear, I simply wish them a day filled with love. I might say to myself something like, "I hope you have a wonderful day filled with loving kindness." When I'm finished, which is within seconds, I usually feel that my heart is ready to begin my day. In some mystical way that I can't explain, those few seconds stick with me for many hours. If you give this little exercise a try, I think you'll find that your day is a little more peaceful.

Excerpted from _Don't Sweat the Small Stuff...and It's All Small Stuff_ by Richard Carlson, Ph.C. Copyright © 1997 by Richard Carlson. Reprinted by permission of Hyperion Books.

3. Review "Spend a Moment, Every Day, Thinking of Someone to Love." What is important to remember?

_____

_____

_____

4. How does the author start each day?

_____

_____

_____

Fill Your Life with Love

I don't know anyone who doesn't want a life filled with love. In order for this to happen, the effort must start within us. Rather than waiting for other people to provide the love we desire, *we* must be a vision and a source of love. We must tap into our own loving-kindness in order to set an example for others to follow suit.

It has been said that "the shortest distance between two points is an intention." This is certainly true with regard to a life filled with love. The starting point or foundation of a life filled with love is the desire and commitment to be a source of love. Our attitude, choices, acts of kindness, and willingness to be the first to reach out will take us toward this goal.

The next time you find yourself frustrated at the lack of love in your own life or at the lack of love in the world, try an experiment. Forget about the world and other people for a few minutes. Instead, look into your own heart. Can you become a source of greater love? Can you think loving thoughts for yourself and others? Can you extend these loving thoughts outward toward the rest of the world–even to people who you feel don't deserve it?

By opening your heart to the possibility of greater love, and by making yourself a source of love (rather than getting love) as a top priority, you will be taking an important step in getting the love you desire. You'll also discover something truly remarkable. The more love you give, the more you will receive. As you put more emphasis on being a loving person, which is something you can control–and less emphasis on receiving love, which is something you can't control–you'll find that you have plenty of love in your life. Soon you'll discover one of the greatest secrets in the world: Love is its own reward.

5. Review "Fill Your Life With Love." What is important to remember?

_____

_____

_____

6. How can you be a source of greater love?

_____

_____

_____

Practice Random Acts of Kindness

There is a bumper sticker that has been out for some time now. You see it on cars all across the nation (in fact, I have one on my own car). It says, "Practice Random Acts of Kindness and Senseless Acts of Beauty." I have no idea who thought of this idea, but I've never seen a more important message on a car in front of me. Practicing random kindness is an effective way to get in touch with the joy of giving without expecting anything in return. It's best practiced without letting anyone know what you are doing.

There are five toll bridges in the San Francisco Bay Area. A while back, some people began paying the tolls of the cars immediately behind them. The drivers would drive to the toll window, and pull out their dollar bill, only to be informed, "Your toll has been paid by the car ahead of you." This is an example of a spontaneous, random gift, something given without expectation of or demand for anything in return. You can imagine the impact that tiny gift had on the driver of the car! Perhaps it encouraged him to be a nicer person that day. Often a single act of kindness sets a series of kind acts in motion.

There is no prescription for how to practice random kindness. It comes from the heart. Your gift might be to pick up litter in your neighborhood, make an anonymous contribution to a charity, send some cash in an unmarked envelope to make someone experiencing financial stress breathe a little easier, save an animal by bringing it to an animal rescue agency, or get a volunteer position feeding hungry people at a church or shelter. You may want to do all these things, and more. The point is, giving is fun, and it doesn't have to be expensive.

Perhaps the greatest reason to practice random kindness is that it brings great contentment into your life. Each act of kindness rewards you with positive feelings and reminds you of the important aspects of life–service, kindness, and love. If we all do our own part, pretty soon we will live in a nicer world.

7. Review "Practice Random Acts of Kindness." What is important to remember?

_____

_____

_____

Excerpted from *Don't Sweat the Small Stuff...and It's All Small Stuff* by Richard Carlson, Ph.C. Copyright © 1997 by Richard Carlson. Reprinted by permission of Hyperion Books.

8. What is the greatest reason to practice random acts of kindness?

_____

_____

_____

Reading Selections

Selection One: **"Love is Real Medicine"**

Dean Ornish

Before Reading

Before you read the story "Love Is Real Medicine" complete the following:

Predict what the topic may be.

Skim the reading to see if you have correctly predicted the topic. Look at the first and last paragraphs, and glance at the first sentences of the other paragraphs.

Think about the topic and relate what you know to "Love Is Real Medicine"

Set a purpose for reading this story. Do you expect to be entertained, to gain knowledge, or to explore an argument?

Words to Preview

strife *(n.)* conflict; struggle *(par.1)*
combing *(v.)* to search thoroughly *(par.1)*
malpractice *(n.)* improper or negligent treatment *(par.2)*
refuge *(n.)* something to which one may turn for help, relief, or escape *(par.3)*
confidants *(n.)* one who secrets or private matters are told *(par.4)*

During Reading

As you read "Love Is Real Medicine," continue to predict where the author is headed, visualize the story, and monitor your understanding. Write your comments, questions, or descriptions in the margin as you read.

Love Is Real Medicine
Loneliness Fosters Cardiovascular Disease. Fortunately, There's an Antidote

Dean Ornish, M.D.

1   People who survive a heart attack often describe it as a wake-up call. But for a 61-year-old executive I met recently, it was more than that. This man was in the midst of a divorce when he was stricken last spring, and he had fallen out of touch with friends and family members. The executive's doctor, unaware of the strife in his life, counseled him to change his diet, start exercising and quit smoking. He also prescribed drugs to lower cholesterol and blood pressure. It was sound advice, but in combing the medical literature, the patient discovered that he needed to do more. Studies suggested that his risk of dying within six months would be four times greater if he remained depressed and lonely. So he joined a support group and reordered his priorities, placing relationships at the top of the list instead of the bottom. His health has improved steadily since then, and so has his outlook on life. In fact he now describes his heart attack as the best thing that ever happened to him. "Yes, my arteries are more open," he says. "But even more important, *I'm* more open."

2   Medicine today focuses primarily on drugs and surgery, genes and germs, microbes and molecules. Yet love and intimacy are at the root of what makes us sick and what makes us well. If a new medication had the same impact, failure to prescribe it would be malpractice. Connections with other people affect not only the quality of our lives but also our survival. Study after study find that people who feel lonely are many times more likely to get cardiovascular disease than those who have a strong sense of connection and community. I'm not aware of any other factor in medicine– not diet, not smoking, not exercise, not genetics, not drugs, not surgery–that has a greater impact on our quality of life, incidence of illness and premature death.

3   In part, this is because people who are lonely are more likely to engage in self-destructive behaviors. Getting through the day becomes more important than living a long life when you have no one else to live for. As one patient told me, "I've got 20 friends in this pack of cigarettes. They're always there for me. You want to take away my 20 friends? What are you going to give me instead?" Other patients take refuge in food, alcohol or drugs: "When I feel lonely, I eat a lot of fat–it coats my nerves and numbs the pain." But loneliness is not just a barrier to fitness. Even when you eat right, exercise and avoid smoking, it increases your risk of early death.

4   Fortunately, love protects your heart in ways that we don't completely understand. In one study at Yale, men and women who felt the most loved and supported had substantially less blockage in their coronary arteries. Similarly, researchers from Case Western Reserve University studied almost 10,000 married men and found that those who answered "yes" to this simple question–"Does your wife show you her love?"–had significantly less angina (chest pain). And when researchers at Duke surveyed men and women with heart disease, those who were single and lacked confidants were three times as likely to have died after five years. In all three studies, the protective effects of love were independent of other risk factors.

Love is Real Medicine.

5   Awareness is the first step in healing. When we understand the connection between how we live and how long we live, it's easier to make different choices. Instead of viewing the time we spend with friends and family as luxuries, we can see that these relationships are among the most powerful determinants of our well-being and survival. We are hard-wired to help each other. Science is documenting the healing values of love, intimacy, community, compassion, forgiveness, altruism and service—values that are part of almost all spiritual traditions as well as many secular ones. Seen in this context, being unselfish may be the most self-serving approach to life, for it helps free both the giver and recipient from suffering, disease and premature death. Rediscovering the wisdom of love and compassion may help us survive at a time when an increasingly balkanized world so badly needs it.

Ornish, a clinical professor of medicine at the University of California, San Francisco, is founder and president of the Preventive Medicine Research Institute. His books include "Love and Survival" and "Dr. Dean Ornish's Program for Reversing Heart Disease." For more information, go to pmri.org or ornish.com.

After Reading
Connecting Meaning

1. What does the author feel is the cause of what makes us sick and what makes us well?

_____

_____

2. What effect can loneliness have on a person's health? What self-destructive behaviors are associated with being lonely?

_____

_____

3. Review and recall the author's examples of how love protects your heart.

_____

_____

_____

Love is Real Medicine.

Selection Two: **"Isn't She Lovely?"**

Brad Lemley

Before Reading

Before you read the story "Isn't She Lovely?" complete the following:

Predict what the topic may be.

Skim the reading to see if you have correctly predicted the topic. Look at the first and last paragraphs, and glance at the first sentences of the other paragraphs.

Think about the topic and relate what you know to "Isn't She Lovely?"

Set a purpose for reading this story. Do you expect to be entertained, to gain knowledge, or to explore an argument?

Words to Preview

symmetrical *(adj.)* evenly balanced *(par.1)*
morphs *(v.)* changes *(par.1)*
mesmerized *(adv.)* hypnotized *(par.1)*
ambiguous *(adj.)* uncertain, doubtful *(par.3)*
arbitrary *(adj.)* determined by chance *(par.4)*
blather *(v.)* talk nonsensically *(par.4)*
transcendence *(n.)* beyond the limits *(par.4)*
allures *(v.)* attracts with something desirable *(par.4)*
garner *(v.)* to acquire *(par.5)*
contentious *(adj.)* controversial *(par.6)*

During Reading

As you read "Isn't She Lovely" continue to predict where the author is headed, visualize the story, and monitor your understanding. Write your comments, questions, or descriptions in the margin as you read.

Isn't She Lovely?

If you think that physical appeal is strictly a matter of personal taste and cultural bias, think again. Who you find attractive, say psychobiologists, is largely dictated by evolutionary needs and hardwired into your brain.

Brad Lemley

1 She's cute, no question. Symmetrical features, flawless skin, looks to be 22 years old–entering any meat-market bar, a woman lucky enough to have this face would turn enough heads to stir a breeze. But when Victor Johnston points and clicks, the face on his computer screen morphs into what a mesmerized physicist might call a discontinuous state of superheated, crystallized beauty. "You can see it. It's just so extraordinary," says Johnston, a professor of biopsychology at New Mexico State University who sounds a little in love with his creation.

2   The transformation from pretty woman to knee-weakening babe is all the more amazing because the changes wrought by Johnston's software are, objectively speaking, quite subtle. He created the original face by digitally averaging 16 randomly selected female Caucasian faces. The morphing program then exaggerated the ways in which female faces differ from male faces, creating, in human-beauty-science parlance, a "hyperfemale." The eyes grew a bit larger, the nose narrowed slightly, the lips plumped, and the jaw contracted. These are shifts of just a few millimeters, but experiments in this country and Scotland are suggesting that both males and females find "feminized" versions of averaged faces more beautiful.

3   Johnston hatched this little movie as part of his ongoing study into why human beings find some people attractive and others homely. He may not have any rock-solid answers yet, but he is far from alone in attempting to apply scientific inquiry to so ambiguous a subject. Around the world, researchers are marching into territory formerly staked out by poets, painters, fashion mavens, and casting directors, aiming to uncover the underpinnings of human attractiveness.

4   The research results so far are surprising–and humbling. Numerous studies indicate that human beauty may not be simply in the eye of the beholder or an arbitrary cultural artifact. It may be an ancient, hardwired, universal, and potent behavior-driver, on a par with hunger or pain, wrought through eons of evolution that rewarded reproductive winners and killed off losers. If beauty is not truth, it may be health and fertility: Halle Berry's flawless skin may rivet moviegoers because, at some deep level, it persuades us that she is parasite-free and consequently good mating material. Acquired, individual preferences factor in, but research increasingly indicates that their influence is much smaller than many of us would care to know. While romantic writers blather about the transcendence of beauty, Elizabethan poet Edmund Spenser more than 400 years ago pegged the emerging scientific thesis: "Beauty is the bait which with delight allures man to enlarge his kind."

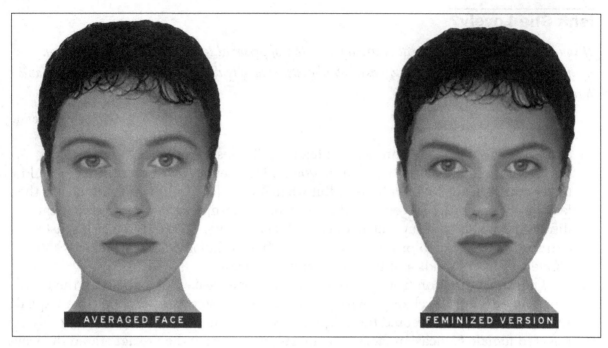

AVERAGED FACE   FEMINIZED VERSION

Courtesy Victor Johnston

Biosycholologist Johnston creates the face on the left by digitally morphing 16 female Caucasian faces. Then he warped it by subtly exaggerating the ways in which female faces differ from males faces, making the brows more arched, the eyes bigger, the nose and jaw narrower, and the lips fuller. Both male and female students judged the resulting face, right, as more attractive. In Johnston's view, the experiment confirms that the hyperfemale embodies even more allure because of her promise of extraordinary fertility.

5   Implications of human-beauty research range from the practical–providing cosmetic surgeons with pretty-people templates–to the political and philosophical. Landmarkstudies show that attractive males and females not only garner more attention from the opposite sex, they also get more affection from their mothers, more money at work, more votes from the electorate, more leniency from judges, and are generally regarded as more kind, competent, healthy, confident, and intelligent than their big-nosed, weak-chinned counterparts. (Beauty is considered such a valuable trait by some that one entrepreneur recently put up a Web site offering to auction off the unfertilized ova of models.)

6 Human attractiveness research is a relatively young and certainly contentious field– the allure of hyperfemales, for example, is still hotly debated–but those on its front lines agree on one point: We won't conquer "looks-ism" until we understand its source. As psychologist Nancy Etcoff, author of the 1999 book *Survival of the Prettiest*, puts it: "The idea that beauty is unimportant or a cultural construct is the real beauty myth. We have to understand beauty, or we will always be enslaved by it."

———————————————————————————————————————**Stop here**

7 The modern era of beauty studies got a big push 20 years ago with an awkward question in a small, airless room at Louisiana State University in Baton Rouge. Psychology graduate student Judith Langlois was defending her doctoral dissertation—a study of how preschool children form and keep friendships—when a professor asked whether she had factored the kids' facial attractiveness into her conclusions. "I thought the question was way off the mark," she recalls. "It might matter for college students, but little kids?" After stammering out a noncommittal answer—and passing the examination—she resolved to dig deeper, aiming to determine the age at which human beings could perceive physical attractiveness.

8 Langlois, who had joined the faculty at the University of Texas at Austin, devised a series of experiments. In one, she had adults rate photos of human faces on a spectrum from attractive to unattractive. Then she projected pairs of high- and low-rated faces in front of 6-month-old infants. "The result was straightforward and unambiguous," she declares. "The babies looked longer at the attractive faces, regardless of the gender, race, or age of the face." Studies with babies as young as 2 months old yielded similar results. "At 2 months, these babies hadn't been reading Vogue magazine," Langlois observes dryly.

9 Her search for the source of babies' precocious beauty-detection led her all the way back to nineteenth-century research conducted by Sir Francis Galton, an English dilettante scientist and cousin of Charles Darwin. In the late 1870s, Galton created crude, blurry composite faces by melding mug-shot photographs of various social subgroups, aiming to prove that each group had an archetypal face. While that hypothesis fizzled—the average criminal looked rather like the average vegetarian—Galton was shocked to discover that these averaged faces were better looking than nearly all of the individuals they comprised. Langlois replicated Galton's study, using software to form digitally averaged faces that were later judged by 300 people to be more attractive than most of the faces used to create them.

10 Human beings may be born "cognitive averagers," theorizes Langlois. "Even very young infants have seen thousands of faces and may have already constructed an average from them that they use for comparison."

11 Racial preferences bolster the idea, say some scientists. History shows that almost universally when one race first comes into contact with another, they mutually regard each other as homely, if not freakish. Etcoff relates that a delegation of Japanese samurai visiting the United States in 1860 observed that Western women had "dogs' eyes," which they found "disheartening." Early Western visitors to Japan thought the natives' epicanthic folds made the eyes appear sleepy and small. In each case, Etcoff surmises, the unfamiliar race most likely veered from the internal, averaged ideal.

12 But why would cognitive averaging have evolved? Evolutionary biology holds that in any given population, extreme characteristics tend to fall away in favor of average ones. Birds with unusually long or short wings die more often in storms. Human babies who are born larger or smaller than average are less likely to survive. The ability to form an average-mate template would have conveyed a singular survival advantage.

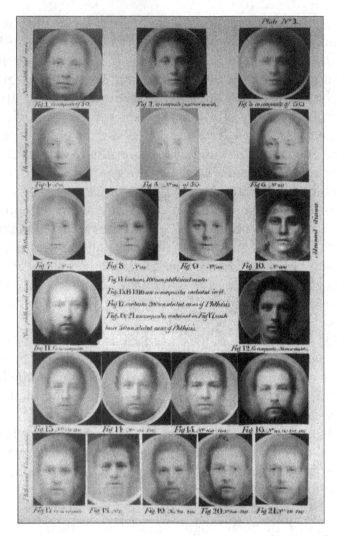

Francis Galton figured that photographically melding the faces of criminals, consumptives, and so on would yield an archetypal image for each group. But, he concluded, the resulting faces were not categorically unique. He also observed that these averaged faces were surprisingly better looking than most of humanity.

13   Inclination toward the average is called koinophilia, from the Greek words koinos, meaning "usual," and philos, meaning "love." To Langlois, humans are clearly koinophiles. The remaining question is whether our good-mate template is acquired or innate. To help solve the mystery, Langlois's doctoral student Lisa Kalakanis has presented babies who are just 15 minutes old with paired images of attractive and homely faces. "We're just starting to evaluate that data," says Langlois.

14   But koinophilia isn't the only—or even supreme—criterion for beauty that evolution has promoted, other scientists argue. An innate yearning for symmetry is a major boon, contend biologists Anders Moller and Randy Thornhill, as asymmetry

can signal malnutrition, disease, or bad genes. The two have found that asymmetrical animals, ranging from barn swallows to lions, have fewer offspring and shorter lives. Evolution would also logically instill an age preference. Human female fertility peaks in the early 20s, and so do assessments of female attractiveness. Between 1953 and 1990, the average age of Playboy centerfold models—who are presumably selected solely for sexual appeal—was 21.3 years. Similarly, Johnston has found that the beauty of a Japanese female face is judged to be at its peak when its perceived age is 22.4 years. Because men are fertile throughout most of their adult lives, their attractiveness ratings—while dropping as they age past their late 20s—remain relatively higher as their perceived age increases. As Johnston puts it, "Our feelings of beauty are exceptionally well tuned to the age of maximum fertility."

15   Still, a species can stagnate without some novelty. When competition for mates is intense, some extreme traits might help to rivet a roving eye. "A male peacock is saying, 'Look at me, I have this big tail. I couldn't grow a tail this big if I had parasites,'" says Johnston. "Even if the trait is detrimental to survival, the benefit in additional offspring brought about by attracting females can more than compensate for the decrease in longevity." The concept seems applicable to humans, too, because it helps to resolve a nagging flaw in average-face studies. In many of them, "there were always a few individual faces in the population that were deemed even prettier than the average," says Etcoff. "If average were always best, how could that be?"

16   Psychologist David Perrett of the University of St. Andrews in Scotland aimed to find out by creating two averaged faces—one from a group of women rated attractive and another from men so judged. He then compared those faces with averaged faces constructed from a larger, random set of images. The composites of the beautiful people were rated more appealing than those made from the larger, random population. More surprising, when Perrett exaggerated the ways in which the prettiest female composite differed from the average female composite, the resulting face was judged to be even more attractive.

17   "It turned out that the way an attractive female face differs from an average one is related to femininity," says Perrett. "For example, female eyebrows are more arched

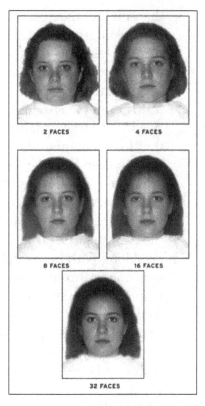

Courtesy Judith Langlois

Is deviation from the average more appealing than just plain averageness? Definitely not, declares researcher Judith Langlois. Indeed, she argues, the more faces you mate together, the more beautiful the image becomes because it literally becomes more average. "Averaging two faces is not enough to make an attractive face," she says. "But when you get up to 32 faces, you end up with a face that is pretty darned attractive." As proof of her premise, she offers the above series of composite faces.

than males'. Exaggerating that difference from the average increases femininity," and, in tandem, the attractiveness rating. In the traffic-stopping female face created for this experiment, 200 facial reference points all changed in the direction of hyperfemininity: larger eyes, a smaller nose, plumper lips, a narrower jaw, and a smaller chin.

18   "All faces go through a metamorphosis at puberty," observes Johnston. "In males, testosterone lengthens the jaw. In females, estrogen makes the hips, breasts, and lips swell." So large lips, breasts, and hips combined with a small jaw "are all telling you that I have an abundant supply of estrogen, so I am a fertile female." Like the peacock, whose huge tail is a mating advantage but a practical hindrance, "a small jaw may not, in fact, be as efficient for eating," Johnston says. But it seems attractive because it emphasizes la difference; whatever survival disadvantage comes along with a small jaw is more than made up for by the chance to produce more babies, so the trait succeeds.

19   Along with his morphing program, Johnston approached the hyperfemale hypothesis through another route. Starting with 16 computer-generated random female Caucasian faces, he had visitors to his Web site rate the attractiveness of each face on a scale of one to nine. A second generation of faces was then computed by selecting, crossing, and mutating the first generation in proportion to beauty ratings. After 10,000 people from around the world took part in this merciless business, the empirically derived fairest-of-them-all was born. Facial measurements confirm that she is decidedly hyperfemale. While we might say she is beautiful, Johnston more accurately notes that the face displays "maximum fertility cues."

20   Johnston's findings have set off a ruckus among beauty scientists. In a paper titled "Attractive Faces Really Are Only Average," Langlois and three other researchers blast the notion that a deviation from the average—what they term "facial extremes"— explains attractiveness better than averageness does. The findings of Perrett and his team, she says, are "artifacts of their methodology," because they used a "forced-choice" scenario that prevented subjects from judging faces as equally attractive. "We did the same kind of test, but gave people a rating scale of one to five," says Langlois. "When you do it that way, there is no significant difference—people would tell us that, basically, the two faces looked like twins." Langlois argues that if extremes create beauty, "then people with micro-jaws or hydrocephalic eyes would be seen as the most beautiful, when, in fact, eyes that are too big for a head make that head unattractive."

As the world becomes more egalitarian, beauty becomes more inclusive

21   But for Etcoff, circumstantial evidence for the allure of some degree of hyperfemininity is substantial. "Female makeup is all about exaggerating the feminine. Eye makeup makes the brow thinner, which makes it look farther from the eye," which, she says, is a classic difference between male and female faces. From high hair (which skews facial proportions in a feminine direction, moving up the center of gravity) to collagen in lips to silicone in breasts, women instinctively exaggerate secondary female sex characteristics to increase their allure. "Langlois is simply wrong," declares Johnston. In one of his studies, published last year in

Reprinted with permission from *Discover* magazine, February 2000, pp. 43–49. © 2000 by The Walt Disney Company.

Psychophysiology, both male and female subjects rated feminized pictures as more attractive. Further, male subjects attached to electrical brain- activity monitors showed a greater response in the P3 component, a measure of emotional intensity. "That is, although both sexes know what is attractive, only the males exhibit an emotional response to the feminized picture," Johnston says.

22   And what about male attractiveness? IT stands to reason that if men salivate for hyperfemales, women should pursue hypermales—that is, men whose features exaggerate the ways in which male faces differ from female ones. Even when adjusted for differing overall body size, the average male face has a more pronounced brow ridge, more sunken eyes, and bushier brows that are set closer to the eyes. The nose and mouth are wider, the lower jaw is wider and longer. Ramp up these features beyond the norm, and you've got a hunk, right?

23   There's no question that a dose of this classic "maleness" does contribute to what is now called handsome. Actor Brad Pitt, widely regarded as a modern paradigm of male attractiveness, is a wide-jaw guy. Biologically speaking, he subconsciously persuades a female that he could chew more nutrients out of a leafy stalk than the average potential father of her children—a handy trait, in hunter-gatherer days anyway, to pass on to progeny.

24   But a woman's agenda in seeking a mate is considerably more complex than simply whelping strong-jawed kids. While both men and women desire healthy, fertile mates, a man can—and, to some extent, is biologically driven to—procreate with as many women as possible. Conversely, a woman "thinks about the long haul," notes Etcoff. "Much of mate choice is about finding a helpmate to bring up the baby." In several studies, women presented with the hypermale face (the "Neanderthal type" as Etcoff puts it) judged its owner to be uncaring, aggressive, and unlikely to be a good father.

25   Female preferences in male faces oscillate in tandem with the menstrual cycle, suggests a study conducted by Perrett and Japanese researchers and published last June in Nature. When a woman is ovulating, she tends to prefer men with more masculine features; at less fertile times in her monthly cycle, she favors male faces with a softer, more feminine look. But amid the hoopla that this widely publicized finding generated, a critical fact was often overlooked. Even the "more masculine" face preferred by the ovulating women was 8 percent feminized from the male average (the less masculine face was 15 to 20 percent feminized). According to Perrett's study, even an averagely masculine face is too male for comfort.

26   To further complicate the male-appeal picture, research indicates that, across the board in mating species, an ugly guy can make up ground with status and/or wealth. Etcoff notes that female scorpion flies won't even look at a male unless his gift—a tasty bit of insect protein—is at least 16 square millimeters wide. The human situation isn't all that different. Anthropologist John Marshall Townsend showed photos of beautiful and homely people to men and women, and described the people in the photos as being in training for either low-, medium-, or high-paying positions—waiter, teacher, or doctor. "Not surprisingly, women preferred the best-looking man

with the most money," Etcoff writes, "but below him, average-looking or even unattractive doctors received the same ratings as very attractive teachers. This was not true when men evaluated women. Unattractive women were not preferred, no matter what their status."

27   It's all a bit bleak. Talk to enough psychobiologists, and you get the impression that we are all rats–reflexively, unconsciously coupling according to obscure but immutable circuitry. But beauty researchers agree that, along with natural selection and sexual selection, learned behaviors are at least part of the attractiveness radar. In other words, there is room for individuality–perhaps even a smattering of mystery–in this business of attraction between humans.

After Reading
Connecting Meaning

1. Using a software program, Johnston changed the look of an "ideal" female face. Describe the look of a "hyperfemale."

   _____

   _____

2. According to this article, is what you find attractive in a woman a matter of personal taste or hardwired into your brain as part of human evolution? Do you agree with the authors?

   _____

   _____

   _____

   _____

3. Review and recall the details of studies that show the positive effects of being attractive.

   _____

   _____

   _____

   _____

Selection Three: **"She's Out There"**

Kyle Western

Before Reading

Before you read the story "She's Out There" complete the following:

Predict what the topic may be.

Skim the reading to see if you have correctly predicted the topic. Look at the first and last paragraphs, and glance at the first sentences of the other paragraphs.

Think about the topic and relate what you know to "She's Out There."

Set a purpose for reading this story. Do you expect to be entertained, to gain knowledge, or to explore an argument?

Words to Preview

filaments *(n.)* evenly balanced *(par.1)*
onus *(v.)* changes *(par.6)*
mustering *(adv.)* hypnotized *(par.12)*
detrimental *(adj.)* uncertain, doubtful *(par.13)*
altruism *(adj.)* determined by chance *(par.20)*
embedded *(v.)* talk nonsensically *(par.25)*
plummets *(n.)* beyond the limits *(par.25)*
trajectory *(v.)* attracts with something desirable *(par.26)*
ambience *(v.)* to acquire *(par.28)*
inquisitiveness *(adj.)* controversial *(par.28)*
conviviality *(adj.)* *(par.39)*

During Reading

As you read "She's Out There," continue to predict where the author is headed, visualize the story, and monitor your understanding. Write your comments, questions, or descriptions in the margin as you read.

She's Out There

Kyle Western

1 Will you meet her?

2   In times of economic distress, women seek emotional safe havens. Here are 13 places—and reasons—she's looking for you.

3   The saddest thing you will ever see in a bar is the lights on at closing time. It's the moment you realize that although you've been bankrolling her martinis since midnight, she won't be going home with you. And why should she? You're a stranger, and this is just a game. When the filaments flicker on, the fantasy ends.

4   "Men are possessed by the myth of the pickup," says David Grazian, Ph.D., an associate professor of sociology at the University of Pennsylvania and the author of *On the Make: The Hustle of Urban Nightlife*. It's in their heads that these bars and clubs are "teeming with anonymous females who are dying to have sex with any guy who is confident enough to talk to them." The reality is that less than 6 percent of women report having had sex with their partners within two days or less of meeting them, and less than 20 percent of adults say they first met their most recent sexual partner in a bar. Perhaps it's the nasty stigma of nightlife: A survey of 1,034 women by StrategyOne, a market research agency, reveals that nearly one in four women would be embarrassed to admit that she met a mate in a bar.

5   So why does the alcohol-soaked pickup scene still exist? Aside from the obvious reasons (tequila, vodka, rum), there's a surprising one as well: inexperience. Men are new to this 21st-century version of the boy-meets-girl game. In 1970, the median age for marriage was 23 for men and 21 for women. Today it's 28 and 26. "It used to be that people felt they'd somehow missed out if they didn't have a spouse by the time they graduated college," says David Popenoe, Ph.D., founder and codirector of the National Marriage Project and a professor emeritus of sociology at Rutgers University. "Today, people feel they need to establish themselves economically first." The postponement of "I do" means most men will be single in their 20s, a trend that populates the bar scene and empties the church aisles.

6   The real world of dating is rough on men. The risk and onus of rejection are almost always on them, because men initiate about 80 percent of encounters. And the competition is brutal for men in their 20s and 30s: For every 100 unmarried women there's an average of 113 unmarried men, according to the U.S. Census Bureau. And those men just aren't doing the job. The Pew Research Center found that about half of young singles reported going on no more than one date in the three months prior to its survey, and 55 percent of singles who were looking for love said it was hard to meet people.

7   But the situation doesn't have to be that bleak. In fact, there's no better time to be single than during an economic recession. A recent eHarmony survey found that one in four single women say that financial stress has increased their interest in a relationship. Compare that with the 61 percent of men who say money worries are causing stress in their love lives. Look at it this way: More women are on the

market, and they're primed to connect. But men are looking to meet them over $12 martinis—and are going home alone and broke. There's an opening here for you: Think patterns, not people. Forget the pickup lines and rely on the new rules of attraction. We can help you with the odds.

RULE 1 Build Your Romantic Network

8 You're 227 percent more likely to meet a potential girlfriend through a friend or family member rather than in a bar, at the gym, or on the street.

9   Malcolm Parks, Ph.D., knows the secret to meeting women: Don't.

10   Instead, meet people.

11   Parks, a University of Washington communication researcher and author of *Personal Relationships & Personal Networks*, has determined that 75 percent of the people who dated extensively the year before said they had help from a friend. In their corner is what Parks calls "the social proximity effect," which holds that the probability of two people meeting is directly proportional to the number of contacts they share. In other words, more friends means more female referrals. "Our research has shown that two-thirds of people who initiate a romantic relationship had met at least one of the dozen or so members of their partner's closest social network prior to meeting their partner for the first time," says Parks, "and nearly half had met two or three." If you know Tom, and Tom knows Betty, then there's a greater chance you'll meet Betty. And if Tom also knows Susan, Heather, and Kimberly . . . well, then you owe Tom a fruit basket.

12   The potential is there, but the problem is that most men's social networks are too small or too stale to be effective. The average guy would have difficulty mustering enough friends to round out a Fave 5, according to a 2006 survey in the American Sociological Review. In fact, our close social networks have shrunk by almost a third since 1985.

13   But it's not just the friend famine that's starving our sex lives. Socially inbred crews are detrimental, too. "In a tightly knit group, you know the same people," says Parks. "Your friends can't introduce you to women you don't already know." That's why access to a new resource, whether it's an unadvertised job opening, a lead on a house listing, or an introduction to a woman you might click with, is more likely to come through casual friends than close ones. It's what social network theorists call "the strength of weak ties," and the greater the number of unique casual connections you have, the better positioned you are to benefit. These types of people are essentially network bridges, says Parks.

14   They connect you to women you might not otherwise have met through your close friends. The secret isn't blind dates and setups; it's party invites and casual introductions.

15   The beauty of forging weak ties is that while others hunt, you gather. To be successful, you need to continually meet new people outside your existing circles in

order to find quantity and diversity in new links. All connections have potential. For example, you may have written off the guy with a wife or live-in girlfriend, but he's the money ball. According to a 2003 study in Social Networks, dating couples share 20 percent to 25 percent of their friends, but that percentage increases to 50 when they start living together. The result: His network is likely to be populated with more women after he moves in with her.

16   We'll supply the fertile meeting grounds. You find the equivalents in your town, and the potential mates who gather there.

Weak-Tie Strongholds

Dallas Sport and Social Club Coed Kickball

17 Team play encourages what sociologists call "situational generalization"—in other words, positive circumstances help people click. "When people are working toward a shared outcome, they're more likely to grow closer together," says Parks. Recreational outfits make it easy to form new connections because individuals can sign up and be assigned to a team without needing to know anyone.

ImprovBoston Theatre Performance Classes

18 Sharing a funny experience can help reduce tension among strangers, according to a 2004 study in Personal Relationships. And improv class will sharpen communications with everyone you encounter.

Durham Bulls Athletic Park (Durham, NC)

19 For the cost of a Yankees ticket (or less), you and your friends can each grab a multigaine package featuring up to 13 MLB minor-league affiliates. Rooting for team sports can boost testosterone levels—yours as well as hers. And T is the libido hormone, so if your team wins, you both win. Try this: Split the cost of an extra package with your friends, and then take turns inviting someone new. It'll expand your weak ties, and the presence of friends creates a "celebrity effect" that can be as desirable as attractiveness or wealth.

Meetup Volunteer Groups

20 Selflessness is sexy. A 2008 study published in the *British Journal of Psychology* showed that women consider altruism more important in a mate than men do. To show your selless stuff, try joining a Meetup volunteer group (volunteerism.meetup.com). This network serves a variety of causes, allows you to select groups with members who share your interests, and lets you see who has signed up for which projects.

RULE 2 Let Chaos Be Your Wingman

21 Less than 1 percent of women say they met their current partner because they were neighbors, compared with 22 percent of women who say their man is from a different part of town.

22   When a team of two physicists and a human-network scientist tells you your life is bland, you know you're in trouble.

23   Northeastern University researchers took their dig in a 2008 study in the journal *Nature*, after they tracked the movements of 100,000 cellphone users for six months. Their finding: People are predictable. Nearly half of their human lab rats kept to a maze that was little more than 6 miles wide, and 83 percent mostly stayed within a 37-mile radius. And they tended to spend the majority of their time in five or fewer places.

24   The result: dating pools the size of shot glasses.

25   In the United States, there's an average of only seven single women between the ages of 20 and 44 per square mile. Now consider your "spots," the places you usually go despite the presence of equivalent alternatives: your Starbucks, your bank branch, your dry cleaner, your gym, your grocery store. These are embedded destinations in other people's travel itineraries, too, meaning they're also their "spots." If everyone repeats routines, as the Northeastern University research suggests, the rate at which you encounter new women plummets.

26   If you stick to a 6-mile orbit, your romantic trajectory is stunted as well. "In the stock market, diversification is critical to reducing risk," says Amir Aczel, Ph.D., a former professor of mathematics and statistics at Bentley University near Boston and author of *Chance*. "In dating, the same rule applies. You should vary the places you go, and when you go there. This diversification will result in increased probability of meeting women who respond well to you."

27   Consider these tweaks to your routine.

Chaos Corners

Santa Monica Farmers' Market

28 Bust out of supermarket hell to join the communal ambience of a farmers' market, where you can tap into a spirit of sociability, exploration, and inquisitiveness. Engage her over the Asian pears, and she'll thank you for the rest of her life. To find a market near you, go to localharvest.org.

Annual Editions

Yelp

29 Yelp.com's 5 million local reviews can lead you to a dry cleaner, cafe, barbershop, or bookstore where all the cool people go. Post your own reviews and you may meet a

fellow critic. The social-networking functions of the site allow readers to swap private messages, post public comments, and classify deserving reviews as funny, useful, or cool, so you can navigate them accordingly.

Waterloo Records (Austin, Texas)

30 Research suggests that people are more attracted to potential partners who share their musical tastes. Itunes has revolutionized the music landscape, but for many passionate music lovers, it can't replace the places like Waterloo and the 700 other independent record stores across the country. Go to recordstoreday.com to find a shop near you.

Ikea

31 Researchers note that shopping trips are fueled by social motives, including the desire for new communal experiences. Big-box stores are socially fertile: More than 10 million people pass through Ikea every week, and U.S. consumers spend an average of 2 to 3 hours each visit. And at Ikea, traffic moves one way, creating a natural movement and pacing that makes it easy to stroll and engage. Think about store or mall flow the next time you're shopping, and patronize spots, like the Apple store, that make kibitzing part of the experience. If you're the active type, L.L. Bean or REI might be a better bet.

RULE 3 Use Spare Time as Showtime

32 Approximately one-fifth of couples first met in public places. But as available free time plummets, you may not get out enough.

33   You're just about as likely to meet a woman during Sunday service at church as you are during "Sexy Saturday" at a club. The takeaway isn't that you need to find God to find a woman. You simply need to be with people, wherever they may gather.

34   Your time to do that is shrinking, according to a 2008 Harris Interactive poll. Americans have just 16 hours a week–down 20 percent from 2007–that are all theirs. With leisure time scarce, many men make the mistake of blocking off a weekend night for dating, says Paul Dobransky, M.D., a Chicago psychiatrist and the director of DoctorPaul.net. "Their lack of success is due to their hyperfocused approach," says Dr. Dobransky. "They see meeting women as something that is done rather than something that naturally happens, which is the way women view it."

35   The single women are waiting, but they're not doing it in front of an LCD screen, where you're more likely to be most nights. On any given day, more women attend or host social events, volunteer, join religious functions, practice hobbies, or go shopping, while the average single guy is home, pathetically alone. Compared with

single women, single men spend 45 minutes more a day watching TV and about 20 minutes more on the computer.

36   It's a surprisingly detrimental decision. A 2008 study in Social Indicators Research reveals that unhappy people watch 30 percent more TV every day than very happy people. "It's possible that TV causes people to be unhappy because it pushes aside time for activities with long-term benefits," says study author John Robinson, Ph.D., a professor of sociology at the University of Maryland and director of the Americans' Use of Time Project. "Or TV viewing is an outlet for people who are already unhappy."

37   Whatever the case, the consequences are clear: If you shut down socially during the week, you're severely undermining your efforts and personal satisfaction. You'll have more success with women if you aim to collect experiences rather than phone numbers. Consider these connection points.

Showtime Showcases

First Fridays at the Natural History Museum of Los Angeles County

38 In a 2008 University of Iowa survey, women ranked a man's intelligence and education higher than his good looks and financial prospects. On the first Friday of the month, stuffy cultural mainstays unbutton their starched shirts a bit, offering gallery tours, cocktails, hors d'oeuvres, and music.

Movies in the Parks (Chicago)

39 In the summer, the park district invites citizens to pull up a blanket and watch movies. The air is warm with conviviality. Many cities offer similar programs. If yours doesn't, volunteer to start one and meet artsy types and wealthy sponsors as you set it up.

Mile High Music Festival

40 "The rhythmic pulse of music lets listeners synchronize with one another, which can increase group cohesion," says Michael Cunningham, Ph.D., a psychologist and professor of communication at the University of Louisville. Concerts are good, but music festivals attract a more diverse crowd because of the different acts and transcend the behavioral norms of everyday life. Visit festivalfinder.com for events near you.

Philadelphia Punk Rock Flea Market

41 Odd? Sure, and that's the point. If you want to meet interesting people, you need to do interesting things.

Bank of America Chicago Marathon

42 No, she's not waiting for you at mile marker 19. The real appeal here is the free training program held several days a week. Studies show that when we anticipate future experiences with someone, we focus on that person's positive qualities to better ensure that those upcoming experiences will be pleasant ones. Go to marathonguide.com for a list of races near you. No training program? Join a local running club.

After Reading
Connecting Meaning

1. List the three rules for men can follow to increase their odds of connecting with a woman.

   _____

   _____

   _____

   _____

2. Describe the "social proximity effect" from Rule One.

   _____

   _____

   _____

3. Review and recall some of the places that may be used to find a date.

   _____

   _____

   _____

   _____

4. Based on the suggestions given in the article, what do you think are the best places to meet someone? What do you think are the worst places? Why?

_____

_____

_____

_____

Portfolio Activities

Integrating Ideas

The selections you have read deal with ideas of love and attractiveness. Describe your ideal of attractiveness. How does it compare to the selections you read? Reflect on these ideas in writing or in class discussion.

Collaborative Activity

Local newspapers contain advice columns that deal with relationships. Each group will choose several letters dealing with love and its problems. Discuss the problem without reading the columnist's reply. The group will draft their own reply in letter form. Compare the group's response to the columnist's response.

Additional Portfolio Suggestion

The more you read, the more comfortable you will be with the reading process. There are many books dealing with the topic of love. Choose one to read that interests you and write a book review. A book review should include a brief summary of the book, your opinion of the book, and why you hold this opinion. Would you recommend the book to others?

Chapter Summary Graphic Organizer

Complete the steps that explain the After Reading process.

After Reading

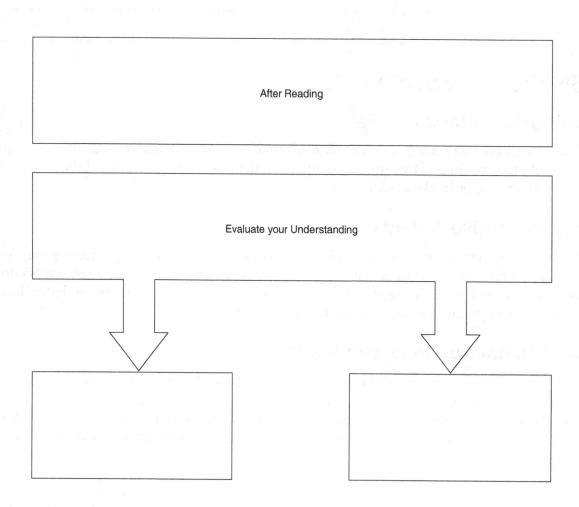

The Reading Process

In this unit, you examined reading as a three step process. By using *before, during,* and *after reading* strategies you are better able to construct meaning from what you read. Your active involvement in this process includes the following strategies.

Before Reading

Preview the reading.

- Read the title.
- Make a prediction about the topic.
- Skim the story.

Connect your knowledge to the author's ideas.

- Think about what you know about the topic.

Establish a purpose for reading.

- Do you expect to be entertained, gain knowledge, or explore an argument?

During Reading

Predict as you read.

- Confirm predictions.

Visualize the story.

- Create mental pictures.

Monitor your comprehension.

- Does this make sense?
- Have a mental conversation about the reading.
- Has your comprehension broken down?
- If so, stop and reread.

After Reading

Evaluate your understanding.

- Review the story.
- Did I meet my purpose for reading?
- Did I understand what I just read?
- Were there any confusing parts?
- Can I relate the information to my knowledge or experience?

Recall.

- What is important to remember?

Unit Review Graphic Organizer

Complete the steps that explain the Reading Process.

The Reading Process

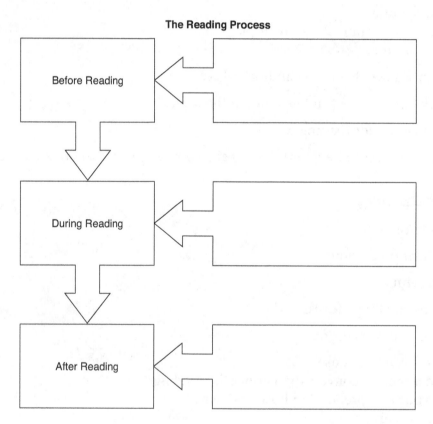

Portfolio Suggestion

Responding to reading in a variety of ways helps you to think critically about what you are reading. A reader response journal is an important way of evaluating your understanding and connecting reading and writing. In a reader response journal, you go beyond writing a simple summary of what you are reading.

- What did you find to be interesting or thought provoking?
- What experiences have you had that you can relate to what you are reading?
- What is your opinion of the reading or the author?
- Can you make a prediction about the story?

You may include any other thoughts about your reading. Other possibilities for reader responses are found in Appendix C.

Want to Know More?

If you are interested in knowing more about relationships, the following books and websites further explore this theme. You can find these books at your local library to read more about relationships or use the internet and check out the websites.

Books

Buscaglia, Leo F. *Living, Loving, and Learning.* New York: Fawcett Books, 1990.

This book is an inspirational treasure for all those eager to accept the challenge of life and to profit from the wonder of love.

Davis, Sampson, George Jenkins, Rameck Hunt, and Lisa Frazier Page. *The Pact.* New York: Riverhead Books, 2002.

Bill Cosby states the following about this book, "Through the strength of their friendship, together these three young men defied the odds. They are an inspiration to young people everywhere, and their message is on that can transform the world."

Giovanni, Nikki. *Selected Poems of Nikki Giovanni.* New York: Wm. Morrow and Company, 1996.

Giovanni has always been first and foremost a lover, and this is a collection of her love in the affirmative musical language of her Black womanhood.

Websites

www.ellisisland.org If any of your family immigrated to the United States in the early 1900s, you may find information about them. The website includes photos of ships, lists of passengers with their ages and original hometowns.

www.marsvenus.com Dr. John Gray wrote a book called, *Men are from Mars, Women are from Venus.* This website talks about his current books and his insights on relationship problems.

www.drphil.com Dr. Phil McGraw provides enlightening information on how to "get real" in relationships and in life. His trademark is his "tell-it-like-it-is" style.

Vocabulary

Theme of Readings: Heroism

"A hero is no braver than an ordinary man, but he is braver five minutes longer."

RALPH WALDO EMERSON

Heroism

For centuries, the concept of heroism applied only to figures of mythology and legend. In Greek and Roman mythology, for example, Hercules was a man of divine ancestry, who showed courage, strength, and boldness. Other cultures have similar "larger than life" figures whose stories were often retold to teach values, create a group identity, and entertain listeners.

As time passed, the need for these stories was still important, but the concept of heroism was extended to real people. George Washington fought for his country, shared the hardships of Valley Forge with his men, and chose becoming president instead of king. He was admired for honesty, courage, leadership, and compassion and came to be viewed as an American hero. Similarly, Charles Lindbergh was called a hero for being the first person to fly across the Atlantic Ocean by himself, and Rosa Parks was hailed for standing her ground against segregation on buses. In all these cases heroes had courage, goals, beliefs, and willingness to make personal sacrifices for what is important.

Heroes are found among family, friends, teachers, and neighbors. A passing motorist pulls an accident victim from a burning car. A twelve-year-old girl saves her little brother from drowning in the local lake. An ordinary person put to a test may accomplish an extraordinary feat. Whoever they may be, heroes will continue to inspire us.

Vocabulary Strategies

The ordinary feat of reading may at times seem extraordinarily difficult if you are not familiar with the words used by an author. You may have ignored a word rather than dust off the dictionary. Sometimes, you feel you know the word but can not clearly express its meaning. Without a clear understanding of the words, you are unable to grasp an author's concepts. Increasing your vocabulary will expand your knowledge and improve your reading.

To improve your vocabulary, you can use a variety of strategies. Through context clues, some sentences will provide enough information to allow you to figure out a word's meaning. The general sense of the reading may also help you to predict the definition of a word. Your knowledge of word parts, roots, prefixes, and suffixes, can be applied to unknown words. No one method will help you learn the meaning of every word, but together these strategies will help you increase your vocabulary.

To help you remember new words, you will want to try recording their meanings in several ways. Graphic organizers (diagrams of words) show definitions, related terms, examples, and concepts. They create a picture of a particular term that will help you to visualize the meaning. Word cards may also be used if they include more than a definition.

These vocabulary strategies reflect the activities that make you an effective reader. You will predict, visualize, and monitor your understanding of words as you apply these strategies to construct meaning for the entire selection.

Unit Objective

At the completion of this unit, you will be able to understand multiple strategies to increase vocabulary knowledge.

Chapter 4

Vocabulary Strategies

Theme of Readings: Contemporary Heroes

"There lives in each of us a hero awaiting the call to action."

H. JACKSON BROWN, JR.

Contemporary Heroes

Contemporary heroes come from all walks of life. They are men and women who have answered their own personal call to action. The stories in this chapter are about heroes both widely proclaimed by the media and virtually unknown.

As part of the Mercury 7 program, John Glenn was among the first group of American astronauts to enter outer space. In 1962, he became the first American to orbit the Earth. He went on to a successful career in government and politics. In 1998, at the age of 77, he braved the dangers of space again and became America's oldest astronaut.

Some heroes may be your neighbor, your friend or someone you have never met. When faced with a life threatening situation such as a burning car, someone may place themselves in harm's way in order to help another. Often they do not see themselves as heroes, only a person who did what was necessary to save a life, even if it meant risking their own life. For those they saved, the people who stepped up to help will forever be heroes.

Heroes do not always come in the two-legged form. After the collapse of the World Trade Center on September 11, 2001, search and rescue dogs were an integral part of the hundreds of volunteers combing the wreckage. Their efforts aided both the rescue and recovery effort.

Under different circumstances, each of these heroes answered a "call to action." They represent only a few of the contemporary heroes who may inspire you to do the same.

Chapter Objectives

After completing this chapter, you will be able to:

1. Use context clues to define a word.

2. Use word parts to construct word meaning.

3. Create graphic organizers to improve vocabulary knowledge.

Focus on Vocabulary Strategies

Vocabulary in Context

When you open a jigsaw puzzle box, a thousand individual pieces wait to be assembled into one scene. Hold up a piece of the puzzle and you can not recognize the finished picture. To help you to figure out where the piece fits, you use clues, such as the shape and color of the piece, the picture on the box, and your own sense of how to put the puzzle together. As you find surrounding pieces, the picture begins to emerge.

When you open a book, you see a thousand different words. It is only when you put these words together while reading that they make sense. Sometimes a word is unfamiliar to you but you can use clues found in the context–the surrounding words, ideas, and punctuation–to understand the meaning of the word.

Using the context clues of definition, explanation, example or illustration, logic, and contrast will help you to give meaning to unfamiliar words. Following are examples of these clues.

Definition/Synonym Sometimes a sentence provides a direct definition or a synonym of the unknown word.

> *Example:* Molly Brown became better known as the "Unsinkable Molly Brown" for her <u>prowess</u>, or superior courage, during the *Titanic* disaster.
>
> *Example:* Florence Nightingale pioneered modern nursing when she established <u>infirmaries</u>, or hospitals, during the Crimean War.

Explanation An explanation of the unknown word may be found in other words in the sentence or paragraph.

> *Example:* Charles Lindbergh gained fame as the first aviator to complete a solo <u>transoceanic</u> flight. His non-stop flight across the Atlantic Ocean began May 20 in Long Island, New York and ended May 21, 1927 in Paris, France.
>
> *Example:* Teddy Roosevelt set a presidential <u>precedent</u>. He was the first president to consider the protection of nature as a function of the federal government.

Example/Illustration An unfamiliar word may be followed by an example or illustration that leads you to its meaning.

Example: Jackie Robinson, the first player to break the color barrier in major league baseball, endured <u>discriminatory</u> acts against him as he grew up. For example, the local swimming pool was "for whites only."

Example: During the Holocaust, many brave men and women risked their lives to provide <u>sanctuary</u> for their Jewish neighbors. Anne Frank and her family were hidden in an attic for a little over two years before being discovered by Nazi soldiers.

Logic   Sometimes a word's meaning may come indirectly from the ideas presented in the sentence or paragraph. Use your own thoughts and experiences as a basis to predict the meaning of the word.

Example: <u>Pandemonium</u> broke loose at the Olympic games when Florence Griffith Joyner (Flo Jo) set a new world record for the women's 100 meter dash in 1988.

Example: Seeing her son trapped under the collapsed wall, his mother <u>hoisted</u> a heavy beam and pulled him to safety.

Contrast   A word's meaning may be found in a sentence or paragraph that states the opposite meaning.

Example: Joe Foss is a relatively unknown World War II hero when compared to <u>prominent</u> heroes such as George Patton and Dwight D. Eisenhower.

Example: The effort to save the miners was <u>herculean</u> when compared to the ordinary work at the mine.

Short Exercises: Context Clues

Rosa Parks is a hero of the Civil Rights Movement in America. Mahatma Gandhi led the people of India in their successful struggle for independence from Britain.

Directions: *Read the following sentences about Rosa Parks and Mahatma Ghandi. Define each of the underlined words using context clues.*

1. In the 1930s, the education that most black children like Rosa Parks received was minimal, leaving many of them only qualified for <u>menial</u> or domestic jobs.

2. In the South, the treatment of blacks on the public bus system was one of the most frustrating of everyday <u>indignities</u>. Black passengers were required to give up their seats for any whites who wanted to sit. Blacks could not sit forward of any white passenger, and were always told to "move to the back of the bus."

_____

3. In 1955, Rosa Parks was arrested for refusing to give up her seat on the bus to a white person. This action was <u>momentous</u>, touching off a thirteen-month bus boycott in Montgomery, Alabama, and giving civil rights activists national attention. Eventually the events in Montgomery led to the Supreme Court decision outlawing segregation on buses.

_____

4. Rosa Parks did not <u>succumb</u> to the hardships put upon her by society. She rose above them and went on with her life.

_____

5. In 1999, President Clinton <u>bestowed</u> the nation's highest civilian honor upon Parks, giving her the Congressional Gold Medal.

_____

6. The British passed many <u>exorbitant</u> laws against the people of India to keep strict control over the country. Ghandi felt these laws were unfair.

_____

7. Many of the protests led by Ghandi were <u>illicit</u> and he had often been jailed.

_____

8. Ghandi was a <u>revered</u> leader with hundreds of followers. He reminded the people of their duty to love one another and to resist the British through nonviolent means.

_____

9. Achieving independence from Britain was not a <u>facile</u> accomplishment. It was seventeen years from Ghandi's first march until the British granted India self-government.

_____

10. Mathatma Ghandi's <u>doctrine</u> or teachings were a great influence on another heroic figure of our time, Martin Luther King.

_____

Word Parts

The use of context clues is one strategy for finding the meaning of unknown words. If the sentence does not contain these clues, you may use your knowledge of word parts to help you to figure out the meaning. Word parts are segments of words that have consistent meanings that can be used to define the whole word. These segments are commonly referred to as prefixes, suffixes, and roots.

Prefix   A **prefix** is a word part added to the beginning of a word that changes the meaning of a word. For example, the meanings of *unicycle, bicycle,* and *tricycle* differ because of the prefixes *uni, bi,* and *tri,* indicating one, two, or three wheels.

Suffix   A **suffix** is a word part added to the end of a word which often changes a word from one part of speech to another. Adding the suffix *-ment* to the verb, *encourage,* changes it to the noun, *encouragement.*

Root   A **root** is a word part or word to which prefixes and suffixes can be added. For example, *graph* is a root that can stand alone as a word. Its meaning can be expanded by adding a prefix, a suffix, or another root, for example, *autograph, graphing, telegraph.*

It is important to note that a certain combination of letters can be a word part in some instance but not in others. For example, the prefix *pre* means "before" as in *preview* or *precaution.* In words such as *precious* and *preach,* the letters "pre" are not a prefix.

The following sentences contain words that have a prefix, root, and suffix.

Reading John F. Kennedy, Jr.'s *biography* was inspiring.
> bio (life) + graph (write) + y
> a story about someone's life

At any time an ordinary person can make the *transformation* to a heroic individual.
> trans (change) + form (appearance) + ation (state of)
> the state of a change of the nature, function, or appearance

As a *prescription* for new parents, Dr. Benjamin Spock, a famous pediatrician, wrote, "Trust yourself. You know more than you think you do."
> pre (before) + scrip (write) + tion (act of)
> act of writing instructions

Hercules, the son of the Greek god, Zeus, was a hero of extraordinary strength who won *immortality* by performing twelve labors demanded by the goddess, Hera.
> Im (not) + mort (death) + al (relating to) + ity (state of)
> relating to the state of not being able to die

Short Exercises: Word Parts

Jonas Salk is recognized as a hero for the development of the first polio vaccine. Dr. Shirley Jackson was appointed head of the U.S. Nuclear Regulatory Commission in 1995, making her the first woman and the first African-American to lead the agency.

Directions: *Read the following sentences about Jonas Salk and Dr. Shirley Jackson. Define the underlined words using your knowledge of word parts. You may refer to the list of common word parts in Appendix E.*

1. Jonas Salk is an American <u>epidemiologist</u> and medical researcher who was born in New York City in 1914.

   _____

2. While still a student, Salk became interested in bacterial vaccines. These vaccines could be made from a preparation of dead bacteria, which would immunize without <u>inducing</u> the infection.

   _____

3. Salk is noted for developing the vaccine that causes the building of <u>antibodies</u> against several types of polio, a crippling disease of the 1950's.

   _____

4. Salk became an <u>international</u> hero as millions of parents were relieved of the anxiety that their child might die or be crippled for life.

   _____

5. Jonas Salk is one of the founders of the field of <u>psychoneuroimmunology</u>.

   _____

6. Dr. Jackson <u>superceded</u> many obstacles in her academic and professional career such as being ostracized by many in her freshman class in 1965 for being one of two black women at the Massachusetts Institute for Technology.

   _____

7. Four years into her post at the Nuclear Regulatory Commission, Jackson had won considerable praise for restoring <u>credibility</u> to a troubled agency.

   _____

8. Rensselear <u>Polytechnic</u> Institute has asked Dr. Jackson to become the head of their institution. This would make her the first African-American woman to head a major research institution.

_____

_____

9. & 10. Dr. George Campbell Jr., president of the National Action Council for Minorities in Engineering stated, "Jackson's <u>visibility</u> and <u>extensive</u> network of scientists will draw more people of color to Rensselear and to the fields of mathematics and science."

_____

_____

Graphic Organizers

By using context clues and word parts you are able to figure out some unknown words as you read. To continue to expand your vocabulary knowledge, you may want to use other effective strategies to learn and remember new words. Graphic organizers are visual representations of the words, their meanings, and related terms.

Concept of Definition Map

One easy and effective organizer is a **concept of definition map** originally developed by Schwartz and Raphael (1985). It helps you to understand a vocabulary word by answering three key questions: What is it? What is it like? What or who are some examples? (Figure 4-1)

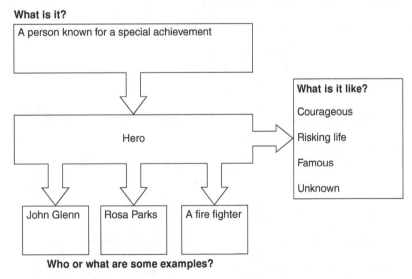

Figure 4-1 Concept of definition map.

Word Maps

A **word map** based upon common word parts can also help you expand your vocabulary. A word map is a chart on which your knowledge of one word part is expanded to a group of other words that use that word part. For example, if you know the word *phobia* means "fear of" you can use that knowledge to figure out the meaning of the word *cardiophobia*, the fear of heart disease, or *technophobia*, the fear of technology. Use an organizer to help learn and remember related words. You may wish to add the definition under each word.

This word map shows words related by the root *phobia*. (Figure 4-2)

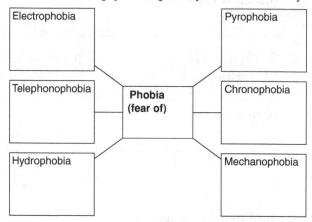

Figure 4-2 Word map for phobia.

Meaning from Context Map

A **meaning from context map** (Figure 4-3) is an adaptation of a Context-Content-Experience graphic organizer developed by Janet Allen for her book *Words, Words, Words* (1999). The meaning from context map develops your understanding of a word based on its use in a sentence or selection.

After reading an unfamiliar word in a sentence, predict what you think it means. Reread the sentence. Does your meaning make sense? If it doesn't, what would make sense in the context of the sentence? Find the actual definition in the dictionary. Apply the word to your life for a personal connection. Use this connection to write an example sentence that shows the meaning of the word.

Context: The war plane was shot down by enemy fire and was forced to *ditch* in the sea.

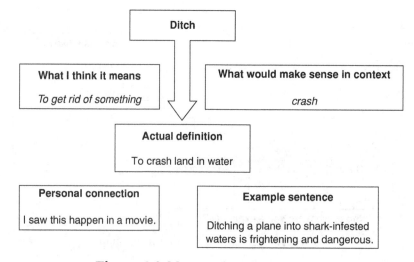

Figure 4-3 Meaning from context map.

Word Cards

Graphic organizers represent one way of increasing your vocabulary knowledge. Another method to learn and remember new vocabulary is the use of word cards. On your card, write a troublesome word, its definition, and pronunciation. To make sure that your word card will be meaningful to you, include one or more of the following: a sentence that uses the word, a visual image (picture) that you associate with the word, or a graphic organizer for the word. Constructing one card for each difficult word, will provide study cards that can be reviewed to increase your vocabulary knowledge.

No one strategy can be used for all words. As you apply these strategies to various readings, you will learn to choose the most appropriate one for the words you need to learn and remember.

Short Exercises: Concept of Definition Maps

Directions: *A model of a concept of definition map was provided previously. Complete the concept of definition maps by filling in the blanks. The first one has been started for you.*

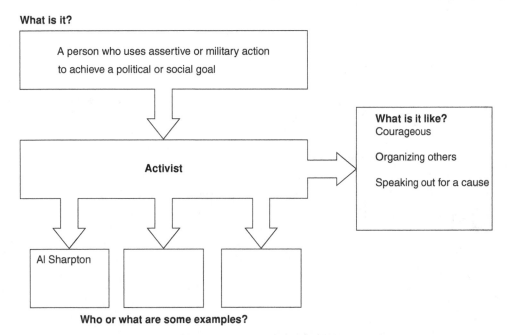

Figure 4-4 Four concept of definition maps to complete.

(continues)

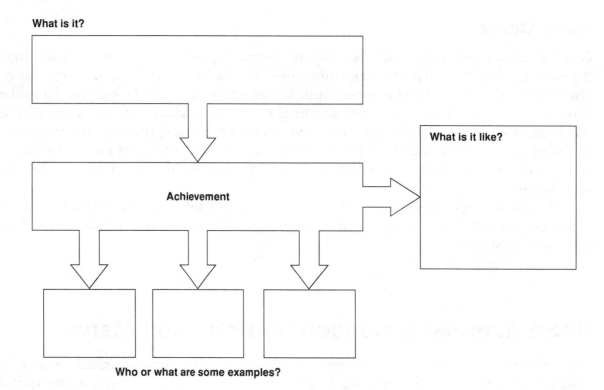

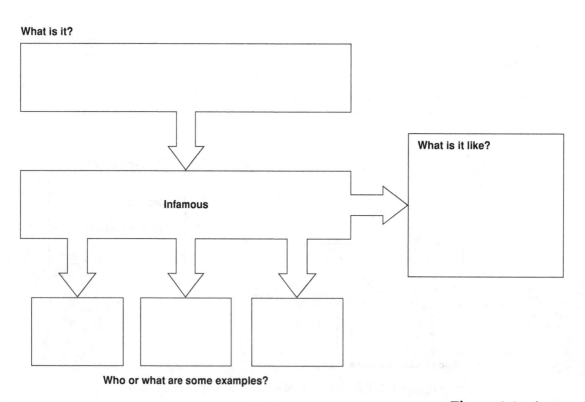

Figure 4-4   *(continues)*

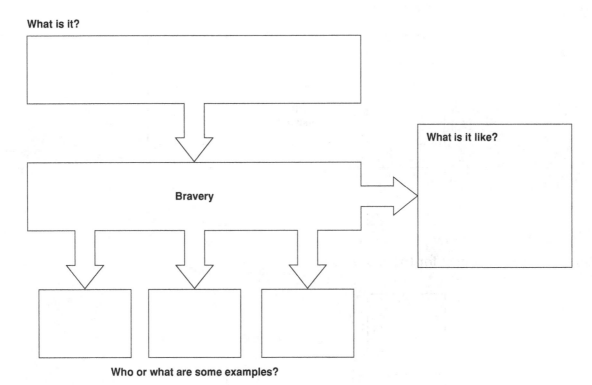

What is it?

Bravery

What is it like?

Who or what are some examples?

Figure 4-4

Short Exercises: Word Maps

Directions: *Fill in these word maps with other vocabulary words that use the common word part at the center. You may wish to add the definition of the word beneath it. You can check your answers using a dictionary. Add more lines as necessary to expand.*

1.

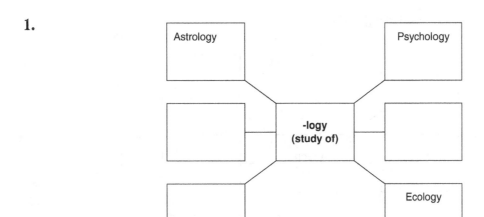

Astrology

Psychology

-logy
(study of)

Ecology

Figure 4-5 Five word map exercises.

(continues)

2.

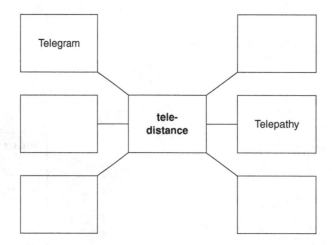

3. Create a word map for the root *port*.

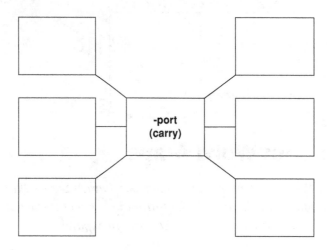

4. Create a word map for the root *graph*.

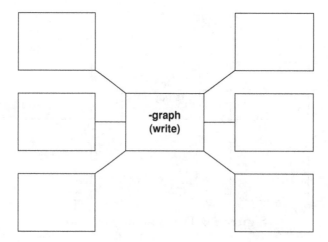

Figure 4-5 *(continues)*

5. Create a word map for -duct.

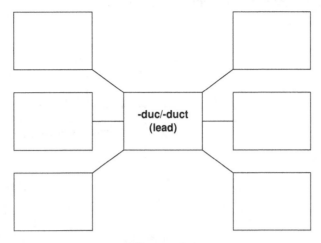

Figure 4-4

Short Exercises: Meaning From Context Maps

Directions: *A model of a meaning from context map was provided previously. Complete the maps by filling in the blanks. The first one has been started for you.*

1. The action of heroes continue to *inspire* us every day of our lives.

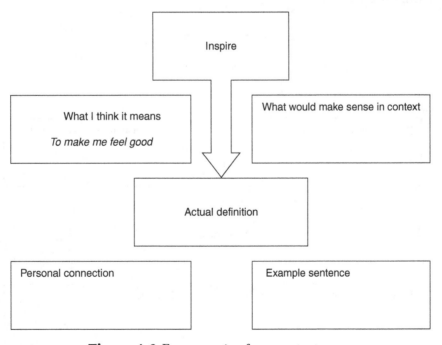

Figure 4-6 Four meaning from context maps.

(continues)

2. In the 1950s Senator John F. Kennedy's activities were interrupted by his *convalescence* after surgery to correct a war injury.

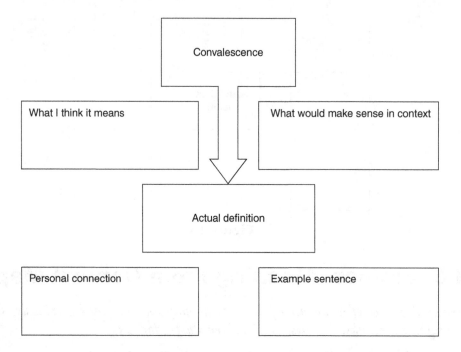

3. People stood *mesmerized* as they watched the police officer pull the accident victim from the burning car.

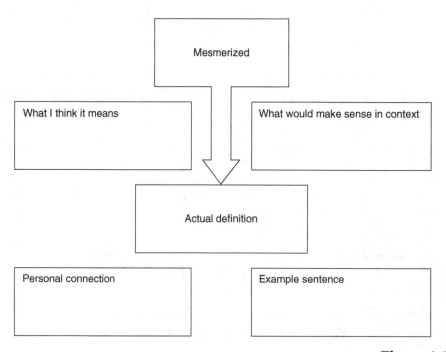

Figure 4-6   *(continues)*

4. During World War II, the Tuskegee Institute trained the first group of black pilots for *aerial* combat. Word

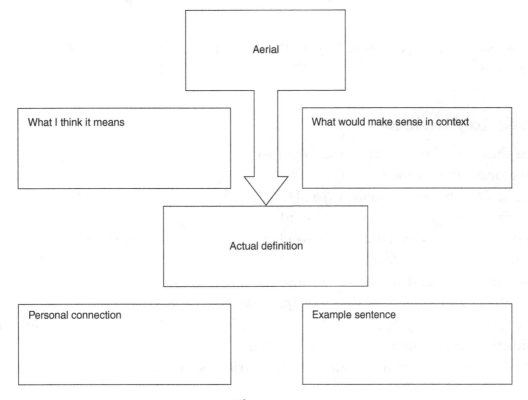

Figure 4-6

Readings Selections

Selection One: **"John Glenn: Man With a Mission"**

William R. Newcott

Before Reading

Before you read the story "John Glenn," complete the following:

Predict what the topic may be.

Skim the reading to see if you have correctly predicted the topic.
Look at the first and last paragraphs, and glance at the first sentences of the other paragraphs.

Think about the topic and relate what you know to "John Glenn."
Is outer space a frontier to explore for people of all ages? Have you

ever thought of being a space pioneer? Relate what you already
know about space exploration and the astronaut, John Glenn, to this topic.

Set a purpose for reading this story. Do you expect to be entertained, to gain knowledge, or to explore
an argument?

Words to Preview

triumphant *(adj.)* celebrating in success *(par.3)*

emblazoned *(v.)* adorned *(par.4)*

insignia *(n.)* a badge or emblem *(par.4)*

scrub *(n.)* a scraggly tree or shrub *(par.6)*

gantry *(n.)* a massive vertical frame used in assembling a rocket *(par.6)*

speculate *(v.)* to guess *(par.11)*

adrift *(adv.)* without direction or purpose *(par.13)*

advocate *(n.)* a supporter or defender *(par.15)*

converged *(v.)* having approached the same point from different directions *(par.20)*

trepidation *(n.)* a state of alarm or dread *(par.22)*

fester *(v.)* to become an increasing source of irritation *(par.24)*

During Reading

As you read "John Glenn," continue to predict where the author is headed, visualize the story, and monitor your comprehension. Write your comments, questions, or descriptions in the margin as you read.

John Glenn

1   JOHN GLENN gazed out the big square window in the orbiter *Discovery* and watched the Earth slide by 345 miles below. A tear came to his eye. And stayed there.

2   "In zero gravity a tear doesn't roll down your cheek," he later recalled. "It just sits there on your eyeball until it evaporates."

> I wonder what zero gravity feels like?

3   He smiled, embarrassed a little. But he was clear-eyed on this day in December 1998, a month after his *triumphant* return to space and just a couple of weeks before his four terms as a United States senator would come to an end. On the walls of his corner office in the Hart Senate Office Building in Washington, D.C., hung

From "John Glenn: Man With a Mission" by William R. Newcott. From *National Geographic*, June 1999 (v195, n6). Reprinted by permission of the National Geographic Society.

mementos of legislative victories, photos of presidential handshakes, tributes to him as America's first man in orbit, in 1962. And everywhere, pictures of his beloved wife, Annie.

4   Sitting across from Glenn, who was illuminated like a museum piece by sunlight slanting through the window, I realized that this was the first time I'd encountered the senator in a suit and tie. For months I'd followed his training at the Johnson Space Center in Houston and at the Kennedy Space Center in Florida, and virtually all he'd worn were blue zippered flight outfits, bulky orange pressure suits, polo shirts *emblazoned* with the mission *insignia*.

5   Even at age 77, John Glenn seemed to be made for an astronaut's gear, and vice versa. Back in the beginning it was that way too.

6   Early on the morning of Glenn's space shuttle flight, I drove through the Florida *scrub* to the Kennedy Space Center by way of the Cape Canaveral Air Station, where the original Mercury rockets were launched. It was still long before dawn as I approached the abandoned site of launch complex 14. The Mercury *gantry* is gone. The blockhouse is a conference center. The ghosts of a space program in its infancy whisper through the sea grapes.

7   Thirty-six years earlier, at this spot on a morning much like this, a man in a silver space suit trudged from a trailer carrying his briefcase-size life-support system, an alien headed for the office. Above him a nine-story-tall rocket groaned under the pressure of refined kerosene fuel and hissed billowing clouds of vented liquid oxygen.

8   A countdown, a roar, a pencil-shaped craft rose into the Florida sky. Five hours later it was all over: John Glenn, the first American to see three sunrises in a single day, sat bobbing in the Atlantic, awaiting pickup by the destroyer U.S.S. *Noa*.

9   He was a national hero. Although two other U.S. astronauts, Alan Shepard and Gus Grissom, had pierced the boundary of space before him in short suborbital flights, Glenn cast a spell on the American people that never quite wore off. There were parades, speeches, honorary degrees, and a medal from the President. But what John Glenn really wanted, and what he genuinely expected, was his next shot. America was going to the moon, and John Glenn planned to be there.

10   "I wasn't concerned when I wasn't put back in the astronaut rotation right away," he says. "They gave me some administrative work to do, and I kept asking about being sent up again, and they kept telling me, 'Headquarters says not yet. Not yet.'"

> It must have been terrible not to be able to go up in space again.

11   Some *speculate* that President John F. Kennedy didn't want to risk losing the space program's greatest hero in an accident.

12   "Unfortunately I never got to ask him," said Glenn. "And I got tired of waiting around. So I left the space program."

From "John Glenn: Man With a Mission" by William R. Newcott. From *National Geographic*, June 1999 (v195, n6). Reprinted by permission of the National Geographic Society.

13   A year later, *adrift* from the Marines for the first time in his adult life, Glenn went into business. He became president of Royal Crown International and eventually achieved political legend status: Four times Ohioans sent him to the Senate.

14   "I figured my time in space had come and gone," he said. "I'd given the space program a good run, I thought, and that was it."

15   He has always remained an *advocate* of NASA and the space program though. Within hours of the space shuttle *Challenger* accident in 1986, Glenn was in Florida with the crew's families to offer sympathy and to lend his support to the space program. His influence has been key in keeping the International Space Station program alive.

16   It was while doing research in support of the space station that Glenn stumbled upon what ultimately became his ticket back.

17   "Over the years," Glenn said, "NASA has observed more than 50 changes that occur in the human body in space. And nine or ten of these are very similar to things that happen in the process of aging. Things like loss of muscle strength. Bone density loss. Cardiovascular changes. Changes in balance and coordination.

> What does cardio-vascular mean?

18   "My idea was to send an older person up and study the body's reaction to space flight—see if there were differences between younger and older people. For example, how long was the recovery period after returning to Earth? Shorter or longer for an older astronaut?

19   "I went over to NASA to talk to Dan Goldin, the administrator. I made no bones about it—I wanted to be the person to do it."

20   As dusk fell over Florida, I wandered to the top of the Kennedy Space Center press mound, a small hill where the NASA public information office and network broadcast booths perch. "Not since the shuttle's return to flight in 1988 have so many members of the press *converged* upon this place … ."

21   The routine on October 29 bore more than a passing resemblance to that Mercury morning in 1962. The drive to the pad, the ride in the gantry elevator, the walk across a metal bridge to the waiting spacecraft. The strap-in, the closing of the hatch, the long wait.

22   A few minutes of *trepidation*—five private planes buzzing into, and finally out of, restricted airspace—and then *Discovery* rose into the afternoon sky on a tongue of fire. As an estimated quarter million observers crawled back home fighting ten-mile-an-hour traffic jams, the shuttle crew orbited the globe at five miles a second.

23   Space travel used to be a young man's game, but when John Glenn went into orbit aboard *Discovery*, four generations of men and women could gaze into the sky and think, That could be me someday. At the same time Glenn was looking down and doing some thinking of his own.

From "John Glenn: Man With a Mission" by William R. Newcott. From *National Geographic*, June 1999 (v195, n6). Reprinted by permission of the National Geographic Society.

24   "It's quite something," he said, "to look down on this blue planet, seeing that little film of air that surrounds it. You fly over the Mediterranean, over the Middle East–and it's so beautiful. You wonder why in the world humans can't solve all the problems they've created and left to *fester* over the centuries.

25   "I was at the Houston airport on my way back to Washington recently when this older guy walked up to me, all excited. He shook my hand and said, 'Boy, you're changing my life!' I said how's that? He said, 'I'm 74, and ever since I was a kid I've wanted to climb Mount Kilimanjaro. I haven't done it, and I kept putting it off. And now I'm gonna do it!' And all the time his wife is standing behind him, just shaking her head.

> John Glenn had an impact on people of all ages.

26   "So I may have killed a man on Kilimanjaro, for all I know. But I've noticed something. I've noticed that maybe because of all this, people are seeing themselves in a way they haven't before. They're realizing that older people have the same ambitions, hopes, and dreams as anybody else. I say you should live life based on how you feel and not by the calendar."

27   The measure of John Glenn's achievements may someday be the familiar sight of grandparents waving good-bye to grandchildren at Gate 36 of the Los Angeles Space Port. And don't be surprised by the gentleman with the sky blue eyes you see in line there.

28   "Annie says no more space travel," Glenn grins. "Well, I've never fully committed to that."

> I think Glenn would go into space again if he could.

After Reading

Word Connections

1. Glenn was "illuminated like a museum piece by sunlight slanting through the window." Which words in this sentence help you to define *illuminated*?

_____

2. Alan Shepard and Gus Grissom completed short suborbital flights even before John Glenn. Define the prefix *sub-*. Create a word map for this word part.

_____

From "John Glenn: Man With a Mission" by William R. Newcott. From *National Geographic*, June 1999 (v195, n6). Reprinted by permission of the National Geographic Society.

Word Map for Sub

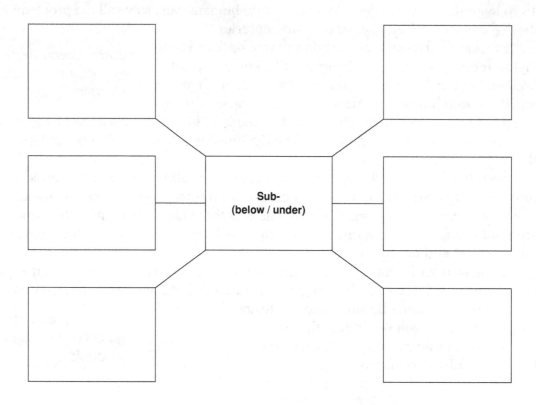

3. Use your knowledge of word parts to help you to define *cardiovascular.*

_____

_____

4. The astronaut in a silver space suit *trudged* from a trailer carrying a briefcase-sized life support system.

   A person who is trudging will walk

   a. quickly.
   b. without worry.
   c. slowly with a heavy step.
   d. with support from others.

5. "The routine of October 29 *bore* more than a passing resemblance to the Mercury morning of 1962." Define *bore* as it is used in this sentence.

_____

Connecting Meaning

1. What careers other than astronaut did John Glenn pursue?

_____

_____

_____

_____

2. What research questions ultimately supported Glenn's ticket back to space?

_____

_____

_____

_____

3. John Glenn's initial space venture was followed by a return to space in 1998 at the age of 77. Why do you think Glenn chose to take this risk again?

_____

_____

_____

_____

Selection Two: **"The Hero Next Door"**

Ellen Michaud

Before Reading

Before you read "The Hero Next Door," complete the following:

Predict what the topic of this article may be.

Skim the reading to see if you have correctly predicted the topic.

Think about your definition of a hero. Do you know anyone you would consider a hero? Do you think anyone can be a hero?

Set your purpose for reading.

Words to Preview

glaciated *(v.)* to cover with a glacier *(par. 1)*

decisively *(adv.)* determined; unmistakably *(par. 5)*

subdue *(v.)* bring under control *(par. 8)*

hone *(v.)* to make more acute, intense or effective *(par. 12)*

prudent *(adj.)* marked by wisdom *(par. 18)*

paradox *(n.)* seemingly contradictory; opposed to common sense *(par. 19)*

succor *(n.)* relief; help; aid *(par. 24)*

During Reading

As you read "The Hero Next Door," continue to predict what may happen next in the article, visualize the story, and monitor your comprehension. Write your comments, questions, or descriptions in the margin as you read.

THE HERO NEXT DOOR

Exactly What is it that Makes Ordinary Folks Risk Their Lives to Save Others?

by Ellen Michaud

1   JOPLIN JAMES, a kindergarten teacher at Shelburne Community School in Vermont, tightened his grip on the seatback rail as the school bus lurched toward a treacherous curve of I-89 sliced between huge walls of glaciated rock. Joplin, along with 60 energetic middle-schoolers and their chaperones, was eager to get home from a week-long school camping trip. But this section of roadway was notorious for accidents, and the teacher silently wished for everyone's safety.

2   As they came through the turn, he saw the accident. A woman had smashed her car into the rocks, the impact tossing her vehicle across two lanes of traffic and onto the median strip. Debris littered the road.

3   The bus braked hard to a stop and, without thinking, Joplin leaped to the ground and ran to the car. "I thought the driver was a goner," he recalls. "Her whole face was bloody, she was unconscious, and the roof was caved in. She had her seatbelt on, but the way she hit ..." He shakes his head. "The hardest part was the kids had to watch."

4   As he paused for a moment to assess the damage, the driver's compartment began to fill with smoke. Joplin ran back to the bus and grabbed a fire extinguisher. "By the time I got back, the engine compartment was full of flames," he says. He emptied the extinguisher over the blaze as other motorists pulled the driver from the wreck.

5   "She was so banged up I questioned the choice to move her," he says. "But it was the right thing to do because the fire reignited and totally consumed the car's interior."

6   Joplin is more comfortable hiking the Long Trail high in the mountains of Vermont or reading *Blueberries for Sal* to his kindergartners than he is being called a hero. But, by anyone's definition, that's precisely what he is. When another human being needed help, he acted decisively and put himself in harm's way.

7   "I'm not a hero," he protests vehemently. "When I think of a hero, I think of that guy who stepped in front of the shooter in Tucson when Arizona Congresswoman Gabby Giffords was shot in January. Now he's a hero!"

8   Joplin is referring to Bill Badger, the 70-something retired army colonel who leaped at the Tucson shooter as he tried to reload, and held onto his gun arm as two others joined him to subdue the man. Six people died that day, including an elderly woman and a young girl, but Badger undoubtedly saved others from violent death.

9   Watching the replay of cell phone images and news media interviews with Tucson survivors, the question became inescapable: What makes a person risk himself to save others?

10   "Helping others in a crisis is a gut response," explains researcher Paul Slovic, Ph.D., a professor of psychology at the University of Oregon and president of Decision Research, a nonprofit institute that investigates human judgment, decision-making, and risk. "We don't fully understand what's going on in the brain, but we're built in a way to respond quickly to emergencies. And in a crisis, we don't sit back and weigh the costs and benefits with pencil and paper. We react in an instant."

11   Essentially, the human default position is to help others.

12   Most people we tag with the label "hero" are professionals who have been trained as soldiers, firefighters, police, paramedics, or search and rescue team members to hone that instinctive, heroic response and put their lives on the line—so in the split-second it takes to decide to either run or help, they'll move forward and do what needs to be done. They'll take the risk, take the bullet, take the consequences.

13   But so, it turns out, will ordinary people on their way to work or picking up milk at the corner market. There's the subway hero in New York City who, after a woman commuter fell from the train platform onto the tracks, jumped onto the tracks himself, pulled her between the rails, and covered her body with his as a train passed over the two of them.

14   There's the letter carrier in Lexington, Massachusetts, who saw a house on fire, ran in, and pulled a 96-year-old man to safety. Before it was brought under control, the blaze engulfed the house and burst through the roof.

15   Then there's the Mississippi football coach who was out fishing with a buddy when he spotted smoke coming from another craft. Acting swiftly, the coach pulled passengers to safety just before the craft burst into flame.

16   And there's the Pennsylvania mom who was picking up some milk from the local stop-and-go when she saw a man grab his former wife and force her into a car. As the man tried to hang on to the woman and get into the car himself, the mom leaped forward, opened the passenger door, yanked the woman out of the car, and pulled her into the store to call police.

---

17   "Every one of us is a hero in waiting," says Scott Allison, Ph.D., a psychologist at the University of Richmond and co-author of *Heroes: What They Do & Why We Need Them*. "We're just waiting for the opportunity to step forward and do something extraordinary."

18   Still, why? Why place oneself in harm's way–often for a complete stranger? After all, it's not rational, and it's certainly not prudent. The explanation may have as much to do with human biology as with altruism, says Allison. "There's research to show that there's a biological, evolutionary tendency toward these actions. We're social animals. And we've learned, or at least our genes have learned, that survival is fostered by social relationships. We've learned that if we're helpful to others, we're more likely to survive ourselves."

19   Selfless selfishness: That does sound like a bit of a paradox, but it may well be that the engine of self-interest–on a genetic level, at least–is what drives our noblest deeds.

20   Another surprising fact about heroism is that it need not be associated with danger or classical ideas of bravery at all. Heroism does not require standing in front of a speeding bullet, leaping through fire, or putting one's life on the line. Indeed, there are many ways to be heroic, and some do so quietly, without any fanfare. Take Mississippi washerwoman Oseola McCarty. Forced to quit school in the sixth grade to care for an elderly home-bound relative, she took in laundry to support herself. Throughout her life, she never owned a car, walked everywhere she needed to go, attended Friendship Baptist Church every Sunday, held her Bible together with tape, and banked just about every dime she ever made. Eventually those dimes added up to $150,000–and Oseola decided to give it all away.

21   "More than I could ever use," the tiny, 87-year-old told *The New York Times*.

22   The money went into a trust and, upon her death in 1999, some went to her church and family, but most went to the University of Southern Mississippi, a nearby school that did not admit children of Oseola's race when she was a girl. The money– quickly matched by a business community humbled by the woman's generosity–was used to provide scholarships for nine African-American children.

23   Or take two nuns in Indianapolis, Sisters Rita Ann Wade and Barbara McClelland, who had seen the largely middle-class eastside neighborhood nearby slide into poverty. Based at the Holy Cross convent, church, and school, they watched as older residents–and some of the young ones, too–became afraid to venture into the increasingly hostile streets.

24   Holy Cross became an oasis of safety and succor. It wasn't unusual for a homeless or hungry soul to come knocking on the convent's back door in the middle of the night. "Holy Cross had a food pantry, and the door to the parish office was right next to our kitchen door," explains Sister Barbara. "So when people got hungry or just wanted to talk, they'd come and pound on our door."

25   She chuckles. "We had one guy who came every night at 2, 3, or 4 in the morning and woke us up."

26   As a result of their nocturnal visitors, the two Sisters jokingly began to refer to their "back door ministry." But they also recognized the very real need for a place

where people in the neighborhood could find food, a place to relax, a place to be heard, a place to be safe—and a couple of loving hearts.

27   The two women approached the problem the way they approached every other challenge: They thought about it, prayed about it, then talked to their spiritual community. The women's order ultimately voted to have the nuns quit their jobs and begin serving the neighborhood on a fulltime basis. Within a year, Sisters Rita Ann and Barbara had rented and renovated a house on the near eastside and named it "Miracle Place" (amiracleplace.org).

28   Today, 11 years later, the house is a hive of activity—and the Sisters have also cleared away a pocket park across the street where kids can play safely. Those who have watched the community evolve say that the Sisters will never tell you the half of what they do nor take the credit for any of it. Yet one look at the door constantly swinging open for neighborhood children, their brothers, sisters, parents, and old folks shows the Sisters are saving lives as fully as if they were snatching victims from a burning building.

29   The point being that heroes come in different forms: the action-hero kind like Joplin James, the secret-giver kind like Oseola McCarty, and the quietly devoted kind like Sisters Rita Ann and Barbara.

30   There's heroism in such small gestures as writing a check to your favorite charity, coaching a little league team, or offering a kindness to a total stranger. "It's all these gifts of self that, put together, really make the biggest difference," says Diane Heavin, co-founder of the Curves fitness centers and a star of the ABC hit television show *Secret Millionaire.*

31   In fact, if you really want to change someone's life, "Think about the last time you put a smile on someone's face," says Heavin. "Then go out there and do it again."

Know an everyday hero in your community? If so, please describe briefly what makes them a hero and share it with us via mail or at saturdayeveningpost.com/heroes.

Ellen Michaud is the author of *Blessed Living a Grateful Life.* Contact her at theblessedblog.com.

After Reading

Word Connections

1. "But this section of roadway was *notorious* for accidents, and the teacher silently wished for everyone's safety." From the context of the sentence, what does the word, *notorious* mean?

   _____

   _____

2. They (heroes) take the risk, take the bullet, take the *consequences.* Create a concept of definition map for the term *consequence.*

Concept of Definition Map for Consequence

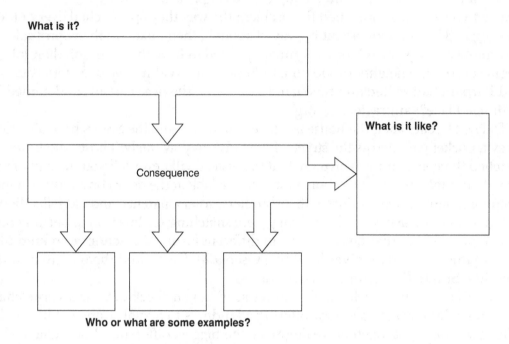

What is it?

Consequence

What is it like?

Who or what are some examples?

3. Several words in the article use the word part *re-*. Identify and define three of those words.

_____

_____

4. From its use in paragraph 26, what does the word *nocturnal* mean?

_____

5. Today, eleven years later, the house is a *hive of activity*. Choose the meaning of the italicized phrase.

   a. Bees are living in the house.

   b. The house is busy with activity.

   c. No one is doing anything there.

   d. The house is too old.

Connecting Meaning

1. What is it that makes ordinary folks risk their lives to save others?

_____

_____

_____

_____

2. In your own words, describe one hero and his/her act of heroism discussed in the article.

_____

_____

_____

_____

3. "The human default position is to help others." What does this statement mean?

_____

_____

_____

4. State the three forms of heroes mentioned in the article.

_____

_____

_____

5. Do you know anyone you would consider a hero? Explain why.

_____

_____

_____

Selection Three: "Animals at Ground Zero" from Best Friends magazine

Before you read "Animals at Ground Zero," complete the following:

Predict what the topic of this article may be.

Skim the reading to see if you have correctly predicted the topic.

Think about this topic. Animals were a valuable part of the rescue effort at Ground Zero. Do you know anything about search and rescue dogs? Do you know a dog that saved someone's life? Think about what you already know about rescue animals.

Set your purpose for reading. Do you expect to be entertained, gain knowledge, or explore an argument?

Words to Preview

ensuring *(adj.)* following as a consequence or result *(par.2)*

chaos *(n.)* total disorder or confusion *(par.2)*

MASH *(n.)* Mobile Army Surgical Hospital *(par.5)*

Belgian Malinois *(n.)* breed of dog similar to the German Shepherd *(par.13)*

FEMA *(n.)* Federal Emergency Management Agency *(par.19)*

deployed *(v.)* stationing people systematically over an area *(par.19)*

During Reading

As you read "Animals at Ground Zero," continue to predict where the author is headed, visualize the story, and monitor your comprehension. Write your comments, questions, or descriptions in the margin as you read.

Animals at Ground Zero

Four-Legged Heroes

1 From the moment the first plane hit one of the Twin Towers, dogs emerged as heroes.

2   On the 70th floor, as soon as he heard the crash and the *ensuing chaos*, Omar Eduardo Rivera, who is blind, ordered his guide dog, Dorado, to go down the stairs to safety without him. He was certain that he could never make it to safety himself. Dorado began to obey him, then turned and came back to his side. For perhaps the first time ever, she would not do what he asked. She was not going to leave without him. So the two set off down the stairs together, and both made it to safety.

3   Eight floors further up, Roselle had been snoozing under the desk of Michael Hingson, a channels manager at a major data storage company who has been blind since birth. Roselle led him down the stairs and across the street to safety.

4   Like Roselle and Dorado, dozens more dogs were about to distinguish themselves in the work that followed. Rescuers had been kept from the scene all day as suffocating smoke and hot ash were billowing through the air. But at 6 P.M., the Suffolk County SPCA team arrived at Ground Zero and began search-and-rescue operations.

Search and Rescue

5 Staffed only by volunteers, the Suffolk crew's regular job was to investigate animal abuse. But recently, they had received legislative funding for a *MASH* unit, a mobile spay/neuter hospital.

6 Roy Gross, chief of the rescue department, took the call from NYPD Emergency Services. The MASH unit was needed, with all their expertise and staff, to help with the rescue dogs. Veterinarians, vet techs, and volunteers were mobilized from all over the city. Half a dozen tents were quickly erected.

7 "Search and rescue units were coming in from all over the country and even Canada," Gross recalls. "When they arrived, the Office of Emergency Management would register them and tell the handlers where to find our MASH unit.

8 "The dogs would come out of the site covered in dust, ash, and debris. We hydrated them with IV fluids, rinsed the dust out of their eyes, bathed them, gave them antibiotics, cleaned and stitched wounds, and fitted them with booties.

9 "In just the first five days, we treated well over 200 dogs. I believe there were about 300 dogs in the perimeter. Some of them came in, and they'd been working so hard, they were about to collapse.

10 "They work as a team. The handler and the dog are like two trained soldiers. It's amazing.

11 "We provided first aid for the handlers, too, because it was just easier that way. They were right there. We treated scrapes and cuts and gave them aspirin, gloves, flashlights, whatever they needed. They came in, they went out; it was just incredible to see. Some of the dogs, they would come out of the site and their back legs were just about to give out on them. I actually saw one come in that we treated and hydrated, and the dog was just *pulling* his handler back to the pile—like he just knew he had to go in there and do his job."

Rescuing the Rescuers

12 Chris Christensen knows about the bond between rescuer and canine partner. The St. Louis police officer couldn't stay at home and do nothing. So he and eight friends piled into cars and drove to New York.

13 On Thursday, September 13, Christensen and Servus, his *Belgian Malinois*, were near the top of a pile of concrete, glass, and twisted steel that was once the World Trade Center. Servus was sniffing for survivors.

14 They continued climbing, following what appeared to be footprints, to a place where there once was an escalator. Suddenly, Servus slid down 20-feet, landing face-first into a pile of white ash. Christensen rushed to his side. At first, he thought the dog had broken a leg, but he quickly saw that the canine had inhaled the ash-like debris in a huge gulp and couldn't breathe. Christensen hauled his 70-pound partner over his shoulders and began running, screaming, "I need help."

15 He was instantly surrounded by a nurse and over a dozen firefighters and police officers. An IV was administered right there on the sidewalk, and a firefighter provided suction. A police officer poured water over Servus, who had begun convulsing from the lack of air. The suction began to work, and what appeared to be liquid concrete streamed from Servus's nose. A paramedic offered a stretcher. Christensen ran down the street with his still-convulsing pet, while the nurse ran beside him with the IV. They flagged down a police car, and with lights flashing and sirens blaring, rushed the animal to a nearby medical center. A team of five

"Animals at Ground Zero" from *Best Friends* magazine, Nov/Dec 2001. Reprinted by permission of Best Friends Animal Sanctuary.

veterinarians and technicians scrambled to save the dog. "In seven minutes, they had him stabilized," Christensen said. After several hours, the dog was ready to be released.

16   "I can't believe I nearly lost him," says Christensen, holding back tears. "There are just no words to describe it."

17   There were, indeed, no words to describe their bond. Servus has saved Christensen's life—twice.

18   "I just couldn't let him die," he says, gratefully.

Diary of a K-9 Team

19 Paul Morgan and Cody spent two days volunteering at Ground Zero with friends Hal Wilson and Sue Nine. FEMA response teams with about 35 search and rescue dogs and cadaver dogs were already on the scene. But it wasn't enough. Usually outside individuals aren't asked to the area for fear of greater injury as the handlers are unknown and the dogs untested. But the rescuers needed all the help they could get. Morgan hooked up with four state police K-9 teams. The FEMA rescue dogs were pulling out for a much needed rest and the two men and their dogs were deployed to the site by a fireman. Here's an excerpt from what Morgan wrote:

20   The troopers and their dogs being relieved were absolutely expressionless, with that thousand-meter stare. As Hal and I were escorted to the pile and up to tons of debris, wrecked police and fire vehicles, hose lines, steel girders, pieces of aluminum, drywall, broken glass, and steel rods, we stumbled a dozen times.

21   A lieutenant brought us to a burned-out rig that had been a hose truck from a rescue unit. It was gray and the cab was cleaned out … no seats, steering wheel, dashboard, nothing. The lieutenant asked Cody and me to climb down into a pit 10-feet deep and search for any signs of life. I called into the back of the hose truck several times, but there was no response. Then Cody, my golden retriever, began scratching the earth and whimpering. I told the firefighters above me, "We have a body down here!"

22   My dog and I were lifted out of the pit by about a dozen firefighters and the digging began with pikes and shovels. Minutes later the call came out … "Body bag!" An orange body bag was sent into the pit and out came a firefighter's remains.

23   A battalion chief asked me, "How good is your dog?" I didn't have to answer. Cody was scratching into a hole on the hose line—he'd found another body. He found three bodies in thirty minutes.

24   But this time I was trapped. I couldn't get out from under the slab. It was like being caught under a stairway in a dark basement. I couldn't go forward and I couldn't back out with my boots caught in some other concrete chunks. Then Cody turned me around, pulling me to the left. He was gasping for air and was desperate to escape from the hold. I held on to his lead and crawled out. Then the firefighters above me pulled me out and lifted Cody to the surface.

25   When I got back to the ruins where the restaurants were, two nurses gave me some water and another gave me a glass of orange juice. My buddy, Hal, and his

"Animals at Ground Zero" from *Best Friends* magazine, Nov/Dec 2001. Reprinted by permission of Best Friends Animal Sanctuary.

dog, Sue, were right behind me. Hal found a metal tray in a trash pile. The dogs needed a awful lot of water. Then out of nowhere, a line of firefighters with dirty, grim faces passed by, each of them pouring out his own water into the metal tray. Another firefighter gave us two sandwiches and some more water. The dogs consumed every drop of water … three or four quarts, and then the buildings began to crumble again. We were ordered out of the pile. It was now 14:30 hours—2:30 P.M.

After Reading

Word Connections

1. "The troopers and their dogs being relieved were absolutely expressionless, with that *thousand-meter* stare." Explain the phrase, "thousand-meter stare."

_____

_____

_____

2. "A team of five veterinarians and technicians *scrambled* to save the dog."

Meaning from Context Map for Scrambled

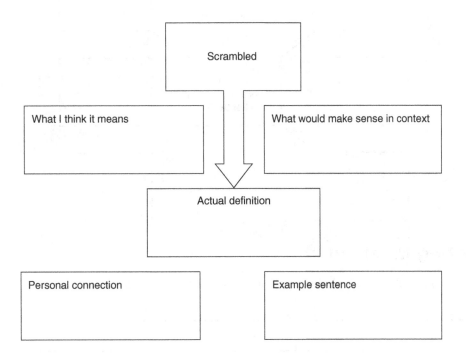

3. In paragraph 15, what does IV stand for?

_____

_____

_____

4. There are three types of working dogs mentioned in this story: guide dogs, search and rescue dogs, and cadaver dogs. Explain what the job of each type of working dog is.

_____

_____

_____

_____

5. Create a word map for suffix *-er*.

Word Map for the Suffix -er

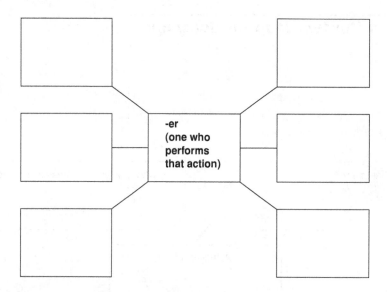

Connecting Meaning

1. Explain three examples of the heroism of the dogs in this selection.

_____

_____

_____

2. Why was it necessary to keep a MASH unit available for the dogs?

_____

_____

_____

_____

3. Recall in detail the problems of Servus in his rescue efforts.

_____

_____

_____

_____

_____

_____

_____

Portfolio Activities

Integrating Ideas

The selections you have read describe the actions of heroes. Although each of their situations was unique, as heroes they share common characteristics. What heroic qualities do they embody? What other traits do you see as heroic? Reflect on these ideas in writing or in class discussion.

Extending Concepts

America's first spacemen and World War II heroes represented America's hopes and dreams. Think about the changes in America since the early 1960's. What are the hopes and dreams of today? Write about a contemporary hero who represents these hopes and dreams.

Collaborative Activity

Who are the heroes of today? Create groups of four students. Each student will survey 25 students with the following questions: Do you have a hero? If yes, who is it? After bringing their results back to the group, the findings will be compiled and presented to the class.

Additional Portfolio Suggestion

To show your understanding of the vocabulary strategies presented, create several concept of definition maps and word maps with words of your choice.

Chapter Summary Graphic Organizers

Complete the graphic organizer by labeling five types of context clues.

Context Clues

Divide the word reviewing into its prefix-root-suffix.

Word Parts

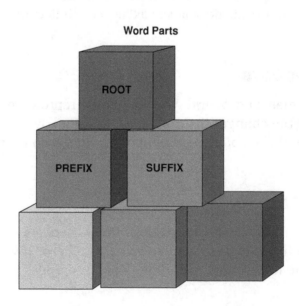

Label the types of graphic organizers that can increase your vocabulary knowledge.

Graphic Organizers

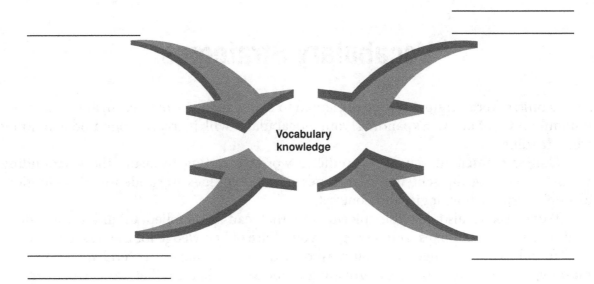
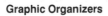

Unit II Review

Vocabulary Strategies

In this unit, several strategies were presented to help you figure out, learn, and remember unfamiliar vocabulary. Expanding your vocabulary will increase your understanding while reading.

Context clues allow you to predict a word's meaning by using the surrounding words or sense of the sentence. Five types of context clues were identified: definition, example, explanation, logic, and contrast.

Word parts also provide information that can be applied to unknown words. Common prefixes, suffixes, and roots give you a base of knowledge for use with new words.

To help you to remember, you may record the meanings in several ways. A **word map** expands the word parts by providing other words that use that part. A **concept of definition map** helps you to understand vocabulary by answering three questions: What is it? What is it like? What or who are some examples? A **meaning from context** map helps you to use a definition in context. These are only three of many graphic organizers that you may use.

As you construct meaning for a reading selection, you will predict, visualize, and monitor your understanding of words as you apply these vocabulary strategies.

Unit Review Graphic Organizer

Label the three types of vocabulary strategies discussed in this unit.

Vocabulary Strategies

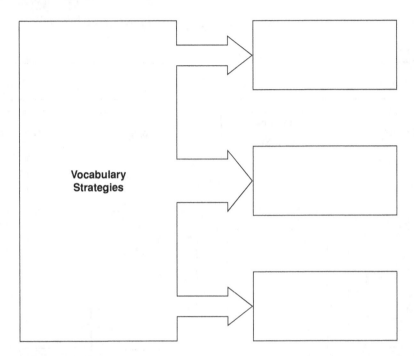

Portfolio Suggestion

Choose a comic book hero such as Batman, Spiderman, or Wonder Woman. Write an essay identifying their heroic qualities. Compare them to real life heroes.

Portfolio Vocabulary Exercise

Think about your concept of hero. Write as many words as you can think of that fit the categories dealing with heroes.

Hero Map

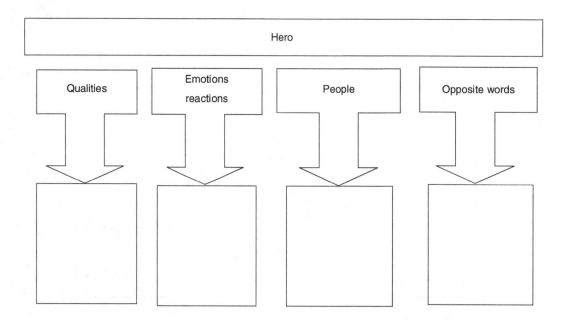

Want to Know More?

If you are interested in knowing more about heroes, the following books and websites further explore this theme. You can find these books at your local library to read more about heroes or use the internet and check out the websites.

Books

Brokaw, Tom. *The Greatest Generation.* New York: Dell Publishers, 2001.
   Tom Brokaw honors the ordinary people who fought World War II and then built America.

Walker, Keith.(editor) and Martha Raye. *A Piece of My Heart: The Stories of 26 American Women Who Served in Vietnam.* New York: Presidio Press, 1997.
   Record the memories of a war in the words of those courageous women who served in Viet Nam.

Warshaurer, Sherry Bennett, Mary Bloom (photographer) and Betty White. *Everyday Heroes: Extraordinary Dogs Among Us*. New York: John Wiley & Sons, 1998.

This book tells the remarkable stories of service dogs who are guides, healers, therapists, and, in many cases, the bridge to a normal, fulfilling life for many patients and owners.

Websites

www.nasa.gov **NASA**.gov brings you images, videos and interactive features from the unique perspective of America's space agency. Get the latest updates on **NASA** missions.

www.ctlegalguide.com/SlideShow/caninetribute.htm This website is a tribute to the canine search and rescue teams.

www.nasar.org The National Association for Search and Rescue, Inc., (NASAR) is a not-for-profit membership association comprised of thousands of paid and non-paid professionals interested in all aspects of search and rescue - the humanitarian cause of saving lives - throughout the United States and around the world. "... that others may live."

www.tdi-dog.org Therapy Dogs International, Inc. (TDI) is a volunteer group organized to provide qualified handlers and their Therapy Dogs for visitations to institutions, facilities, and any other place where Therapy Dogs are needed.

Google the term *everyday heroes* to find multiple stories of heroism.

Unit III

Main Ideas

Theme of Readings: Fear

"You can measure people ... by the way they respond to challenge."

DWIGHT D. EISENHOWER

Fear

Fears ... We all have them. When we are young, we lie in bed frozen with fear of the dark or an open closet door, sure an unseen monster is coming to get us. We may be afraid of a neighbor's dog, a crash of thunder, a bad dream, or an unfamiliar place. As we grow, our fears change. With or without good reason, some of us are afraid of spiders, flying, public speaking, new technology, illness, or death. Others fear crowds, confined spaces, high places, or guns. It is human nature to have some fears, even in adulthood.

For most people, fears are simply part of life. Some of them are justified; they come and go as life changes. There are true dangers in the world which one needs to be on guard against. Sometimes, however, fears become so overwhelming that they are paralyzing and cross the line into phobia. Phobias are such intense fears that they are no longer manageable. A phobia keeps a person from going on with everyday life. For example, people commonly fear dentists but will go regularly anyway to keep their teeth healthy. A dental phobic experiences extreme, paralyzing fear at the thought of a visit to the dentist's office and will avoid this situation if at all possible. Likewise, someone may be nervous about flying but will nonetheless get on the plane headed for their dream vacation in Hawaii. A person with a phobia of flying is limited to trips by land, rail, or water: phobias restrict life experiences.

While some people's lives are made narrow by fears, others relish the excitement and challenge of coming face-to-face with danger in their work or leisure time. Policemen, firemen, astronauts, and military personnel, for example, often get great satisfaction from their difficult jobs. They still feel fear on occasion, but ideally they have the bravery, experience, training, equipment, and teamwork to bring threatening situations to a good conclusion.

Other people enjoy pursuing death-defying sports or hobbies, for example sky diving, mountain climbing, or tornado chasing. A great number of us like the excitement that comes from watching others face fearful situations or from experiencing as spectators "safe" danger. We as a nation spend many entertainment dollars to see action/ adventure and horror movies, attend car races, watch "X-Game" extreme sports events, and go on ever-more-frightening roller coaster rides.

People with common fears, those with phobias, and those who challenge themselves to confront fear, each handle fear differently. How you deal with your fears depends on your experiences and your personality. If you are like most people, your fears and your attitude toward them will have had a significant impact, either positive or negative, on your life.

Main Ideas

As a student, you may hesitate to participate in a class discussion about a reading. You may not be clear on its main points. By using the *before, during,* and *after* reading strategies, your understanding will improve.

1. Before you read, you predict the topic of the reading. Ask yourself, "*Who or what is this paragraph or selection about?*"

2. While you read, you establish a mental conversation to keep yourself focused on the reading and connected to the topic. Ask yourself, "*What does the author want me, the reader, to understand or remember about this topic? What is the author's main idea?*" Whether directly stated or not, the main idea is supported by details that allow you to better understand or visualize the reading. Identify the examples, explanations, or facts which support the author's main point. Major supporting details establish the main idea while minor details simply add interest.

3. After you read, the topic, main idea, and supporting details will come together as you evaluate your understanding. Ask yourself, "*Were there any confusing parts? What is important to remember?*"

Having the ability to identify the topic, main idea, and supporting details will enhance your comprehension and make you a more effective reader.

Unit Objectives

After completing the unit, you will be able to:

1. Identify the topic of a selection.

2. Determine the stated or unstated main idea of a paragraph or longer selection.

3. Recognize the major and minor supporting details of a paragraph or longer selection.

Chapter 5

Topics and Main Ideas

Theme: Phobias

"The oldest and strongest emotion of mankind is fear."

H. P. LOVECRAFT

Phobias

We all have fears, but at what point do they interfere with our lives? Many of us jump at the sight of a spider crawling on our leg. A very bumpy plane ride may make us nervous. But what if a fear becomes so intense that normal life is impossible? Then a fear would have become a phobia.

A phobia is an intense and persistent fear of a specific object, situation, or activity. The anxiety is usually out of proportion to the real situation, and the victim is fully aware that the fear is irrational. Because of this fear, the phobic person leads a restricted life. A salesperson who is terrified to fly has to limit business to areas which can be visited by land, rail, or water. A person with an extreme fear of elevators must use the stairs to get to a friend's tenth-floor apartment.

Phobic anxiety is different from other forms of anxiety because it is focused on a particular object or event. When confronted with the object of their phobia, people often experience physical symptoms. A rapid, pounding heartbeat, stomach disorders, nausea, diarrhea, frequent urination, choking feelings, flushing of the face, sweating, trembling, and faintness are some common symptoms.

Through various types of therapy, some phobic people are able to confront their fears. More commonly, however, they avoid the situation or object that causes the fear—an avoidance that limits the phobic's life experiences.

Chapter Objectives

After completing this chapter, you will be able to:

1. Identify the topic of a paragraph or longer selection.

2. Determine the stated main idea of a paragraph.

3. Determine the stated main idea of a longer selection.

Focus on Topics and Main Ideas

When you were little, did you ever wonder how something worked? For example, the telephone was a fascinating item. It rang, you could talk into it, and you could hear someone else talk to you. You may have taken the telephone receiver and pulled out the parts to figure out how it worked. To understand how something works, you sometimes have to examine the parts. The topic and the main idea are the parts you need to identify to get a better understanding of what you are reading.

Topic

The topic is the general subject of a paragraph or longer selection. You can usually express it in one or two words. Using *before reading* strategies, you can identify the topic of what you are reading by previewing the title, skimming the reading, and asking yourself, "*Who or what is this paragraph or selection about?*"

Stated Main Idea

After confirming the topic, read the selection. While reading, ask yourself, "*What does the author want me, the reader, to understand or remember about this topic?*" The answer is the main idea of the paragraph or selection.

Authors will often state the main idea they are trying to convey in one or two sentences towards the beginning of the paragraph or longer selection. This statement is referred to as the main idea statement or the topic sentence. While the main idea statement is frequently found early in the reading, there is no rule as to where the main idea statement will be located. The author may place it in the beginning, middle, or end of a paragraph or selection. As you read, look for a stated main idea.

To sum up, find the topic of the selection by asking yourself, "Who or what is this paragraph or selection about?" To determine the main idea, ask yourself, "What does the author want me, the reader, to understand or remember about this topic?"

To understand the difference between topic and stated main idea, read the following paragraph.

> Phobias are very treatable. In *Prevention* magazine (July 1992), a psychologist reports as many as 90 percent of people with phobias recover or show significant

progress after treatment. Effective therapies include relaxation techniques, thinking about the reality of the situation and gradual exposure to the source of fear. People with mild phobias often treat themselves using self-help groups and books. With more intense phobias, a few sessions with a good therapist will often relieve the problem. Severe phobias may require more intensive therapy.

What is the *topic* of this paragraph?

The topic is phobias, a brief answer to the question, *"Who or what is this paragraph a bout?"* Notice that the term *phobias* as mentioned five times by the writer.

What is the *stated main idea* of the paragraph?

The main idea statement "Phobias are very treatable" answers the question, *"What does the author want the reader to understand or remember about the topic of phobias?"* The main idea statement tells us that phobias can be treated.

Short Exercises: Topics and Main Ideas

Directions: *Read each paragraph. State the topic in one or two words. Underline the sentence that contains the main idea.*

1. A phobia is a real fear, but it is a reaction that is out of proportion to a specific situation or thing. Phobias cannot be voluntarily controlled, and they lead to total avoidance of the feared situation. One classic case of phobia concerns Professor William Ellery Leonard, who was terrified by a locomotive when he was a child. This had such far-reaching effects that his phobia virtually kept him a prisoner in the university town where he taught. Professor Leonard described seizures that terrified him. When his anxiety attacks occurred, he had to retreat to what he felt was a safe place.

   Taken from *Fears and Phobias* by Margaret Hyde

   Topic:_____

2. Almost everyone knows the look and sound of fear. Suppose a cry pierces the distant air. You can tell from the sound that someone is frightened even though you have no idea what is causing the fear. You can picture the distorted face of the person. The eyes are open, and the muscles of the lower eyelids are tense. The upper eyelids are raised, and so are the eyebrows. Eyebrows appear to be straightened, and there are horizontal wrinkles across the forehead. This is the physical face of fear.

   Taken from *Fears and Phobias* by Margaret Hyde

   Topic:_____

3. Antianxiety and depression drugs such as Xanex and Prozac can prove useful in treating phobias, but many therapists say their use should be limited and not form the basis for treatment. "We don't want to cover over people's fears with drugs," says Dr. Natalie Schor. "Our goal is to allow phobics to experience some anxiety so they

can learn to be less afraid." Conventional psychoanalysis, she and other phobia experts note, is useless in treating these problems. What seems to work best—and treatment for phobias yields the highest rate of success of any type of psychotherapy, with more than 90 percent of patients finding some relief—is a combination of cognitive and behavioral approaches, with supporting medication if necessary.

Taken from a 1994 *Cosmopolitan* article written by Stephen Rae

Topic:_____

4 Technophobia—fear of technology—is another common problem, and one that's growing. "People aren't just afraid of computers," says Larry Rosen, a psychology professor at California State University in Dominguez Hills. "These days, almost everything in your house has technology: computers embedded in the VCR, microwave, coffeepot. We're finding that people are uncomfortable with all of them." Up to 25 percent of the population "are technophobes," Rosen adds. "They avoid technology at all costs. If you force them to use something that involves it, they'll have all the symptoms of a true anxiety reaction: sweaty palms, nervousness, quickened heartbeat. Maybe their mind goes blank."

Taken from a 1994 *Cosmopolitan* article written by Stephen Rae

Topic:_____

5. Some people are so consumed by a fear of dentists that they develop dental phobia. Although dentistry has changed over the years, a few people who have had a negative experience will never go back for dental care. These men and women are so afraid of a dentist that they avoid them at all costs. The lack of care can result in missing teeth, bad breath, and poor health due to dental infections. Hopefully as dentistry becomes more and more pain free, this phobia will disappear.

Topic:_____

6. Every year in November, the Butterball company and the Federal government provide a hot line for information for anyone cooking a Thanksgiving turkey. Excessive worrying over being able to cook a turkey properly is known as turkey phobia. Will the bird be done? How do you stuff it? Will it taste good to all of your special guests? This turkey cooking anxiety affects thousands. Everyone wants to have the perfect holiday and a delicious turkey for this day.

Topic:_____

7. Coulrophobia, or fear of clowns, seems to be relatively common but no one knows the reasons why many people fear clowns. Circus entertainers delight and entertain young children. Yet clowns have also been characters in horror films or murder mysteries. Is it the makeup that prevents someone from seeing who is really there? Is

it the fear of the unknown or unreal? Those who suffer from coulrophobia feel anxious at a circus. To ease anxiety, sitting far away from the center ring or near an aisle for a quick escape may allow a person to enjoy the show.

Topic:_____

8. Do you shake and feel dizzy when you experience heights? Is there a feeling of panic when you are on a ladder or the 102nd floor of a building? You may want to cling to something nearby or avoid any situations that will bring you to new heights. You cannot trust your balance. You cannot even ride a horse as they seem too "high." It could be a case of acrophobia or the fear of heights.

Topic:_____

Reading Selections

Selection One: **"A Virtual End to Stage Fright"**

Heidi V. Anderson

Before You Read

Before you read "A Virtual End to Stage Fright," complete the following:

Predict what the topic may be.

Skim the reading to see if your prediction was correct.

Think about what you already know about virtual reality exposure therapy. Have you ever heard of VRE therapy? Do you have stage fright? How do you cope with it?

Set your purpose for reading. Do you expect to be entertained, to gain knowledge, or to explore an argument?

Words to Preview

augmenting *(v.)* to make greater; increase *(par. 3)*
anecdotal *(adj.)* characterized by short stories of interest *(par. 4)*
efficacy *(n.)* power to produce a desired effect *(par. 4)*
logistics *(n.)* the handling of the details of an operation *(par. 10)*
intuitively *(adv.)* known through insight *(par. 13)*

A Virtual End to Stage Fright.

During Reading

As you read "A Virtual End to Stage Fright," continue to predict events, visualize the story, and monitor your comprehension. What is the author telling you about VRE therapy and its uses?

Virtual End to Stage Fright

Sophisticated New Technology Spells the End of Podium Panic

by Heidi V. Anderson

1 On the surface, the successful executive was an accomplished public speaker: Confident and composed, he exhibited a firm grasp of his material and spoke with intelligence and ease. For decades he'd delivered speeches to all types of audiences, from small groups of colleagues assembled in conference rooms to upwards of 200 strangers in convention halls. But what the audience members didn't know was that heavy doses of medication accounted in large part for his relaxed manner.

2   Finally, enough was enough—he decided to end his paralyzing stage fright for good. So he entered a novel treatment program that uses virtual reality exposure therapy, or VRE therapy, to overcome phobias. After a dozen or so sessions, his comfort level with giving speeches and presentations notably increased—and his need for a chemical crutch saw a corresponding drop.

3   Augmenting traditional therapy for phobias with high-tech tools, including a headset that places wearers in a simulated environment, VRE therapy is an innovative treatment for a number of pathological fears, including aviophobia (fear of flying), acrophobia (fear of heights), and glossophobia (fear of public speaking).

Virtual Therapy, Real Results

4 While no long-term studies have demonstrated the effectiveness of VRE therapy for glossophobia, the anecdotal evidence of its efficacy is strong.

5   "It has tremendous power, and once clients experience VRE therapy they'll rarely do a speech without it," says psychologist Robert H. Reiner, the executive director of Behavioral Associates, a practice specializing in cognitive behavioral therapy located on Manhattan's Upper East Side, and a faculty member in the Department of Psychiatry at New York University Medical Center.

6   "As psychologists we generally don't speak in terms of treatment cure, but in these cases, we are able to do just that," he says. "Executives who have been too anxious to give presentations suddenly become effective public speakers; travelers who refused air travel are becoming frequent fliers."

7   To understand why VRE therapy shows such promise, look no further than the traditional methods of treating a fear of public speaking. Many who experience anxiety when faced with a public-speaking experience have attended Toastmasters,

A Virtual End to Stage Fright.

a non-profit organization that helps individuals improve communication skills. Members meet once a week for about an hour and practice conducting meetings, giving impromptu speeches, and presenting prepared speeches.

8   But for those whose reluctance to speak in public goes beyond a mild anxiety, such an experience can be far too overwhelming. Many who fall into this group choose traditional therapy, in which they work with a trained clinician to learn how to overcome such fears.

9   According to Page Anderson, an assistant professor in the department of psychology at Georgia State University, the process of overcoming a particular fear includes gradual and controlled exposure to the source of the fear, in which the exposure is repeated and prolonged.

10   But when the fear under consideration is that of public speaking, logistics often get in the way. It's expensive and difficult to gather a real audience, and it's also a challenge for the therapist to "control" that audience—for example, having them look bored or interested at appropriate moments—during a session. Therefore, some therapists have their patients try to visualize speaking in front of an audience.

11   "We used to have clients imagine the problem, but many couldn't imagine it well enough," says Brenda Wiederhold, executive director of the San Diego, Calif.-based Virtual Reality Medical Center. "Now, we can have them feel more like they are really in that scenario with VR. If you don't feel the fear, you can't get over it."

> If you don't feel the fear, you can't get over the fear.

12   An additional difficulty is that a stigma against seeing a therapist may keep some from seeking treatment.

13   "Some people aren't so keen to go to a therapist. But many are accustomed to using a computer to help in their everyday lives," says Anderson, who was formerly the director of clinical services at Virtually Better, a Decatur, Ga.-based company that designs VRE software. "Also, it's intuitively appealing. The virtual audience can be a gentle way to face their fears. It's real but not real at the same time."

Step by Careful Step

14   VRE therapy varies from clinic to clinic, but the general procedure is the same. The first step for many patients is to learn general anxiety management skills. Reiner notes that the physiological response to the fear of public speaking is slightly different from other fears he treats. This fear produces a "fight or flight" response, and the body goes into overdrive; blood flows from the hands and feet to the center of the body, and patients sometimes hyperventilate as their breathing shifts from their abdomen to their chest.

15   And, since the human brain is associative—i.e., the brain associates the public-speaking situation with this reaction—the condition will only get worse without help.

A Virtual End to Stage Fright.

16   The help takes the form of a therapist working with the patient to slow down his breathing. Reiner says he shows patients how to breathe from the diaphragm, at a slow rate of about six to seven times per minute. How long it takes to become comfortable with new relaxation techniques depends upon the patient, and Anderson typically spends her first four sessions with a patient working on building these coping skills.

17   Next comes the virtual reality portion of the therapy. The patient puts on a headset—also called a head-mounted display or "glasses"—that looks a bit like an old-fashioned stereo headset, only one that fits over the top of one's head and eyes. Some therapists also attach biofeedback equipment so they can monitor heart rate and other physiological responses; others simply observe the patient's breathing patterns, rate of perspiration, and other physical signals.

> The behavior of the virtual audience varies, depending on where the patient is in treatment.

18   Via the headset, the patient sees a three-dimensional world. She is onstage, usually behind a podium, with a curtain facing her, a slide projector and clicker next to her, and a large screen at her back. To make the situation as realistic as possible, the software has a feature that allows it to work with a presentation designed by the patient; the therapist can import a PowerPoint or other presentation so that the patient is presenting an actual talk she might be giving in the future to a live audience. Then, the therapist "loads up" the audience. The audience varies, depending on where the patient is in the treatment hierarchy.

19   For example, the first time a patient tries out the software, only a handful of people may be in the audience. They may be smiling, laughing, or otherwise showing enthusiasm for the talk. In many cases, the patient creates a list of questions that she'd like someone in the audience to ask, and the therapist then poses those questions in this controlled setting.

20   Over time, the therapist typically introduces more challenging situations. For instance, for a patient who wishes to work on assertiveness, the therapist may have an audience member ask a question at an inappropriate time. Before the VRE session, the therapist and the patient discuss how the question might be handled; during the VRE session the patient can practice asking the audience member to hold that question until the Q&A period at the end of the talk.

21   The effectiveness of virtual reality exposure therapy for glossophobia remains to be proven. While it shows great promise and therapists who have used the treatment speak well of it, there is a lack of data supporting its efficacy. But a couple of studies could soon remedy this.

22   One, funded by the National Institutes of Health, involved 10 participants who went through eight individual sessions over the course of eight to 10 weeks. It is just wrapping up its first phase. Another study, conducted at theUniversity of Houston's College of Technology in the fall of 2002, divided students in a communications

---

A Virtual End to Stage Fright.

class into two groups, each of which contained students with high, medium, and low levels of speaking anxiety.

23   Although neither study is ready to release results, both found the therapy promising enough that follow-up, larger-scale studies are planned.

Heidi V. Andersonis a Boulder, Colo.–based free-lance writer whose work has appeared in Smart Computing, PC Novice, and Editor & Publisher. She can be reached at hmcl@hbsp.harvard.edu

---

The word *glossophobia* is derived from *glosso*, a learned borrowing from Greek meaning "tongue," and *phobia*, a fear or anxiety that exceeds normal proportions or has no basis in reality, according to *Webster's Encyclopedic Unabridged Dictionary*. Glossopohobia falls into the category of social anxieties, and it's one of the most common fears in the United States.

But unfortunately, most people with social anxiety don't seek help. The reason? They don't know where to go for help, according to a study that examined responses from more than 6,000 people who participated in National Anxiety Disorders Screening Day.

Web Resources

www.virtuallybetter.com Visit the Virtually Better Web site for more information on VRE therapy for glossophobia and for a list by location of clinics offering this therapy.

After Reading

Word Connections

1. What do *glossophobes* fear?

_____

2. "After a dozen or so sessions, his comfort level with giving speeches and presentations notably increased–and his need for a chemical *crutch* saw a corresponding drop." What does the word *crutch* mean is this sentence? What are some other definitions of the word *crutch*?

_____

_____

3. Patients dealing with fear of public speaking aspire to become more assertive. Create a concept of definition map for *assertiveness. (par. 20)*

A Virtual End to Stage Fright.

Concept of Definition Map for Assertiveness

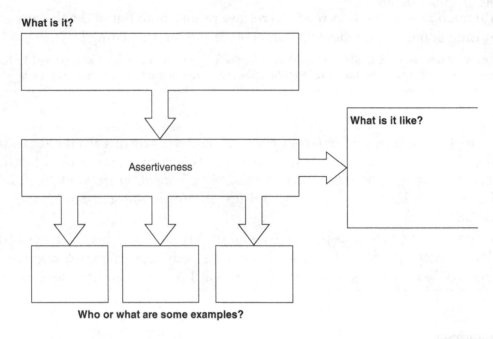

What is it?

Assertiveness

What is it like?

Who or what are some examples?

4. Fear produces a "fight or flight" response and the body goes into overdrive. Some people *hyperventilate* as their breathing shifts from their abdomen to their chest. What does *hyper-* mean? Give an example of a time you or a friend *hyperventilated*?

_____

_____

_____

_____

5. When using VRE therapy, some therapists also attach *biofeedback* equipment to their patients. What does *biofeedback* mean?

_____

_____

Connecting Meaning

1. The fear of public speaking can affect your success at work and other areas of your life. What is the stated main idea of "A Virtual End to Stage Fright?"

_____

_____

_____

_____

2. Describe the general procedure (step by step) of virtual reality exposure therapy.

_____

_____

_____

_____

_____

3. Is there any evidence available to show the effectiveness of VRE therapy?

_____

_____

_____

_____

Selection Two: **"Red Flag"** from "Five Who Conquered Fear"

Cathy Perlmutter

Before You Read

Before you read "Red Flag," complete the following:

Predict what the topic may be.

Skim the reading to see if you have correctly predicted the topic.

Think about the topic. How do you react to injections, violent movies, and the sight of blood? Do you avoid them? Does your heart race uncontrollably? Do you get nauseous or faint? Relate what you know or have experienced to this selection describing how a teenager's phobia affected her life.

Set your purpose for reading. Do you expect to be entertained, to gain knowledge, or to explore an argument?

Words to Preview

queasy *(adj.)* nauseous, uneasy, troubled *(par. 1)*
onset *(n.)* beginning *(par. 3)*
fiasco *(n.)* complete failure *(par. 10)*
neurologist *(n.)* doctor who deals with nervous system disorders *(par. 11)*
hierarchy *(n.)* ranking from highest to lowest or lowest to highest *(par. 12)*
provoking *(adj.)* troubling the nerves or peace of mind *(par. 12)*
squeamish *(adj.)* easily nauseated or sickened *(par. 19)*

During Reading

As your read "Red Flag," continue to predict events, visualize the story, and monitor your comprehension. What is the author telling you about blood and injury phobia?

Red Flag

1 Injections, violent movies, and the sight of blood make many people *queasy*. But for some, the problem gets out of hand. It's called a "blood and injury phobia." Blood and injury phobia is a little different, though. Like other phobic reactions, it starts with a rapid rise in heart rate. But then, blood pressure and heart rate drop dramatically, and the person usually faints.

2   Sarah McKinley, 17, a high school senior, faced down a severe phobia of this kind with the help of the staff of the Center for Stress and Anxiety Disorders at the State University of New York at Albany. (We've changed Sarah's name.)

3   Although Sarah was young, the sudden *onset* of her phobia is exactly like that of many older adults, notes the Center's Dr. Albano. "It even happens in physicians, who after years of treating injuries suddenly start fainting at the sight of them."

4   In grammar school, if we had to watch a gory film, I closed my eyes during the bloody parts. That wasn't unusual; everyone else did the same thing as I did.

5   But then, one day about a year ago, I was sitting in homeroom, reading a newspaper, when I saw a photograph of bloody palm prints on a wall. I looked at it and passed out. That was the first time.

6   The school sent me home. I knew that looking at the photograph had completely grossed me out, but I didn't worry about it too much.

7   Then came a sort of turning point. In a social studies class, they showed us an incredibly bloody movie about the Civil War. A soldier was blown up, and I fainted right there.

8   After that I started fainting about once a week. Then twice a week, then every day, then four or five times a day. The Gulf War was going on at that time, so magazines

and newspapers were full of bloody images and ideas. In English class, we'd read stories in which people were injured, and those scared me. In biology class, talking about body parts made me faint. I think my imagination was too vivid. My mom and I drove by an auto accident once, and even though I couldn't see the injuries, I imagined them, and fainted. I couldn't look at any kind of raw meat.

9   It got so bad that when a teacher handed me back a math test with corrections written in red ink, I thought of blood. The next thing I knew, I was lying on the ground.

10   No one was really sure what was going on. Early on, I was brought to an emergency room. What a *fiasco*. The guy kept asking me if I was pregnant! Then he decided there was nothing wrong with me. Another doctor told my parents I'd have to be on medications for the rest of my life.

11   We went to a *neurologist*, and he said my brain was fine. He said I needed to see a psychologist, that what I actually had was a phobia. My parents found the Center for Stress and Anxiety Disorders.

12   They asked me to write out a *hierarchy*, starting with the situation I found least anxiety *provoking*, and working all the way up to the scariest. At the bottom of my list I wrote down things like, looking at a Band-Aid and seeing something red. At the top, the scariest things I listed were seeing someone bleeding and watching a gory movie.

13   The psychologists told me that most people with phobias must be taught to relax in scary situations. But people who faint need to learn the opposite response—how to tense up our bodies and keep them tense, so our blood pressure doesn't drop and we don't pass out.

14   First I practiced tensing and holding with separate muscle groups, like the hands, the arms, and the legs. Then I learned to tense and hold all the muscles at the same time. I learned to do it sitting, standing up, in a variety of positions.

15   Then the therapists asked me to choose music that made me feel cheerful. I picked Billy Joel music and brought in my favorite tape. That's when we were ready to start working on the hierarchy list.

16   At first I had to write the word blood over and over again. I'd tense all my muscles, and sometimes they'd play the Billy Joel music that I liked. We'd do that until I was completely comfortable writing "blood" and then move up to the next level. They'd bring in pieces of raw meat, scary pictures, gory movies. I'd tense and listen to the music.

17   By the end of about three months, I wasn't fainting anymore and could do all the things on my hierarchy without feeling nervous.

18   My final tasks were to have my blood drawn and to watch a hip operation. When I went to get my blood drawn, the doctor couldn't find my vein, so he let me draw his blood! I was fine, even though I probably hurt him! And I actually found the hip operation interesting. I think the therapist who came along with me was more upset

than I was. He'd never seen an operation, and I noticed he kept his arms folded, which is one way of doing the tension exercise without anyone knowing.

19   I'll probably always be a little bit *squeamish* about blood and injuries. But nowadays, it's no big deal.

After Reading

Word Connections

1. "In grammar school, if we had to watch a gory film, I closed my eyes during the bloody parts." What synonym for *gory* is given in this sentence?

2. The situation that I found to be the most *anxiety* provoking was going to the dentist for a root canal.

Meaning from Context Map

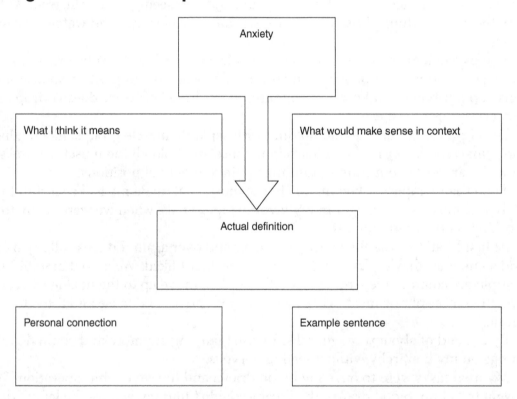

3. Sarah wrote out her hierarchy of anxiety provoking situations. Write your own *hierarchy* of situations that frighten you from the least frightening to the most frightening.

_____

_____

_____

Connecting Meaning

1. What is the stated main idea of "Red Flag"?

_____

_____

2. How does the main idea relate to the title?

_____

_____

3. Name three items that caused an extreme reaction in Sarah, items which most people handle without unusual upset.

_____

_____

_____

4. Most people with phobias must learn to relax. What was different about Sarah's treatment?

_____

_____

_____

Selection Three: **"Foresight Conquers Fear of the Future"**

Edward Cornish

Before Reading

Before you read "Foresight Conquers Fear of the Future," complete the following:

Predict the topic.

Skim the reading to see if you have correctly predicted the topic.

Think about the fear of the future and how foresight can eliminate that fear. Are you fearful about your future? Do you have foresight? Are there ways to improve your foresight?

Set your purpose for reading. Do you expect to be entertained, to gain knowledge, or to explore an argument?

Words to Preview

foresight *(n.)* the act of looking forward *(title)*

shambles *(n.)* a scene or a state of great disorder or confusion *(par. 1)*

lamentations *(n.)* the act of regretting strongly *(par. 4)*

besieged *(v.)* to cause worry or distress *(par. 4)*

anarchy *(n.)* absence of order *(par. 4)*

hedonism *(n.)* the doctrine that pleasure is the sole or chief good in life *(par. 4)*

unprecedented *(adj.)* having no an earlier occurrence of something similar *(par. 11)*

transformation *(n.)* the act, process or instance of change *(par. 11)*

conundrum *(n.)* difficult problem *(par. 14)*

During Reading

As you read "Foresight Conquers Fear of the Future," continue to predict events, visualize the story, and monitor your comprehension. What does the author want you to know or remember about foresight?

Foresight Conquers Fear of the Future

Today's youth are growing up in the midst of radical social and economic transformations. Now is the time to develop the most critical skill for effectively managing their careers and personal lives: Foresight.

Edward Cornish

1   "I'm scared," the young man confessed. "I'm starting my eighteenth year in a world that makes no sense to me. All I know is that this world I'm living in is a shambles and I don't know how to put it together."

2   The young man bared his soul to an invisible audience during a radio call-in show. Other callers agreed with his dismal assessment of the state of the world. Nobody offered an answer for his fears.

3   Bill Moyers, the TV interviewer, happened to be listening that night and was profoundly affected by what he heard.

4   "Such lamentations," Moyers commented later, "are deep currents running throughout the liberal West today. Our secular and scientific societies are besieged by violence, moral anarchy, and purposelessness that have displaced any mobilizing vision of the future except hedonism and consumerism."

5   Moyers put his finger on what may be a key challenge faced by many young people today: their inability to think realistically, creatively, and hopefully about the future. Instead, these young people suffer from what can be described as "futurephobia."

6   Some futurephobes have an acute version of this malady, like the young man described by Moyers, but most futurephobes simply focus on their immediate circumstances and drift into the future without thinking much about it at all. Either way, they may drift into financial or other kinds of trouble.

7   The connection between poor foresight and serious problems is widely recognized by psychologists and sociologists. Yale sociologist Wendell Bell asserts that some authorities "go so far as to claim that all forms of deviant, criminal, and reckless behavior have the same fundamental cause: the tendency to pursue immediate benefits without concern for long-term costs, a disregard for inevitable and undesirable future consequences."

8   Successful self-management, says Bell, requires understanding and giving appropriate value to the likely consequences of your actions. If you have little or no foresight, you cannot think realistically and creatively about your future, so you cannot steer your career and personal life toward long-term success.

9   Poor foresight can threaten not just the careers of emerging adults, but even their lives. Young people lacking foresight are prone to act recklessly—drive too fast, use drugs, play with guns, commit crimes, and even kill themselves (or others).

10   On the other hand, when young people do manage to develop good foresight, they can think realistically, creatively, and hopefully about the future. So empowered, they can aim their careers toward achievable goals and cheerfully accept the burdens of responsibility and self-discipline required for success. Barack Obama is a recent example of foresight-empowered success.

The New Urgency of Foresight

11   Older people are prone to dismiss the problems of youth as just a normal part of growing up, but the fact is that today's youth are coming of age in a world undergoing an unprecedented transformation powered by multiple technological

---

Foresight Conquers Fear of the Future.

revolutions. These technological advances, all occurring simultaneously, are overturning the world's economies and undermining long-established institutions, careers, and lifestyles.

12   Amid such turbulence, making a good decision concerning one's career or private life can be highly problematic, and the demographic group most acutely affected are young people moving into adulthood. These emerging adults have entered a time of life when parents and teachers have diminished power to guide them, so young people must make critical decisions by themselves at a time when their experience of the world is limited and their brains are still immature. (Foresight, scientists say, is largely a function of the brain's prefrontal cortex, which does not reach maturity until about age 25.)

13   Adding to the challenge of making appropriate decisions in today's world is the fact that knowledgeable and trustworthy advisors are now less available to emerging adults. In bygone days, most young people lived in villages or small towns where people got to know each other well, enabling the elders to offer wise counsel for a young person trying to find a suitable job or marriage partner.

14   In today's highly mobile mass society, young people roam the world and can choose among thousands of potential careers and mates in countless different locations. In principle, the abundance of choice offers wonderful opportunities, but it can pose a baffling conundrum for an emerging adult with little experience of the world.

15   Making matters worse for many young people, technological advances have eliminated most of the jobs that could be learned quickly and paid enough for an 18-year-old to live on and maybe support a family. Now, getting a decent job is likely to require years of training at a college or university during which time the student earns little or no money and may go heavily into debt.

Improving Youth Foresight

16 Ironically, it was fear of the future that led to some of our most useful foresight tools.

17   Relatively little was done to create a science of foresight until after World War II, which had led to the development of rockets and atomic bombs. Frightened that the Soviet Union might use the new superweapons, the U.S. Air Force established the RAND Corporation in Santa Monica, California, as a "think factory." The main task of RAND's scientists and scholars was to think about future wars—how to fight and win them.

18   To fulfill their mission, the RAND scientists had to think seriously about the future, and in the process they developed a variety of methods for thinking more scientifically about the future than had ever been done before. Mathematician Olaf Helmer and his RAND colleague Norman Dalkey developed the Delphi technique, a way to refine and synthesize scientists' forecasts of future technological developments. In addition, Herman Kahn developed his scenario technique for exploring the implications of possible future events. The scenario method is now widely used in government and business.

Foresight Conquers Fear of the Future.

19   Meanwhile, Arnold Brown, Edie Weiner, and others refined ways for identifying and analyzing social trends. Today trend analysis is widely recognized as one of the most useful ways for identifying significant developments in technology and society and anticipating outcomes.

20   Many of the methods developed since World War II can now be used in simplified forms by young people and by teachers or others trying to help young people gain a practical understanding of what is happening in the world now, where things are going, and the opportunities that young people have to make valuable contributions to human welfare as well as succeed in their chosen careers and personal lives.

21   The task now is to make foresight into a recognized life skill that can empower young people to think more clearly, constructively, and hopefully about the future. The World Future Society has already initiated several projects for improving youth foresight, and more are under development.

22   Young people interested in participating in a Society conference now can attend at a reduced rate of $125 ($150 on site) and many members have been donating funds to cover one or more full scholarships for young people.

23   In addition, the Society recently sponsored a High School Essay Contest, and the first group of winners was announced in July. Other programs will be instituted as funding becomes available.

24   If we can equip today's young people with good foresight, we can all be much more optimistic about their future and ours.

After Reading

Word Connections

1. "Other callers agreed with his *dismal* assessment of the state of the world." What is the meaning of *dismal*?

   _____

   _____

2. Paragraph 4 states "young people suffer from what can be described as 'futurephobia'." What is *futurephobia*? Are you a futurephobe? "Why or why not?

   _____

   _____

   _____

   _____

_____

Foresight Conquers Fear of the Future.

3. The author uses the words inevitable and inability in the selection. Each word has the prefix *in-* which means not. Inevitable means not capable of being avoided. Inability means not able to do something. Identify two prefixes that mean *not* and provide an example word for each prefix.

_____

_____

_____

_____

4. The television interviewer was *profoundly* affected by what he heard.
   Profoundly **means**
   a. superficially
   b. deeply
   c. shallow
   d. depthless

5. What does the word *baffling* mean? Write a sentence using the word *baffling*.

_____

_____

_____

Connecting Meaning

1. What is the main idea of "Foresight Conquers Fear of the Future?"

_____

_____

_____

2. According to the author, young people who lack foresight are more prone to act how? Give at least three examples.

_____

_____

_____

_____

3. As stated in the selection, who is an example of "foresight-empowered success?"

_____

_____

4. Identify jobs that have been eliminated by modern technology.

_____

_____

5. After World War II, the RAND corporation established a "think factory." What was the main task of this "think factory?"

_____

_____

6. Identify three methods of thinking developed by the "think factory."

_____

_____

_____

Portfolio Activities

Integrating Ideas

Using virtual reality and psychological therapy, patients in these readings were desensitized of their fears. Do you think anyone is really cured of a phobia? Reflect on the causes of phobias. Are they genetically or environmentally caused? Support your answers with examples in writing or in class discussion.

Extending Concepts

In "Red Flag," Sarah used music to help relieve her anxiety. In writing, describe the kinds of music you use to relieve anxiety. What other reasons do you have for listening to music? Describe your favorite music and how it affects your state of mind.

Collaborative Activity

In groups, discuss and record reactions and feelings towards fearful and gory situations. View a movie that reflects the theme of this chapter, for example "Arachnophobia," "Vertigo," or one of the "Friday the Thirteenth" series. Discuss the main idea of the movie and reactions to the fearful and gory situations within the film.

Additional Portfolio Suggestion

Using Internet access, search the web for information about phobias. Compile a list of phobias and their descriptions.

Chapter Summary Graphic Organizer

Complete the graphic organizer with the questions that you should ask yourself when looking for the topic and main idea.

Topics and Main Ideas

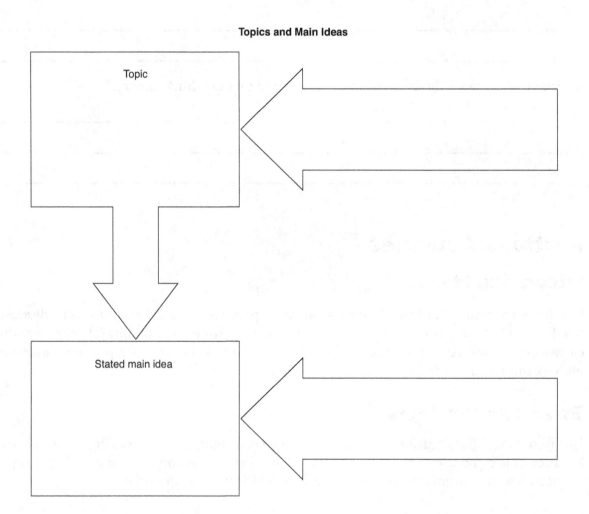

Topics and Main Ideas

Chapter 6

Unstated Main Ideas

Theme of Readings: Taking Risks

"A good scare is worth more to a man than good advice."

EDGAR WATSON HOWE

Taking Risks

How many risks have you taken in your life? Many would say that everything is a risk. Getting up in the morning, driving in traffic, living in urban areas, playing the lotto, falling in love are all risks. You can lose money, time, love, trust, or life itself by taking risks. But is there anything to gain? Take all risks away and life is no longer an adventure. You can not grow or experience what life has to offer without risks. Because of this fact, people commonly accept a number of risks as part of life.

The majority of people feel that acceptable risks are those that do not risk bodily harm. Some people, however, thrive on taking chances. Street luge competitors combine traditional luge and skateboarding as they race down a street flat on their back at 60 mph. Although they wear protective helmets, street lugers lack brakes, seatbelts, and seats. Bungee jumpers secure elastic cords to their ankles and leap hundreds of feet before enjoying the sudden recoil. To provide the ultimate skiing experience, heli-skiers are lifted by helicopter to mountain tops that are not able to be reached by any other means. For casual observers, these thrill-seekers seem to have no fear. In reality, risk-takers don't feel an absence of fear but rather a fear overcome or enjoyed. The challenge satisfies their quest for the exciting adrenaline rush.

Some people choose professions that place them at extraordinary risk. Police officers and firefighters place their life at risk as part of their job. Bomb squads handle bomb threats and possible explosive devices. Medical specialists working with deadly viruses run the risk of contracting fatal diseases. Likewise, scientists who chase tornadoes to record information for study place themselves in incredible danger.

The risks you have taken in life may not be this extreme. The level of acceptable risk differs for everyone. Fearsome or fearless, we choose a variety of experiences to make our life a unique adventure.

Chapter Objective

After completing this chapter, you will be able to determine the unstated main idea of a paragraph or selection.

Focus on Unstated Main Ideas

Are you able to figure out what is being implied but not directly expressed in each of these situations?

- It's the week before Valentine's Day and a woman stops to gaze at every diamond ring she sees in jewelry store windows at the local mall.

- A father places a "Warning–Health Hazard" sign on his teenager's bedroom door.

- A dog sits by the door with a leash in his mouth.

In life we often have to figure out what is being implied but not stated. In reading a paragraph or selection, the same is sometimes true. Often an author will not state the main idea in one or more sentences, but will expect you to figure it out from the information given. In these cases, you must draw a conclusion that is implied but not directly stated.

Whether the main idea is stated or unstated, identify the topic of the paragraph by asking yourself, "*Who or what is this paragraph or selection about?*" As you read, ask yourself, "*What does the author want me to understand or remember about the topic?*" If there is not a single sentence that answers this question, look at all of the important information in the reading and draw your own conclusion about the main idea. Your conclusion is the unstated main idea, which you will then express in one or two sentences.

As you read the following paragraph, draw your own conclusion about the main idea. Compare your answer with the one given.

> Years ago, planning a vacation meant deciding whether to go to the beach, visit out of state relatives, or tour historical landmarks. If adventurous, a person might have chosen to go camping or fishing. Today people plan vacations around activities such as rock climbing, bungee jumping, or white water rafting. An adventurous vacationer may go ice climbing, shark diving, or attend an outdoor survival school.

Who or what is this paragraph about?
The topic of this paragraph is vacations. All four sentences relate to this topic.

What does the author want me to remember about this topic?
The types of vacations have changed over the years. The words *years ago* and *today* establish a comparison with types of vacations given for each time frame.

Short Exercises: Unstated Main Ideas

Directions: *Read each paragraph. Identify the topic and express the author's unstated main idea in a complete sentence.*

1. Expert parachutists on graphite boards twist and turn while free falling 13,000 feet. Sky surfing did not exist in 1990. Today it attracts thousands of devotees. BASE jumping (**B**uildings, **A**ntennas, **S**pans, **E**arth) involves parachuting off fixed objects such as radio towers or bridges. It was officially established in 1980 and now lures hundreds. Ten years ago rock climbers numbered in the tens of thousands. Currently, an estimated half-million Americans enjoy clinging to cliffs.

   Topic: _____

   Main Idea: _____

   _____

2. Tie a secure, super strong, elastic cord around your ankles, close your eyes, and jump hundreds of feet into the air. Suddenly the elastic snaps back and you enjoy the weightless recoil of a bungee jump. For many, this amusement park activity leads to a trip to the doctor or chiropractor to help relieve neck or back pain. Others are not so lucky. In 1997, trapeze artist Laura Patterson, died when a bungee cord broke during rehearsals for a Super Bowl halftime show. Yet the sport of bungee jumping is still pursued.

   Topic: _____

   Main Idea: _____

   _____

3. A person who wouldn't even think about taking a physical risk may stand in front of a large audience to sing. Another may never skateboard but will invest thousands of dollars on a stock tip. A third person is frightened by the thought of parachuting out of a plane but will change careers without a moment's hesitation. Which kind of risk would you take?

   Topic: _____

   Main Idea: _____

   _____

4. With winds approaching 300 miles per hour, a storm bears down on Wichita Falls, Texas. The awesome power of a Texas tornado draws a photographer from Australia to witness its fury. Multiple Texas tornadoes attract a team of meteorologists from Japan to collect data. An Oklahoman scientist establishes a base in Lubbock, Texas,

to study the legendary storms of the state. Even filmmakers focus on the state of Texas to illustrate the power of deadly and destructive tornadoes.

Topic:_____

Main Idea:_____

_____

5. Early explorers took extreme risks to discover new lands. Ancient Hawaiian kings surfed in the treacherous waters off the island shores. In the early 1900s, people went over Niagara Falls in a barrel or stood on the wing of a flying biplane in search of new thrills. The French used the word extreme in the 1970s to describe a type of back country skiing that was so dangerous that if you fell, you died. In the 1990s, those who seek excitement practice skateboarding, BMX bike riding, street luging, and wakeboarding.

Topic:_____

Main Idea:_____

_____

6. Roger Stoneburger started bungee jumping in 1980, before it was regulated. He loves skiing off cliffs, riding his mountain bike from great heights into airbags and jumping off bridges. Lately he gained a foothold in his dream job–the stunt industry–with an offer to double for John Malkovich and do stunt work on Don Johnson's CBS show, "Nash Bridges."

Adapted from "You Can Buy A Thrill: Chasing the Untimate Rush"
by Rebba Piirto Heath

Topic:_____

Main Idea:_____

_____

7. ESPN's Extreme Games series and recent movies like Point Break and Drop Zone glorify extreme sports. Interest in mountaineering seems to pick up after articles and films like Cliffhanger. National advertising spots have sold everything from salsa chips to carrier services using the visual impact of extreme sports. "You can't watch a day of TV without seeing someone jumping out of an airplane," says Chris Needels, executive director of the U. S. Parachute Association. Stoneburger worked as a consultant on a recent Frito-Lay spot that showed Chris Elliot jumping from a blimp to dip a Tostito chip into a jar of salsa on the middle of the football field.

Adapted from "You Can Buy A Thrill: Chasing The Ultimate Rush"
by Rebecca Piirto Heath

Topic:_____

Main Idea: _____

_____

8. "Five...our...three...two...one...see ya!" and Chance McGuire, 25, is airborne off a
   650-ft. concrete dam in Northern California. In one second he falls 16 ft., in two
   seconds 63 ft., and after three seconds and 137 ft. he is flying at 65 m.p.h. He prays
   that his parachute will open facing away from the dam, that his canopy won't
   collapse, that his toggles will be handy and that no ill wind will slam him back into
   the cold concrete. The chute snaps open, the sound ricocheting through the gorge
   like a gunshot, and McGuire is soaring, carving S turns into the air, swooping over a
   winding creek. He lands, packs his chute, and lets out a war whoop. It is a cry of
   defiance, thanks, and victory.

   Adapted from "Life on the Edge" *Time Magazine*

Topic:_____

Main Idea: _____

_____

9. America was founded by risk takers fed up with the English Crown. It was expanded
   by pioneers who risked life and limb to settle in new areas. Lewis and Clark,
   Thomas Edison, Frederick Douglas, Teddy Roosevelt, Henry Ford, and Amelia
   Earhart bucked the odds and took perilous chances.

   Adapted from "Life on the Edge" *Time Magazine*

Topic:_____

Main Idea: _____

_____

10. At 47, Vicki Hendricks has laughed in the face of death more than once. Her idea of
    a good time is running with the bulls in Spain or white-water rafting in Mexico. She
    wanted to go to a great white shark dive next month but that conflicted with the
    national free-fall convention, a gathering of skydiving enthusiasts, which she plans to
    attend.

    Adapted from "The Type T Personality" by Debbie Geiger

Topic:_____

Main Idea: _____

_____

Reading Selections

Selection One: **"On Her Own Terms"**

Nancy Prichard

Before Reading

Before reading "On Her Own Terms," complete the following:

Predict what the topic may be.

Skim the reading to see if you have correctly predicted the topic.

Think about the choices you have made in your life. Have you ever struggled against the odds? Were you comfortable with the outcome? Alison Hargreaves followed her dreams with disastrous results. Think about whether or not the risk is worth the outcome.

Set your purpose for reading. Do you expect to be entertained, to gain knowledge, or explore an argument?

Words to Preview

K2 *(n.)* the world's second-highest and the most deadly mountain *(par.2)*

diminish *(v.)* to make smaller *(par.2)*

insurmountable *(adj.)* impossible to overcome *(par.2)*

supplementary *(adj.)* something added to make up for a deficiency *(par.2)*

desolate *(adj.)* deserted *(par.3)*

plummet *(v.)* to fall straight down *(par.4)*

anorak *(n.)* a heavy jacket with a hood *(par.5)*

surmise *(v.)* to make a guess *(par.8)*

mar *(v.)* inflict damage, spoil *(par.8)*

profoundly *(adv.)* deeply *(par.9)*

inequity *(n.)* injustice; unfairness *(par.9)*

reticent *(adj.)* inclined to keep one's thoughts and feelings to oneself *(par.10)*

hypocrisy *(n.)* the practice of stating beliefs or feelings that one does not possess, falseness *(par.13)*

legacy *(n.)* something handed down from an ancestor *(par.14)*

During Reading

As you read "On Her Own Terms," continue to predict where the author is headed, visualize the story, and monitor your comprehension. What does the author want you to know about Alison Hargreaves and her accomplishments?

On Her Own Terms

1   Her critics felt that she took unacceptable risks, but Alison Hargreaves stayed true to her dreams. In the end, she lost her life—but not the respect she'd earned as one of the world's most accomplished mountaineers.

2   Alison Hargreaves was a true hero, a fact that her tragic death on K2, the world's second-highest and most deadly mountain, does not *diminish*. Struggling against seemingly *insurmountable* odds, the 33-year-old Scot, a mother of two, firmly established herself as an elite mountain climber. She became the first person ever to solo the six classic north faces of the Alps in one season, and the second to climb Mount Everest unassisted by *supplementary* oxygen or partners. By following the call of her lofty ambitions, she became not just a first-rate female alpinist, but one of the top mountain climbers in the world.

3   The events surrounding her death are sketchy—but ultimately not surprising. K2, a mountain in Pakistan's Karakoram Range, has earned its deadly reputation by killing one in three climbers who attempt its *desolate* peak (Everest, by contrast, is fatal to about one out of 10 climbers, and McKinley to one out of 250).

4   Hargreaves had beaten the odds for nearly two months, battling K2's infamous weather in numerous unsuccessful bids for the summit. She was ready to give up and return home to Scotland. But at the last minute, as the Pakistani porters were packing up the base camp, she and her climbing partner, Rob Slater, decided to stay and launch one final attempt. On August 13, Hargreaves, Slater, and four other climbers reached the top of K2. They radioed base camp to announce their success. Then things went horribly wrong. In less than an hour the wind increased to hurricane force and the already-bitter temperature *plummeted*. The summit team was not heard from again.

5   Details of the accident remain a mystery, but two Spanish climbers who had stayed in camp 4 (the last camp before the final push to the summit) confirmed Hargreaves's death. After losing their tents to the wind, the Spaniards bowed to life-threatening cold and exhaustion and began a grim retreat down the mountain. On the descent, they discovered one of Hargreaves's boots, her *anorak*, and her harness. Farther down they saw signs that at least three climbers had fallen from the summit ridge, a distance of nearly 4,000 feet. They *surmised* that the climbers had been blown off the top shortly after they relayed news of their success to base camp. As the Spaniards descended to camp 3, they discovered Hargreaves's body, but they were forced to leave it unburied and abandon a further search for bodies in order to save their own lives.

6   In all, K2 claimed seven of the world's top climbers that night: Hargreaves, three Spaniards, a New Zealander, an American, and a Canadian who turned back earlier than the others but died later at camp 2. They climbed for a variety of shared reasons: a love of the mountains, a passion for adventure, the camaraderie and teamwork, and perhaps the opportunity to gain recognition in the sport they had chosen. Hargreaves's motivation was an echo of her summit partners'; the mountains sent out an irresistible call that she gladly answered.

7   But in a very real way, Hargreaves's experience differed *profoundly* from that of her companions. No matter how great her passion and expertise, she was viewed—and

"On Her Own Terms" by Nancy Prichard. From *Women's Sports and Fitness*, Nov-Dec 1995, v17 n8 p41(3). Reprinted by permission of Nancy Prichard.

judged—first as a woman and a mother. "It's strange," says Karen Dickinson of Mountain Madness, the Seattle guide service that was instrumental in relaying news from the K2 base camp to friends, family, and the public. "Many male climbers have families, but that never seems to be an issue when they're taking huge risks in the mountains. When the seven on K2 were killed, no one asked if the others were fathers; discussion centered on the fact that Alison was a mother."

8   It wasn't the first time. When Hargreaves ascended the north side of the Eiger in 1988, her success was *marred* by controversy over the fact that she was more than five months pregnant at the time. "I was pregnant, not sick!" she countered. "In fact, I'd never felt healthier or more energetic in my life." But her reasons had less to do with pregnancy than with a far-reaching personal philosophy. "What kind of mother would I be if I sacrificed climbing for my children? It's what makes me me, and what makes me the good mother that I am."

9   Whether one agrees with Hargreaves's point of view may be less relevant than the issue of why male climbers—and other risk takers—aren't held to the same standard. Even those who question the choices made by Hargreaves see *inequities* in the criticism launched at her. John Harlin, editor of *Summit Magazine*, was ten years old when his father died during an attempt on the Eiger. He knows both the sorrow of losing a parent and the joy of ascending a mountain. "Being a parent is an enormous responsibility," he says. "When I heard of Alison's leaving her kids at camp when she went up to solo, I didn't like the sound of it, but I would hesitate to condemn her more than I would a male climber."

10   Others have been less *reticent* in their criticism, and Hargreaves's role as a parent continued to overshadow her successes as a climber. Few critics, too, felt it important to note that the children were hardly abandoned but left in the care of their father, Jim Ballard. This was not lost on Hargreaves. "My husband is wonderful with the children," she said flatly. "It's lousy that people don't credit him with his role in parenting. For now, we've chosen our responsibilities, and it works."

11   In spite of her numerous achievements, it wasn't until May of '95, with her oxygenless solo ascent of Mount Everest, that Hargreaves finally gained broad acceptance from the climbing community. For once, the news reports preceded her name not with "Mother of two ..." but with "Mountain climber Alison Hargreaves...." It was a hardwon victory for a woman whose accomplishments had been so monumental.

12   "At times I feel victim to the sexual politics *inherent* in the sport," Hargreaves said not long before her death. "Men don't like seeing women bettering them at high-altitude climbing. That's not what drives me to climb, but it does provide fuel, if just to set the record straight about what people are capable of."

13   Hargreaves's capabilities were not in question, and in the final analysis she should be credited with being a fine mountaineer—one who lost in a high-stakes match but who played the game as well as anyone. Perhaps more important though, she brought to light a glaring *hypocrisy*. "I'm doing something that I'm good at and can hopefully make a living at someday," she said. "It shouldn't matter if I'm female or male, or a mother or not. What should matter is that I do my best with what I have, with what I am."

"On Her Own Terms" by Nancy Prichard. From *Women's Sports and Fitness*, Nov-Dec 1995, v17 n8 p41(3). Reprinted by permission of Nancy Prichard.

14   She wasn't alone in that belief. "Alison made great strides in alpinism, breaking barriers, and setting new standards for women as well as men," says Lydia Brady, the only other woman to have reached the summit of Everest without oxygen. "Not only did she establish herself as a barometer for female alpinists, but she proved herself equal to, or better than, contemporary male alpinists—and on her own terms." In the end, that may be Alison Hargreaves's greatest *legacy*.

After Reading

Word Connections

1. "By following the call of her lofty ambitions, she became not just a first-rate female alpinist, but one of the top mountain climbers in the world." What is the definition of *alpinist*?

   _____Mountain Climber_____

2. Using context clues found in paragraph five, determine the meaning of *surmised*.

   _____Good guess_____

3. Create concept of definition map for *ascend*.

   _____Rise_____

Concept of Definition Map for Ascend

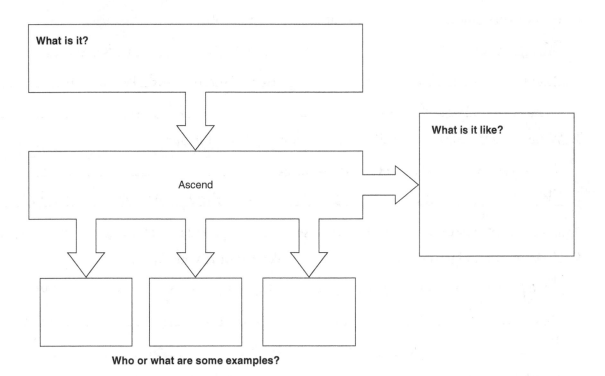

Who or what are some examples?

---

4. Several different prefixes that mean *not* are used in "On Her Own Terms." Identify at least five words that use these prefixes.

Incomplete, o   unburied

5. The speeding car plummeted

   a. across the street.

   b. down into the ditch

   c. to win the race.

   d. up a steep hill.

Connecting Meaning

1. What does the author want you to understand about Hargreaves' mountaineering accomplishments?

   That Hargreaves' ambition was to Sulfill her dream and made other woman to be more ambition with their lifer and is equal or greater then a male alpinists

2. What overshadowed Hargreaves' successes as a climber?

   Hargreaves viewed as a mother who shouldn't risk her children's life in order to fulfill her dreams. And believe to abandon her children with the father in order to climb mountains

3. What does the author identify as Hargreaves' greatest legacy?

   Hargreaves was viewed as a To inspire more woman such as Lydia Brady to reach the top of a mountain and be as equal or greater then a male.

4. How do you judge the risks Hargreaves took? Support your opinion.

   The way I see Hargreaves, she's a strong woman to overcome the K2's deadly weather for the most part and living up to her dream. However, I thought Just as well as other people to have a mother leave and never return to her family. Everyone needs a mother and wife but I can't Judge a person's action to do whatever they want to do.

Selection Two: **"Riders on the Storm: Tornado Chasers Seek the Birthplace of an Elusive Monster"**

Howard B. Bluestein

Before Reading

Before Reading "Riders on the Storm" complete the following:

Predict what the topic may be.

Skim the reading to see if you have correctly predicted the topic.

Think about violent storms. Have you ever experienced a violent thunderstorm, hurricane, or tornado? Have you experienced or seen photos of the damage done by tornadoes? Relate what you know about tornadoes to this selection about scientists who chase tornadoes to increase their knowledge.

Set your purpose for reading. Do you expect to be entertained, to gain knowledge, or to explore an argument?

Words to Preview

troposphere *(n.)* the lowest region of the atmosphere *(par.1)*
stratified *(v.)* formed in layers *(par.1)*
elapsed *(v.)* passed; slipped by *(par.3)*
array *(n.)* impressively large number *(par.3)*
dissipates *(v.)* vanishes *(par.4)*
spawn *(v.)* to produce *(par.5)*
barrage *(n.)* a rapid discharge *(par.6)*
elusive *(adj.)* tending to escape the understanding of *(par.9)*
verified *(v.)* determined the truth or accuracy *(par.9)*

During Reading

As you read "Riders on the Storm," continue to predict what may happen next in the article, visualize the story, and monitor your comprehension. What information does the author want you to remember about tornado chasers?

Riders on the Storm

1 It was April 26, 1991, and high over central Oklahoma an intriguing kind of hell was about to break loose. The early-morning transmissions from the National Weather

Service weather balloons had been encouraging. As the balloons climbed through the *troposphere*, their instrument packages recorded sharply dropping temperatures, increasing wind speeds, and rapid shifts in wind direction. Meanwhile, somewhere between three and eight miles up, an intense disturbance in the wind field was approaching from the southwest on a collision course with warm, moist air flowing northward across the Great Plains from the Gulf of Mexico. The collision would ignite thunderstorms. With luck, the thunderstorms would tap the potential energy of the *stratified* air to trigger more powerful storms known as super-cells: vast rotating mazes of updrafts and downdrafts that stretch 50,000 or 60,000 feet upward into the atmosphere, produce magnificent hailstones, and give rise to many of the most powerful tornadoes on earth.

2   As my team members and I pulled out of the parking lot of the University of Oklahoma at Norman, we thought about those tornadoes. At this time of year the five of us–the driver, Herb Stein; three of my graduate students from the School of Meteorology; and I–thought about little else. Inside the twelve-passenger van our broadband radios, miniature television, and cellular telephone kept up a steady two-way buzz of weather-related chatter. Stored in the rear, where there had been a row of seats, were coils of electrical cables, two tripods, a video camera, data-logging equipment, and a low-power Doppler radar capable of measuring wind speed in rain, hail, and airborne debris at a range of up to three or four miles.

3   Riding along, we kept up running commentaries into small cassette recorders on our laps. Starting at departure time, just after noon, the tapes would later enable us to reconstruct the trip: hours and minutes *elapsed*, mileage readings, road signs, changes of direction, cloud sightings, and, incidentally, mood swings. For example: The National Severe Storms Forecast Center in Kansas City issues a tornado watch for parts of Kansas and Oklahoma. Inside the van, spirits rise. Along the Kansas-Oklahoma border we spot a promising *array* of towering cumulus clouds. Spirits soar. The clouds bubble upward but fail to turn into thunderstorms. Spirits sag. And so on throughout the afternoon.

4   4:15 P.M.: Good news comes in over the National Oceanic and Atmospheric Administration weather band. Back in Norman, the National Weather Service's Doppler radar has detected severe thunderstorms brewing back in northern Oklahoma. Herb Stein makes a U-turn and heads us toward the closest storm. 4:53 P.M.: We catch the storm. Beneath its base, southwest of the precipitation core, a small funnel cloud is forming. The funnel quickly *dissipates*–no tornado this time–and we follow the storm eastward. To the south a new storm has developed, and we spot two more short-lived funnel clouds. 5:47 P.M.: Yet another funnel appears, this time off to the east. We head toward it but change our minds when another severe-thunderstorm warning suggests even better hunting to the south.

5   (Later we would learn that the storm we had abandoned continued into southern Kansas, where it gave rise to a large tornado just south of the small town of Winfield. Meanwhile, not far from where we turned back from Kansas, an even worse storm sprang up. It *spawned* a tornado that cut across Wichita and nearby Andover, killing seventeen people and wreaking more than $150 million worth of damage.)

"Riders on the Storm: Tornado Chasers Seek the Birthplace of an Elusive Monster" by Howard B. Bluestein. From *The Sciences* magazine, March-April 1995, v35 n2 p26(5). This article is reprinted by permission of *The Sciences* and is from the March/April 1995 issue.

6   Approaching our new target storm from the north, we enter Billings, Oklahoma. We pass through town amid the eerie blast of tornado sirens. A *barrage* of wind-driven hailstones, some as big as baseballs, slams into the van. With such a thick curtain of precipitation blocking the view, we could drive right into a tornado without seeing it. We retreat eastward and get ahead of the advancing precipitation core of the storm. Then we see it: the outline of a funnel, possibly a large tornado, off to the southwest. As we head south to investigate, doubt disappears. The tornado—a huge black cylinder jutting upward into the sky—crosses Interstate 35, the north-south highway to Kansas, toppling everything in its path.

7   Near Red Rock, Oklahoma, Stein stops the van, but before we can unload the radar and the video camera, he orders us back inside. The tornado is heading straight for us. Now it is our turn to be chased! We speed south, out of the path of the tornado, set the radar up on its tripod and watch in awe as the funnel crosses the road to our north, strewing debris over a damage path half a mile wide. The wind is so fierce that two people have to lean on the radar to keep it from blowing over; the camera cannot be set up at all and must be held by hand. Just a mile north of us, a house is blown off its foundation; half a mile from us, snapped utility poles tumble onto the road. As the tornado moves away from us, its damage path widens to a mile. Later analysis of the data will show that the Doppler radar detected wind speeds of between 270 and 280 miles an hour, the fastest tornado winds ever measured by an instrument.

8   Even for an experienced storm chaser, the Red Rock tornado was an extraordinary event. People who drive thousands of miles in pursuit of tornadoes might see at most a few a year; people who do not chase them probably will never see any at all. That is why we tornado scientists sometimes envy our colleagues who concern themselves with fixed objects of study such as rocks, microscope slides, or the moon.

9   Our subjects are more like living creatures—enormous shy animals that appear, fleetingly and unpredictably, at places they choose. Because tornadoes are so *elusive* and so dangerous, much of the progress in tornado studies has taken place far from the tornadoes themselves, either at the end of a radar beam or over highly simplified models run on computers or in the laboratory. But radars must be cross-checked against reality; models and laboratory experiments must be *verified*. Ultimately, there is no substitute for ground truth; someone must go to the storm.

After Reading
Word Connections

1. Using context clues, define *supercell*.

   Potential energy of the stratified air to trigger
   more powerful storms

"Riders on the Storm: Tornado Chasers Seek the Birthplace of an Elusive Monster" by Howard B. Bluestein. From *The Sciences* magazine, March-April 1995, v35 n2 p26(5). This article is reprinted by permission of *The Sciences* and is from the March/April 1995 issue.

2. Define *running commentaries* by using the context of paragraph three.

Recording while running

3. The researchers were disappointed when the tornado funnel *dissipated,* leaving nothing behind.

Meaning from Context Map for Dissipate

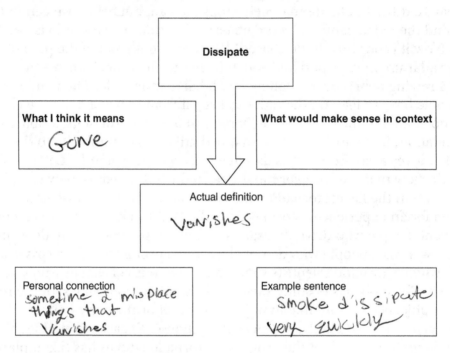

Dissipate

What I think it means
Gone

What would make sense in context

Actual definition
Vanishes

Personal connection
sometime I misplace things that Vanishes

Example sentence
Smoke dissipate very qwickly

4. The angry vandal was *strewing debris* all over the house. The vandal was

  a. putting things back where they belonged.

  b. taking the trash to the curb.

  c. placing pictures of his family throughout the house.

  d. throwing garbage all over the place.

5. Tornadoes are described as elusive and dangerous in this selection.

Explain some things in your life that are *elusive.*

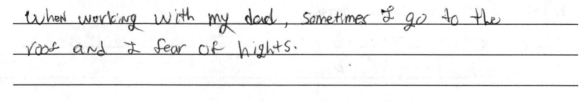

When working with my dad, Sometimes I go to the roof and I fear of hights.

Connecting Meaning

1. With today's advanced technology, why is it necessary to risk lives chasing tornadoes?

   they view tornadoes as enormous shy animals that
   appear fleetingly & unpredictably

2. Why are running commentaries recorded by the scientists?

   to keep track of the tornadoes

3. Describe the Red Rock tornado.

Portfolio Activities

Integrating Ideas

In the readings, each risk taker made individual choices that endangered their lives. If their choice resulted in injury or death, it would have a lasting effect on spouses, family, or friends. What would you consider as acceptable risks for your spouse? What would you consider as acceptable risks for parents of young children? Reflect on these ideas in writing or in class discussion.

Extending Concepts

How does risky behavior differ in men and women? Are men or women more likely to take physical risks? emotional risks? financial risks? career risks? In writing, state and support your opinion on gender differences in risk taking.

Collaborative Activities

Given an unlimited budget, plan the riskiest vacation that you would venture. Investigate activities, locale, equipment, and costs.

Additional Portfolio Suggestion

"Remember that great love and great achievements involve great risk."

H. Jackson Brown, Jr.

Think about this quotation. Reflect on what it means to you. You may record your thoughts through an essay, poem, music, or art.

Chapter Summary Graphic Organizer

Complete the graphic organizer by listing the two steps that help you to determine the unstated main idea.

Unstated Main Ideas

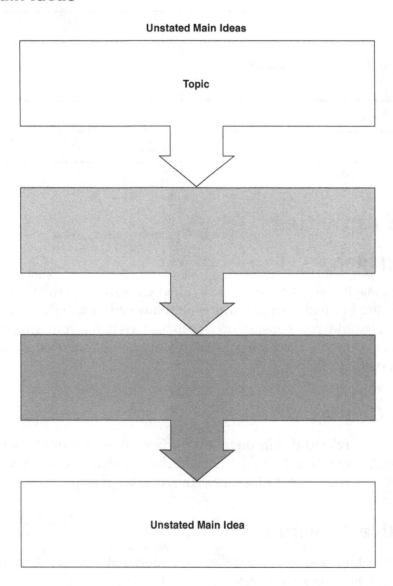

Unstated Main Ideas

Topic

Unstated Main Idea

Chapter 7

Supporting Details

Theme of Readings: Value of Fear

"The only thing we have to fear is fear itself . . ."

FRANKLIN DELANO ROOSEVELT

Value of Fear

Given that fear is an unpleasant and undesirable sensation, does it have any value or is it only the remnant of our caveman days? Twenty-five thousand years ago, humans survived because of fear. Fear activated a physical response that aided survival. Imagine yourself as a caveman out picking berries when suddenly you come nose to nose with a ferocious wolf. At the sight of the wolf, your fear triggers the fight or flight response. Your hypothalamus sends a message to your adrenal glands and within seconds your body becomes supercharged. Extra energy, sharpened senses, and faster responses result from adrenaline produced by your adrenal glands. You narrowly escape death by running faster than you ever have before.

In the present day, you have the same internal body parts and you still have the fight or flight response. Threatening situations cause the same physical responses but today's wolves are more often internal than external. You react to the threat of layoff from your job, the threat of your spouse leaving you, or the threat of an angry confrontation. Not truly life threatening, these situations cause your fight or flight energy to turn inward and cause stress. If you can overcome your fears of non-life threatening situations, you will gain the courage to enrich your life.

Sometimes, however, fear signals should not be ignored. Life threatening situations still exist in today's society. By learning to trust your instincts and intuition, by recognizing those situations that are dangerous, and by learning to distinguish between true fear and baseless worry, you can embrace fear as a gift.

Chapter Objectives

After completing this chapter, you will be able to:

1. Identify the supporting details.

2. Label supporting details as major or minor.

Focus on Supporting Details

You and your best friend are invited to a party on Friday night but you can't go because you have to work. When you see your friend the next day and ask "How was the party?" Your friend replies, "It was great!" and turns to walk away. You get the point–it was a good party–but you need more information. What made it a good party? Your friend tells you there were a lot of people, the food and music were terrific, and some funny things happened. You now understand why the party was great but you want to know more of the details. Who was there? What kind of food was served? Was the music a DJ or a band? What were some of the funny things that happened?

Major Details

The topic of this conversation is the party. The main idea is that the party was great. The major supporting details are the sentences that explain, clarify, and/or prove the main idea. Major supporting details are essential for understanding the main idea. When your friend explained there were a lot of people, the food and music were terrific, and some funny things happened, you are being presented with the major details. To help identify the major details, ask yourself *"How does the author support the main idea by explanation, clarification, or proof?"*

Minor Details

Even though these major details explain the main idea, to create a mental picture you need more than an outline of the images. You need minor details as well: examples, definitions, or statistics that illustrate the major details and add more interest and variety to the material. Minor supporting details clarify and explain the major supporting details. They are answers to the questions: Who was at the party? What did you eat? What kind of music was there? To help identify the minor details, ask yourself *"How does the author illustrate the major details?"*

Read the following paragraph. Then use the guide questions to help you to identify the topic, main idea, and supporting details.

Fear is a great motivator. It motivates children to follow their parents' rules. The threat of being grounded for a week will often ensure that curfew is kept. Schools also use fear as a motivator. The threat of failure or detention is the reason why some students complete their homework and behave in the classroom.

Who or what is this paragraph about?
The topic is fear.

What does the author want the reader to remember or understand about the topic?
Fear is a great motivator.

How does the author support the main idea?
The author states that both parents and schools use fear as a motivator.

How does the author illustrate the major details?
The threat of being grounded and the threat of failure or detention illustrate how parents and schools use fear.

You may find it helpful to create a map when determining the main idea and supporting details.

Map of Main Idea and Major/Minor Details

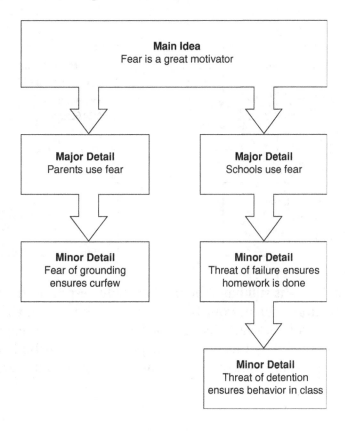

Short Exercises: Supporting Details

Directions: *Read each of the following paragraphs. Identify topic, main idea, and major and minor supporting details by using the guide questions above. Then complete the map or outline provided with your answers.*

1. In early man, fear was a tool for human survival through the fight or flight response. The sight of a threatening situation, like a man-eating tiger, caused the hypothalamus gland to release a rush of adrenaline. Adrenaline caused the man to run faster, jump higher, see better, and think faster than only seconds earlier. In addition, to help humans survive life threatening circumstances, the fight or flight response caused all unnecessary body functions to stop. Digestion stopped and the immune system was temporarily shut down.

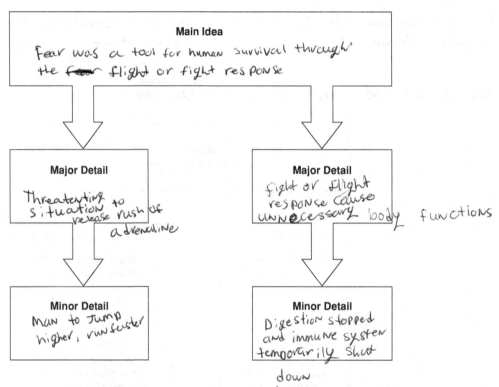

Main Idea

Fear was a tool for human survival through the ~~fear~~ flight or fight response

Major Detail

Threatening situation to release rush of adrenaline

Major Detail

fight or flight response cause unnecessary body functions

Minor Detail

Man to jump higher, run faster

Minor Detail

Digestion stopped and immune system temporarily shut down

2. In today's world, humans still have the fight or flight response. In response to a "threatening" situation, such as your boss calling you into the main office when layoffs are expected, your body activates its fight or flight response. Since you can not fight or flee, the energy produced by this response is pent up in your body causing a physical reaction. Your heart races, your blood pressure rises, and your palms sweat.

Topic: _Fight or Flight_

Main Idea: _Humans still have the fight or flight response_

Major Detail: _Your heart races_

Major Detail: _your blood pressure rises_

Minor Detail: _your palms sweats_

3. Fear in the workplace can be used to a manager's advantage. To make fear work, a manager must set up clear expectations and definite consequences for his employees. For instance, an employee must maintain a sales quota. If the sales quota is not met, the employee will face the reduction of sales territory as a consequence.

Topic: _Fear in the workplace_

Main Idea: _Fear in the workplace can be used to a manager's advantage_

Major Detail: _Set up clear expectations and difinite consequences for his employees_

Minor Detail: _An employee must maintein a sales quota_

Minor Detail: _____

4. Films and novels capitalize on fear as entertainment. Stephen King has enjoyed phenomenal success as a writer of horror fiction. Books like *The Shining, Cujo,* and *Firestarter* are among his best selling novels. Horror films have also been a successful means of entertainment. Thousands have flocked to scream in fear at movies like *The Haunting* or *Friday the Thirteenth.*

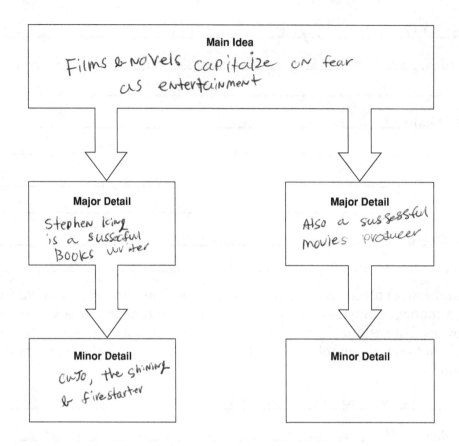

Main Idea

Films & novels capitalize on fear as entertainment

Major Detail

Stephen king is a successful Books writer

Major Detail

Also a successful movies producer

Minor Detail

cuJo, the shining & firestarter

Minor Detail

5. Fear plays a role as an internal motivator. The fear of not being accepted by others causes people to take actions they may not have on their own. For example, a particular brand of jeans or sneakers may be purchased to be accepted as part of the group. People are also driven by the fear of being unsuccessful in their career. For example, they work long hours and take on extra responsibilities to establish their success.

Topic: Fear

Main Idea: Fear plays a role as an internal motivator

Major detail: Not being extpe accepted

Minor detail:

Major detail:

Minor detail: _____

_____

6. To consumers, roller coasters and haunted houses are fright fests. But to a proprietor, the fear that these attractions produce can be a profitable business. A dazzling, "scared to death" attraction drives up the season's gate admissions. It creates a good word-of-mouth publicity that attracts new customers to come and try it out. It also draws repeat customers who want to relive the thrills and chills.

What is the topic of this paragraph?

~~Consumers~~ Roller Coasters & haunted houses

What is the main idea of this paragraph?

To consumers, roller coasters and haunted houses are fright
fests.

_____

How does the author support the main idea? (major details)

To a proprietor, the fear that these attractions produce
can be a profitable bussiness

_____

How does the author illustrate the major details? (minor details)

Dazzling "scared to death" draws out customers who
want to have thrills and chills.

_____

7. Horror films can give a teenager a temporary feeling of loss of control which may be healthy. For example, a teenager who goes to a horror movie experiences a safe and sometimes much needed escape. Horror critic, Douglas E. Winter says, "We love to see something so grotesque and unexpected that it makes us scream or laugh … secure in the knowledge that in the fun house of fear, such behavior is not only accepted but encouraged."

Adapted from "The Thrill of Chills" by Ellen Blum Barish

What is the topic of this paragraph?

Horror films

What is the main idea of this paragraph?

Horror films can give a teenager a temporary feeling of
loss of control

_____

_____

How does the author support the main idea? (major detail)

_____

_____

_____

_____

How does the author illustrate the major details? (minor detail)

We love to see grotesque and unexpected that makes

us scream and ~~laugh~~ laugh

_____

_____

8. Fear has created another valuable use for the technology of virtual reality. Fear has extended virtual reality programs beyond entertainment. Today virtual reality (VR) programs are used in the psychological treatment of phobic victims. In a therapeutic VR program an "online shrink" leads the phobics into a controlled VR environment. There they can safely experience what they fear and thereby ease the problem. The fear of flying and the fear of heights are two of the phobias being treated in this manner.

What is the topic of this paragraph?

_____

What is the main idea of this paragraph?

_____

_____

_____

How does the author support the main idea? (major detail)

_____

_____

_____

How does the author illustrate the major detail? (minor details)

_____

_____

_____

_____

Reading Selections

Selection One: **"Everything You Always Wanted to Know About Fear (But Were Afraid to Ask)"**

David Cornfield

Before Reading

Before Reading Everything You Always Wanted to Know About Fear complete the following:

Predict the topic.

> Truely understanding what fear really is

Skim the reading to see if you have correctly predicted the topic.

> It seems correct.

Think about the feeling of fear. How do you deal with fear? Relate what you know to the author's information.

> Try to be calm and don't let the pressure get to you and realese your ~~fear~~ fear

Set your purpose for reading.

Words to Preview

untempered *(adj.)* unaffected *(par.1)*
inhibition *(n.)* act of holding back *(par.1)*
impenetrable *(adj.)* impossible to enter *(par.2)*
palpable *(adj.)* capable of being touched *(par.3)*
inarticulate *(adj.)* unable to speak clearly *(par.4)*
paradoxically *(adj.)* seemingly contradictory statement that may nonetheless be true *(par.6)*
repertoire *(n.)* range or number of skills, aptitudes, or accomplishments *(par.7)*

visceral *(adj.)* relating to or situated in the soft internal organs of the body *(par.8)*
pervasive *(adj.)* being present throughout *(par.11)*
embark *(v.)* to set out on a venture *(par.12)*

During Reading

As you read "Everything You Always Wanted to Know About Fear" continue to predict and visualize the information, and monitor your comprehension. What does the author want you to know or remember about fear?

Everything You Always Wanted to Know About Fear

1   During the summer of 1983, I created a series of six masks as part of a workshop on clowning. Working the clay with my eyes closed, the masks emerged as powerful expressions of my unconscious mind, *untempered* by *inhibitions* from my rational mind.

2   Each mask was the starting point for the development of a clown personality. Five led quickly and easily to a story and a character. The sixth seemed *impenetrable*. I left the workshop having found only five of my six clowns, and, on returning to my office, I managed to hang the masks so that the sixth was hidden from view.

3   I still have that mask. Looking at it now, the fear it expresses is almost *palpable*. The eyes are wide open and startled, the hair stands on end, the mouth is gasping. Yet at the time, I refused to acknowledge my terrified clown. I wanted him out of sight and out of mind.

> This is the face of fear.

4   Denying fear is not unusual. In our society, to be afraid is considered shameful. Many people hide their fear, from themselves and from others. Yet, fear has survival value. It is there to warn us about danger so that we can take precautions to minimize risk. Ignored, it tries to protect us by finding ways to prevent us from taking risks. It blinds us to an opportunity or makes us arrive late or makes us forget an important detail or makes us *inarticulate* or ... the variations are endless.

5   In my work as a coach for people making the transition to self-employment, the issue of fear is of central concern. An entrepreneur is someone who is able to take risks. If fear prevents you from taking risks, you will not succeed as an entrepreneur. Period. It doesn't matter how marketable your ideas are or how well you understand business concepts. To survive as an entrepreneur, you have to learn how to live with rising levels of fear and not be immobilized.

> Does fear ever immobilize you?

6   The best way to deal with fear is to stop pretending to be fearless. *Paradoxically*, the more you deny fear, the more likely it is to dominate you. Tune into your fear, give it a voice, enter into a dialogue with it, do what you can to reduce the risk, and you will find yourself more able to take risks.

"Everything You Always Wanted to Know About Fear (but Were Afraid to Ask)" by David Cornfield as published on website www.soulmaking.com/fear.htm. David Cornfield is a psychotherapist based in Toronto, Canada who specializes in helping clients meet the challenges that arise mid-career, mid-relationship, and mid-life. For more information about David and the work he does, visit www.soulmaking.com.

7   Listening to fear is more easily said than done. We all have a *repertoire* of defenses that help us deny our emotions. Addictive behaviors are all based in a desire to avoid feeling, and as we know, they are hard to shake. If you avoid feeling your fear by lighting up a cigarette or by getting busy, you have lost the opportunity to respond to your fear. Learning to deal with our fear reduces our need to resort to addictive behaviors.

8   Fear is *visceral*. One way we deny our fear is to numb our bodies with muscle tension and shallow breathing. Over time, numbness becomes chronic. In this depressed state, we don't feel fear, but neither do we feel enthusiasm or pleasure. The fear hasn't gone away. We just don't feel it. And if we don't feel it, we can't listen to it. To prevent fear from stopping us in our tracks, we need to learn to relax our bodies, deepen our breathing, open up to feeling. Body-based expressive psychotherapy and relaxation techniques such as massage and yoga are ways to regain lost feeling so that we can be more responsive to our legitimate fears.

> Fear can be felt by our bodies.

9   Not all fears are legitimate. Legitimate fear is fear that pertains to a real danger in the present. Some fear is an understandable but incorrect response to inadequate information. Ignorance breeds fear. The more informed you are, the easier it is to decide if the danger is real and what precautions you need to take to reduce the risk. If you have a fear about something, get more information.

> What causes fears?

10   Some fears belong to unfinished situations from the past. For example, if you were hurt by a man with a beard, you may be triggered into fear every time you see a bearded man. There are a number of ways to deal with old fears. One is to finish the unfinished business in therapy, diminishing its power to distract you from responding to the present. Another is to use meditation to develop your capacity to view your fear with detachment so that you become aware when it is irrational. It also helps to get the perspective of other people—people in a support group or friends whom you really trust.

11   Some fear is *pervasive* low-level fear that you carry around with you regardless of present circumstances. If you were abused as a child or overprotected by fearful parents or even if your parents weren't there to back you up, you may feel inadequate and just want to hide away. Again, counseling can be useful to help heal wounds that diminished your self-esteem and hindered your full growth as a human being.

> The memories of childhood often cause fears for adults.

12   Keep in mind that emotions come in pairs. Hurt and anger go together. So do shame and desire. Behind fear lies excitement. As Sam says to Frodo in *The Lord of the Rings*, the stories that stay in the mind are about ordinary folks who say yes to the adventures that lie in their path, those who go ahead despite the dangers. Risk is a call to adventure. If you listen to your fear and do what needs to be done to avoid unnecessary danger, you enable yourself to *embark* on the exciting adventure that is your life.

> Risks are part of life.

"Everything You Always Wanted to Know About Fear (but Were Afraid to Ask)" by David Cornfield as published on website www.soulmaking.com/fear.htm. David Cornfield is a psychotherapist based in Toronto, Canada who specializes in helping clients meet the challenges that arise mid-career, mid-relationship, and mid-life. For more information about David and the work he does, visit www.soulmaking.com.

After Reading

Word Connections

1. Define *legitimate fear*. Give one example of a legitimate fear.

   Being clearly scared

2. Using the context of paragraph five, define *entrepreneur*.

   Someone who take risks without fear holding you back.

3. The prefix *in-* was used several times in the reading, for example, inadequate. Create a word map for the prefix *in-* which means not.

Word Map for in-

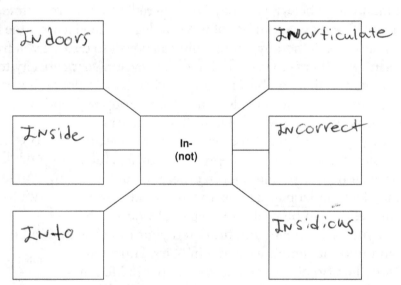

4. Explain the phrase, "Ignorance breeds fear."

   Without aware being scared then the fear can control you.

5. To get their perspective on things that scare them, the reporter interviewed ten students. By getting their *perspective* the reporter learned about the students'

   a. medication.
   b. telephone messages.
   c. overtime money.
   d. views or opinions.

Connecting Meaning

1. What is the main idea of paragraph four?

   In our society, to be afraid is considered shameful.
   Many people hide their fear, from themselves and from
   others.

2. What is the main idea of paragraph eight?

   Fear is visceral

3. Describe what the author thinks is the best way to deal with fear.

   We need to learn to relax our bodies, and to admit
   your fears to have more open ~~minded~~ minded or have higher
   self esteem.

4. State at least two ways to deal with old fears.

   To finish unfinished businesses, Use meditation it's power
   to develop your capacity to view you' fear with
   detachments.

Selection Two: **What Are You Afraid Of? Eight Secrets that Make Fear Disappear. Part 1**

Rick Chillot

Before Reading

Before you read the second half of "What Are You Afraid Of?" complete he following

Predict the topic.

A story that tells different examples of fear

Skim the reading to see if you have correctly predicted the topic.

Think about being afraid and fear. How do you make fear disappear? Relate what you know about being afraid and fear to the selection.

face the fear head on and admit that you are afraid.

Set your purpose for reading.

hurtling *(v.)* moving with great speed or haste *(par.1)*
flaw *(n.)* a defect or imperfection *(par.1)*
rerouting *(v.)* sending on a different course *(par.2)*
impending *(v.)* about to take place *(par.2)*
encoded *(v.)* put into code *(par.2)*
instinctive *(adj.)* arising from impulse or instinct *(par.2)*
surly *(adj.)* gruff, irritable or short-tempered *(par.5)*
cites *(v.)* mentions as support or proof *(par.7)*
simulated *(v.)* used as a substitute *(par.8)*

During Reading

As you read, continue to predict and visualize the information and monitor your comprehension. What does the author want you to know about how to get rid of your fears?

What Are You Afraid Of? Part 1

1 Fear talks to us. You say you'd like to hop on a plane and visit your sister in Dubuque. Fear answers back: Are you crazy? Go *hurtling* through the sky enclosed in a tube at 600 miles an hour? You say you'd like to go camping. Wait a minute, fear says. Aren't those woods full of snakes and bears and blood-sucking ticks? We

---

all hear that inner voice at some time or another. But how do you shut it up? Sometimes you don't want to. Fear isn't a character *flaw*—it's a survival mechanism. "If we didn't have the ability to be afraid, we'd be walking off cliffs and in front of cars," says Richard Surwit, PhD, vice chairman of research of the department of psychiatry and behavioral sciences at Duke University in Durham, NC. Like an over-protective big brother, fear looks out for us, stepping forward when we're about to get into trouble.

2   And it does more than warn us. By making your heart beat faster, *rerouting* the flow of blood to your muscles, and triggering other physiological changes, fear prepares you to deal with an *impending* threat. Fear is so important to our survival that it even becomes *encoded* in our memories: Cast your mind back to that time you were chased by an angry dog, and your heart immediately begins to pound at the recollection. Particularly important fears may be almost *instinctive*. Fear of snakes, for example, turns up in people who've never seen a real one.

3   But that same big brother who looks out for our welfare sometimes gets in our way. "Everyone's afraid of tornadoes," says Dr. Surwit. "But do you avoid going to the Midwest because there are tornadoes there? Does your fear of elevators prevent you from getting a job on the 30th floor of an office building? If fear is preventing you from doing what you want to do in life, it's a problem."

4   For the solution, we found out what makes fear tick—and what tricks will turn it off.

Secret #1

It Doesn't Matter Why You're Scared.

Strategy

5 Stop looking for the answer. Does your fear of dogs date back to that *surly* Doberman that lived next door when you were a kid? Are you afraid to talk in public because of a bad experience in a school play? There's a real temptation to try to trace our fears back to their origins in the hopes of tearing them out by the roots. But in fact, that kind of digging rarely turns up anything useful.

6   "The stories we tell about how we've become fearful are often not true. We just don't remember these things accurately," says Steven E. Hyman, MD, director of the National Institute of Mental Health (NIMH) in Bethesda, MD. "And they're not particularly helpful." You don't need to know exactly how or when you developed your fear of swimming or heights or thunderstorms to put that fear to rest, Dr. Hyman says. So why spend time and effort trying to figure it out? You're better off working on ways to overcome the fear.

Secret #2

Fear Is Erased by Knowledge.

Strategy

7 Find out about what scares you. "One of the main components to fear is uncertainty, or perhaps more accurately, unpredictability," says S. J. Rachman, PhD, author of *Fear and Courage* (W. H. Freeman and Company, 1995) and professor of psychology at the University of British Columbia in Vancouver. "When the situation becomes predictable, the fear diminishes." Which makes perfect sense when you realize that fear is a protective mechanism. In the absence of any other information, fear clicks on to steer you clear of a worst-case scenario. The more accurate and realistic your information is, the better this approach will work. As an example, Dr. Rachman *cites* the use of videotapes to prepare children about to enter the hospital for surgery. "They show an actual child being treated in an actual hospital, and that helps a great deal."

Secret #3

Training Breeds Confidence.

Strategy

8 Learn how to do it. How can you help being afraid when one mistake can blow up in your face—literally? To find out, Dr. Rachman studied military bomb disposal operators. He found that their ability to work fearlessly with deadly explosive devices stemmed directly from their theoretical and practical training. The trainees worked with *simulated* explosive devices that became increasingly realistic as their instruction progressed. In the final stage, a mistake sets off a siren—not an explosion, but heart-stoppingly loud. "The closer the preparation comes to the actual situation, the more effective it is. At the end of it, the operators are extremely confident, and it's not misplaced," Dr. Rachman says.

9 True, you may not be planning to disarm bombs any time soon. But if there's something you'd like to try but are too scared to attempt, you can train for it. Whether it's swing dancing or mountain climbing, by the time the lessons end, your fear will be replaced with confidence.

Secret #4

Courage Is Contagious.

Strategy

10 Catch it. As anyone who's told ghost stories around a campfire knows, one jumpy person can give a whole group the jitters. But you may not realize that the opposite is also true. "People can pick up or model courageous or fearless behavior," says Dr. Rachman. "Watching somebody else behave bravely in a situation that's worrying

you will definitely help." So if you're nervous about flying, plan a vacation with a friend who can be your courageous role model. Before your skiing lessons, spend some time watching the expert slopes.

After Reading

Word Connections

1. Fear was compared to an "*overprotective big brother.*" How did the author define this idea?

   That your insticts will be proctecting you from any danger. Fear is something that the mind will avoid any problems and protect you from any danger

2. We all hear an *inner voice.* Explain an *inner voice.*

   Somewhere in your mind, you have second thoughts about the decisions you are about to choice. Fear isn't a character flaw, It's a survival mechanism.

3. Complete a word map for the prefix *re-* which means *again.*

Word Map for re-

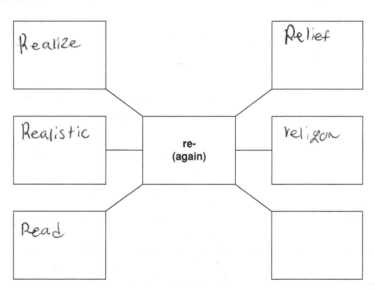

Realize

Relief

Realistic

re-
(again)

religon

Read

4. The doctor cited examples of ways to lessen fear. Define cite and list two homonyms (words that sound the same but have different meanings) and their meanings for cite.

   Realize & Realistic: Realize; to understanding

   Realistic; Something that's very real and not fake

5. In an *simulated* situation

   a. a person has to eat.

   b. a person experiences something like the real thing.

   c. a person is blindfolded.

   d. a person cannot drink.

Connecting Meaning

1. What is the main idea of "What Are You Afraid of?

   Fear speaks to us

2. Name two secrets that help to eliminate fear.

3. Describe one of the "secrets" that make fear disappear.

4. Give an example of how courage can be contagious.

_____

_____

_____

Selection Three: What Are You Afraid Of? Eight Secrets that Make Fear Disappear. Part 2

Rick Chillot

Before Reading

Before you read the second half of "What Are You Afraid Of? complete the following:"

Predict the topic.

Skim the reading to see if you have correctly predicted the topic.

Think about being afraid and fear. How do you make fear disappear? Relate what you know about being afraid and fear to the selection.

Set your purpose for reading.

Words to Preview

conversely *(adj.)* opposite *(par.1)*
cognitive *(adj.)* relating to the process of knowing *(par.2)*
behemoths *(n.)* huge animals *(par.3)*
domain *(n.)* territory over which control is exercised *(par.3)*
anticipation *(n.)* act of feeling or realizing beforehand *(par.6)*
ursine *(adj.)* characteristic of a bear *(par.6)*
debilitating *(v.)* making feeble *(par.9)*

During Reading

As you read, continue to predict and visualize the information and monitor your comprehension. What does the author want you to know about being afraid and fear?

What Are You Afraid Of? Part 2
Secret #5

Talking Helps.

Strategy

1 Open up. It's hard to imagine anything more frightening than a terminal illness. "When you're looking at death, at its door, what I always suggest is to talk,' says Alyssa Byrd, a registered nurse who counsels terminally ill patients at Lehigh Valley Hospice in Allentown, PA. Similarly, when you're facing a major crisis, opening up about your fear can ease your distress even if you can't change the situation. *Conversely,* trying to keep your fear under wraps isn't likely to help. "Suppressing fear is not a very effective technique," says Dr. Rachman.

Secret #6

Simple Mind Games Work.

Strategy

2 Use your imagination. What happens when the big moment comes and, despite your knowledge and training and all the other preparation you've done, your mouth still goes dry and your hands still shake? First, remind yourself that stage fright isn't the end of the world. "Even very accomplished actors or public speakers often have anxiety prior to going on stage. And they deal with it in a variety of ways," says Dr. Surwit. Many of their tricks are variations of the old standby: imagining the audience members naked (or in their underwear if you're more prudish). Why does it work? "People become anxious when they feel the audience is dominant or judgmental," Dr. Surwit explains. "This is a *cognitive* trick that changes the dominance ratio." When you're the only one dressed, you become the dominant one, and your fear goes away. A similar approach that Dr. Surwit recommends is imagining that you're speaking to children or any other non-threatening group.

Related Article: Jim Gorman: "Know the Bear"

3 For months, he dreamed of monsters: hairy, sharp-toothed, barbclawed *behemoths* who could chew him like a stick of gum. The bad dreams were disturbing–but even worse, these monsters were real. And Jim Gorman was going to spend a night in their *domain*–alone.

4   As a senior editor at Backpacker magazine, Jim Gorman knew that an article about someone who faced his fear of bears by camping in Alaskan bear country would make a great story. But as the guy who had to actually do it, he had nightmares. "Since I was the one on staff who had the most fear of grizzlies, I was naturally the person to write the story," he says. "But I had really nasty dreams."

5   But by the time he actually hiked into Chugach State Park near Anchorage, AK, Gorman says he felt confident enough to enter bear country on his own. (He

notes that solo hiking is not a good idea if you're not an experienced hiker.) What made the difference? Learning about the bears that scared him and acquiring the skills for hiking in their territory. While visiting with a team of bear biologists in preparation for the article, Gorman saw bears in the wild and learned firsthand that the average bear is more frightened of humans than a squirrel is. "The more I understood the way bears think, the better I felt." As a result, Gorman says his days of scheduling camping trips for bear-free zones are over. "I used to think twice about camping in Yellowstone. Now I wouldn't hesitate to go there."

Secret #7

It's the Big Picture That's Scary.

Strategy

6 Focus on the details. Of course, not all fear is in *anticipation* of some upcoming event. What do you do when a bear pops out from behind a tree, and there's no biologist around to calm your fears with a lecture on *ursine* behavior? "During intense fear, people tend to lose their focus on what they were doing and become overwhelmed," says Dr. Hyman. "The thing to do in this situation is to focus on the little things."

7 That means, figure out what you have to do, then do it one step at a time. Get through your speech paragraph by paragraph; swim to shore stroke by stroke. Call it the "don't look down" principle: If you were walking a tightrope, you wouldn't look at the ground below you. You'd concentrate on putting one foot in front of the other until you got to the other side.

Secret #8

It's Okay to Get Help.

Strategy

8 Talk to your doctor. When is it appropriate to see a psychologist or psychiatrist to help you get over your fear? First off, if your symptoms are severe, you may be suffering from anxiety disorder, in which case you should definitely seek help, says Dr. Hyman. "If the feelings of fear are pervasive–you have them much of the day, most days, and they last for more than a few weeks–you should get treatment," he says. One of the more severe anxiety disorders is panic disorder: panic attacks marked by sudden bouts of intense fear accompanied by rapid heartbeat and short-ness of breath, often without an external cause.

9 But even if your fear isn't *debilitating*, you may find it useful to seek help if it's preventing you from doing what you want or need to do. "We're talking about 10 to 12 focused sessions aimed at getting rid of your symptoms," says Dr. Hyman. That's not to say that you can't beat your fears on your own though. "As long as you don't have an out-of-control anxiety disorder, I think many people can face their fears and recognize that a lot of them are irrational. People can literally, by understanding what they're afraid of, make themselves braver."

Related Article: Susan Wightman: "Learn Before You Leap"

10 "When they opened the door at 3,000 feet, I was ready to back out," says Susan Wightman. "But I talked myself back into it." That was Wightman's first skydive. Since then, she's made more than 900 others.

11   But just how, that first time, did she know she could jump out of a plane and touch down safely 3,000 feet later? Wightman credits the 6-hour training course she took before the jump. And as an instructor, she says that it's that detailed training that gets first-time jumpers through the experience. "We place them in a suspended harness, we do training exercises providing them with all kinds of different scenarios in which they can practice emergency procedures, and we repeat, repeat, repeat. And eventually because of that education, one feels more confident and in control of the skydive." When it's time for that first plane ride, everyone gets jittery, Wightman says. "I reassure them that they've done everything very well, and that I'm confident that they can do it," she says. She also gets them to focus on the most important skills they learned in class. Usually, that does the trick.

After Reading

Word Connections

1. Trying to keep your fear under wraps doesn't work. *Suppressing* fear is not a very effective technique.

Meaning from Context Map for Suppressing

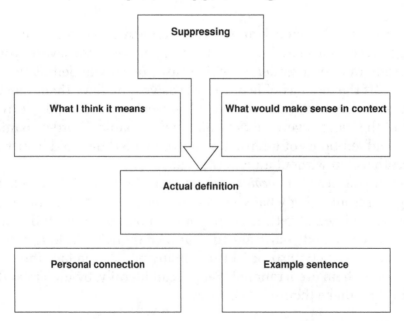

2. "This is a *cognitive* trick that changes the dominance ratio." What does *cognitive* mean?

_____

_____

_____

3. Explain the "don't look down principle."

_____

_____

_____

4. Explain the difference between a psychologist and psychiatrist.

_____

_____

_____

5. By having her own detailed *procedure*, the skydiving instructor is
   a. using a step by step process to teach.
   b. allowing students to try their own techniques.
   c. just letting things happen.
   d. waiting on the ground for students.

Connecting Meaning

1. What is the main idea of paragraph six?

_____

_____

_____

2. How did Jim Gorman lessen his fear of grizzly bears?

_____

_____

_____

3. Do you think people are able to make their fears disappear if they work at it? Give an example of how you made a personal fear disappear.

_____

_____

_____

Portfolio Activities

Integrating Ideas

The three readings focus on the value of fear and ways to deal with fear. Do you think that fear is valuable? How do you deal with fear? Relate your ideas in writing or in class discussion.

Extending Concepts

Describe in writing a situation when you or someone you know dealt with true fear. What role did intuition, instinct, and adrenaline play in the response?

Collaborative Activities

How much of fear is a result of media hype? Amazon.com in September 2011 identified over 21,000 books about fear and 31,000 with violence in the title. Television news and newspapers report story after story about fearful situations. As a group, decide which medium you wish to research. Explore whether or not the medium is "creating" fear in society. Present the group's findings to the class.

Additional Portfolio Suggestion

Read a book about reducing fear, such as _Gift of Fear_ or _Protecting the Gift: Keeping Children and Teenagers Safe (and Parents Sane)_ by Gavin De Becker. When you have completed it, write about those suggestions discussed in the book that you would use to deal with fear.

Chapter Summary Graphic Organizer

Complete the graphic organizer by adding the guide questions you should ask yourself when identifying the major and minor details of a selection.

Supporting Details

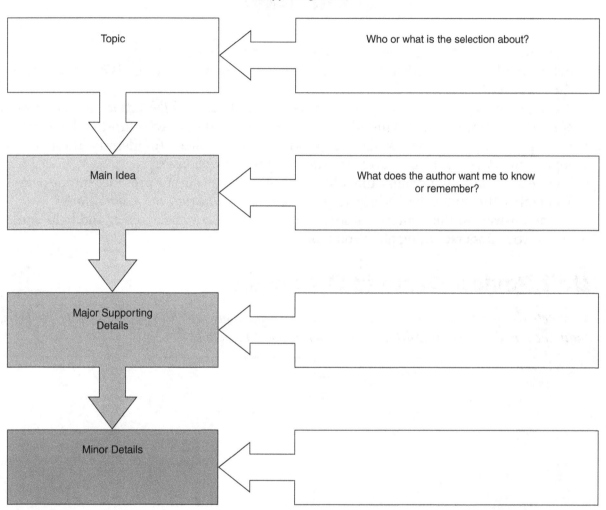

Unit III Review

Main Ideas

In this unit, you continued to work with the reading process.
*   Before reading, you predicted the topic of the selection by asking: *Who or what is this reading about?*
*   As you read, you connected to the topic by asking: *What does the author want me to know or remember about this topic?* This allowed you determine the stated or unstated main idea.
*   Examples, explanations, or facts support the main idea. To identify these major supporting details ask: *How does the author support the main idea?*
*   To illustrate the major details and add more interest, the author provides minor details. To identify the minor details ask: *How does the author illustrate the major details?*

The answers to these guide questions enhance your comprehension and help you to evaluate your understanding after you read.

Unit Review Graphic Organizer

Complete the graphic organizer by writing the guide questions that help you to identify the topic, main idea, major supporting details, and minor supporting details.

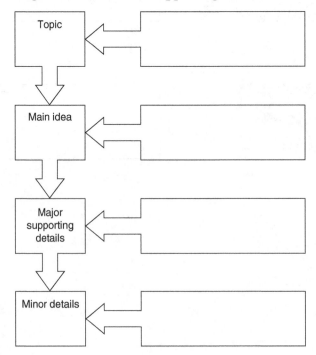

Portfolio Suggestion

To develop lifelong reading habits, it is important for you to read extensively and begin to recognize your reading preferences. A reading log is an excellent place to collect information about your habits and preferences in reading. A chart may be used to keep track of different kinds of information such as date, title, author, genre, pages and comments. See Appendix G.

Portfolio Vocabulary Exercise

Think about your concept of and experience with fear. Write as many words as you can think of or find for each category.

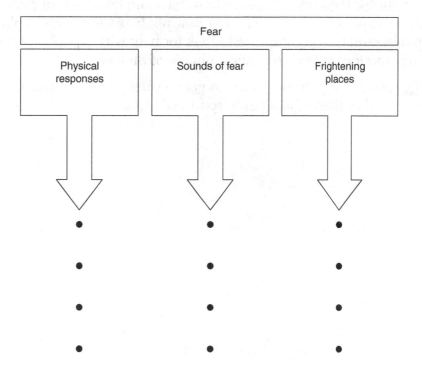

Want to Know More?

If you are interested in knowing more about fear, the following books and websites further explore this theme. You can find these books at your local library to read more about fear or use the Internet to investigate the websites.

Books

The Pop-Up Book of Phobias, Greenberg, Gary. New York: Rob Weisbach Books, 1999. Gary Greenberg is a stand-up comic and writer based in Manhattan. Fear of heights, fear of spiders – everyone is afraid of something. These pop-ups place you in the hot seat.

Dangerous Games: Ice Climbing, Storm Kayaking, and Other Adventures from the Extreme Edge of Sports, Todhunter, Andrew. New York: Doubleday, 2000. Andrew Todhunter is fascinated by risk and danger and the people who engage in these activities. This book is a collection of stories about these risk-takers.

Fear Less, de Becker, Gavin. New York: Little Brown & Company, 2002. Gavin de Becker, a famous author, wrote several books on fear. This book answers the questions many Americans have been asking since September 11, 2001. It offers recommendations that can enhance our national security and individual safety.

Websites

www.phobialist.com There are hundreds and hundreds of phobias. This website lists the phobias. It also tells you how phobias were named, phobia categories, phobia treatments, and sites to look for help with a phobia. Look here for lots of information, unless you have a phobia of phobias!

Google images of extreme sports to get a visual sense of some of the risky behaviors involved in these challenging sport activities.

Unit IV

Patterns of Organization

Theme of Readings: Social Issues

"Fear less, hope more;
Whine less, breathe more;
Talk less, say more;
Hate less, love more;
And all good things are yours."

SWEDISH PROVERB

Social Issues

This unit explores a number of issues and questions that concern us as members of today's society.

Career Selection: What is a good job, and what are some effective ways of finding one? For those with a college education and a resourceful outlook, there are a wealth of fulfilling possibilities. The key to finding "a good fit" is to assess one's skills and strengths, identify potential opporunities and learn the process of job hunting.

Health Issues: How is lasting health achieved and maintained? Everyone wants to enjoy the best of health at all ages. Educating oneself about both physical and mental health issues is an important step in the process.

Censorship: As a society, how can we balance free speech rights with other rights and responsibilities? An explosion of controversial material on the Internet has raised troubling issues. Many people wonder how best to weigh the First Amendment right for free expression with, for example, the need to guard national security and the need to protect children from obscenity.

Violence: What can best be done about violence in our society? Violence enters our lives through experience, movies, video games, and television news reports, threatening our sense of security. The quality of life is diminished when homes, streets, schools, and workplaces do not feel safe and may not be safe.

Patterns of Organization

An effective reader makes sense of what is read by being able to identify the topic, main idea, and supporting details. To relate the supporting details to the main idea, authors often choose organized patterns. This unit will examine patterns of organization: chronological order and listing, definition and illustration/example, comparison and contrast, and cause and effect.

To assist the reader, authors use words that signal these patterns of organization. Signal words provide clues about the author's choice of organization. Certain signal words are common to several patterns. The author may also apply a combination of patterns within a reading to make the main idea as clear as possible. By recognizing signal words and organizational patterns, it is easier for readers to understand the author's ideas and information.

The following guide questions will help you to analyze and determine the pattern of any paragraph or reading.

What is the main idea of this paragraph or reading?

What are the common signals used in this paragraph or reading?

What details support the main idea?

What is the pattern of organization?

Unit Objectives

After completing the unit, you will be able to:

1. Identify signals for patterns of organization.

2. Determine the patterns of organization.

3. Identify the supporting details that determine each pattern of organization.

Chapter 8

Chronological Order and Listing Patterns

Theme of Readings: Career Exploration

"Find a job you like and you add five days to every week"

H. JACKSON BROWNE, JR.

Career Exploration

Most people entering the workforce today will change their career at least twice during their lifetime. Whether you are looking for your first job or changing careers, you need to research your qualifications, career opportunities, and the job search process.

Career exploration begins with self exploration. You need to know your strengths, interests, habits, skills, and weaknesses. These insights will guide you in your choice of careers. Finding the right career does not have to be achieved alone, however. Networking with parents, family, and friends can be valuable because of their past and present job experiences. Internships set up by local colleges and businesses can give you a chance to try out a possible field or type of job and see if you like it. Career counselors are good at guiding you to understand the available opportunities and the best choices for you. Books, articles and websites are other helpful sources of information in the job search.

Ultimately, decision about which career to pursue is yours. Choosing a satisfying career that you enjoy will have a profound impact on your life.

Chapter Objectives

After completing this chapter, you will be able to:

1. Identify the signal words used for the chronological and listing patterns.

2. Distinguish between chronological order and listing patterns.

3. Identify the major supporting details of the reading that determine the chronological or listing patterns.

Focus on Chronological Order and Listing Patterns

Authors often choose to relate the supporting details to the main idea by using organized patterns. By recognizing the patterns of organization, it is easier for readers to understand the author's ideas and information.

Chronological Order Pattern

Chronological order organizes information according to the time order in which it occurs. The *order* of events or ideas is important to this pattern. If the events or ideas are taken out of sequence, the reading will no longer make sense. This pattern is often used to tell a story, to relate historic events, or to give directions. For example, the chronological order pattern would be used in a handbook for new employees that may tell the history of the company, safety procedures, or directions to operate equipment.

Common Signals   **Signal words** that may provide clues to the chronological order pattern are:

first	before	next	when	soon
second	during	then	while	later
third	after	finally	now	until

Dates and times   may also be used to determine this pattern.

Read the following paragraph. Then read the guide questions and answers that follow. In the future, these guide questions will help you to analyze and determine the pattern of any paragraph or reading.

> Effective job search strategy requires that you set objectives and plan specific times to complete each one. First schedule planning time. Then, maintain a list of activities. Write up a weekly calendar and enter each item by day or hour. Next start a notebook with one section for contact names, addresses, and phone numbers and another section for notes about different companies.
> —from *Career Fitness Program* by Sukiennik, Bendat, and Raufman

What is the main idea of this paragraph?
The main idea is found in the first sentence. "Effective job search strategy requires that you set objectives and plan specific times to complete each one."

What are the common signals used in this paragraph?
The words *first, then, next,* and *finally* indicate a sequence of activities and identify the major supporting details.

What details support the main idea?
The major supporting details are (1) schedule planning time, (2) maintain a list of activities, (3) start a notebook, and (4) review your progress.

What is the pattern of organization?
This paragraph shows a pattern of chronological order because the order of activities is important.

Listing Pattern

Authors will sometimes use a list of details, reasons, or examples to support the main idea. In contrast to the chronological order pattern, the order in which the details are listed in the reading does *not* affect the main idea. For instance, an employer may distribute an ad that lists required qualities of prospective employees: "Applicants must be 18 years or older, drive a car, and have a high school diploma." The order in which the requirements are listed does not affect the meaning of the ad.

Common Signals   **Signal words** that may provide clues to the listing pattern are:

first	also	second	many	several
next	another	third	a few	too
finally	in addition	lastly	then	a number of

Details may also be **numbered** or **bulleted** by the author in a listing pattern. **Commas, semicolons,** or **colons** may also signal this pattern.

Read the following paragraph. Then read the guide questions and answers that follow. In the future, these guide questions will help you to analyze and determine the pattern of any paragraph or reading.

Employment will continue to shift from the goods-producing to the service sector of the economy, but the shift will be less pronounced than during past years. The bulk of employment growth will be in three industries: health services; retail trade, including eating and drinking places; and business services, including temporary help services, computer and data processing services and services to buildings.

–from *1996 Information Please Almanac*

What is the main idea of this paragraph?
The main idea is found in the first sentence. "Employment will continue to shift from the goods producing to the service sector of the economy."

What are the common signals used in this paragraph?
The use of a colon, semicolons, and commas in the second sentence indicates the listing pattern.

What details support the main idea?

The major supporting detail is that employment growth will be in health services, retail trade, and business services. The minor details are "including eating and drinking places" and "including temporary help services, computer and data processing services and services to buildings." These phrases illustrate the major detail by providing additional information.

What is the pattern of organization?

This paragraph shows a listing pattern because order is not important to the list of industries.

Determining the Pattern in Longer Selections

It can be helpful when reading longer selections to see if the author uses the chronological order and listing patterns. In longer selections, take note of the headings of the selections that often signal major details. Authors also use or mix several types of organizational patterns within a selection. Look at the entire selection for an overall pattern. Use the same guide questions that you used for single paragraphs.

Short Exercises: Chronological and Listing Patterns

Directions: *Read each paragraph and complete the questions that follow.*

1. Fred DeLuca, President and CEO of Subway, began his entrepreneurial spirit before he was 10 years old, picking up two-cent returnable bottles around his Bronx housing project. At 17 years old, DeLuca opened his shop, Pete's Super Submarine Sandwiches, with $1000 borrowed from a family friend. By 1982, he owned two hundred stores. In August 1997, there were more than 12, 500 Subway stores in over fifty countries. DeLuca's accomplishments over the past thirty years have placed him at the top of a company that now boasts annual sales in excess of three billion dollars.
   –from "Advice From the Top and How to Get There"
   by Brian Caruso and Diane P. Licht

   What is the main idea of this paragraph?

   _____

   _____

   What are the common signals used in this paragraph?

   _____

   _____

What details support the main idea?

_____

_____

_____

What is the pattern of organization?

_____

2. The face of the cable industry changed when Robert L. Johnson launched Black
Entertainment Television [BET] back in 1980 and there's been no looking back for
him since then. Johnson is the chairman and CEO of BET Holdings, Inc. which is
based in Washington, D.C. Now he oversees four major cable channels. Black
Entertainment Television, BET On Jazz: The Cable Jazz Channel TM, BET Movies
and BET Action Pay-Per-View, as well as other BET interests outside of the cable
industry.

–from "Advice From the Top and How to Get There"
by Brian Caruso and Diane P. Licht

What is the main idea of this paragraph?

_____

_____

What are the common signals used in this paragraph?

_____

_____

What details support the main idea?

_____

_____

_____

What is the pattern of organization?

_____

3. Working out of your home can be a great solution for certain people. You need to
ask yourself, "Does this work style fit in with what I want and how I am most

efficient? If you do work out of your home it is important to remember the following guidelines.

- Maintain a presence at the main office. Report in often and let your boss know you are alive and productive.

- Treat your study (or wherever you work) like a real office. Close the door at 6:00 PM and don't open it until you are beginning work the next morning.

- Get dressed as you would for work, and be consistent with your hours. Act like you are at the office and not at home, and you stand a good chance of actually being productive.

–from "Conference Calls in Your Pajamas" by Bradley Richardson

What is the main idea of this paragraph?

_____

_____

What are the common signals used in this paragraph?

_____

_____

What details support the main idea?

_____

_____

_____

What is the pattern of organization?

_____

4. Opportunities for internships have always existed in fields such as medicine and education; now they are common in the liberal arts as well. Two trends in the past decade have led to this. First, tuition costs have risen fast, and families that might have spent $100,000 or more on an education want to know there's a job at the end of it. Second, corporate downsizing has forced hiring practices that have made internships attractive to many employers. "Internships have become the way to look someone over without making a major investment," says Ann Petelka, senior personnel manager at D'Arcy, Masius, Benton, and Bowles, a New York based ad conglomerate that offers jobs to more than 70 percent of its interns.

–from "Working for Credit: How to Make the Most Out of a Semester-Long Internships" by Jo Ann Tooley

What is the main idea of this paragraph?

_____

_____

What common signals are used in this paragraph?

_____

_____

What details support the main idea?

_____

_____

_____

What is the pattern of organization?

_____

5. In August 1977, a young mother with no business experience opened the first Mrs. Fields Cookie store in Palo Alto, California. Debbi Fields, the founder of Mrs. Fields Cookies, has achieved great success through her worldwide chain of cookies and baked goods. Her company began franchising in 1990. Today she has over 650 domestic locations and over 65 international locations in 11 different countries.

www.mrsfields.com

What is the main idea of this paragraph?

_____

_____

What are the common signals used in this paragraph?

_____

_____

What details support the main idea?

_____

_____

_____

_____

What is the pattern of organization?

_____

Reading Selections

Selection One: **"For Liberal Arts Majors Only: The Road To Career Success"**

Robin Ryan

Before Reading

Before you read "The Road To Career Success," complete the following

Predict the topic.

Skim the reading to see if you have correctly predicted the topic.

Think about your future career choices. If you are pursuing a degree in liberal arts, what kind of job are you preparing for? Do you know how to get the job when you have decided what you want to do? As you read, explore some of the strengths and skills you may have not recognized in yourself.

Set your purpose for reading.

Words to Preview

networking *(n.)* an informal system where persons assist each other *(par.4)*
predicament *(n.)* a situation, especially an unpleasant one *(par.5)*
ensuring *(v.)* making sure or certain; insuring *(par.6)*
predicament *(n.)* a situation, especially an unpleasant one *(par.7)*
delve *(v.)* to search deeply *(par.8)*
pursue *(v.)* to strive to gain or accomplish *(par.10)*

During Reading

As you read "For Liberal Arts Majors Only: The Road to Career Success," continue to predict and visualize the information, and monitor your comprehension. Look for signals for the chronological order or listing pattern. What is the author telling you about finding a career for liberal arts majors?

For Liberal Arts Majors Only

1 Microsoft. Nike. American Airlines. Nordstrom. Coors. MTV. Magnet companies attracting tens of thousands of resumes. But your degree is in liberal arts—would a magnet company hire you? And an even bigger question—what would you do for them? Important questions. Do you have the answers? Have you begun to consider the endless list of career choices and fields that you could go into? Do you know what steps to take to land that job once you decide exactly what you want to do? Let's begin by exploring your career options and then look at some of the strengths and skills you may not have even recognized you have to offer to an employer.

> What is a magnet company?

A World of Opportunity You May Not Have Considered

2 Some of the liberal arts grads I've worked with over the years were just as confused about their career options as you might be. They just didn't know about all the fields or kinds of jobs that they could investigate.

3   Dave, for example, had his heart set on working for Nike. He loved sports and had played college baseball. Nike was his place—he just knew it. Problem was, Nike didn't know it. Dave was an English major and never defined what job he could do for them. When a family friend arranged for a meeting with an accountant that worked at Nike, Dave hoped the man would find him a job at the company. Dave never told the man the type of job he could do, never asked questions about Nike's communications department, never inquired about who else he should talk to at the company. The result: Nothing happened after that meeting. It wasn't the Nike employee's job to figure out what career Dave could do, it was Dave's. Not having a clear idea of the types of jobs you can do is a critical error; lots of new college grads are fuzzy about their options because they don't understand their skills and don't know how those skills fit into a variety of careers.

> It takes a lot of work to find a job.

4   I began to work with Dave shortly after the Nike meeting, focusing him on his stronger skills—writing, editing, and computer skills. He began working temporary jobs and started *networking* with other alumni. Through networking, he learned about a position at a publishing company. He landed a job as editorial assistant at a company that published comic books and was coming out with a new baseball video game. Dave found a terrific job once he directed his skills to what he could do for an employer instead of what an employer could do for him.

5   In another instance, Allison, a history major who graduated from one of the West Coast's top colleges, thought that finding a job would be easy. She wanted to work on planning events. Unfortunately, no one would hire her. She sent out hundreds of resumes but got no interviews. When she called employers, everyone said the same thing—experience. Since the only events Allison had ever planned

Reprinted from Job Choices in Business: 1998 with permission of the National Association of Colleges and Employers, copyright holder.

were a few *sorority* functions, I suggested that she volunteer to do an internship for six weeks. There she could learn about the meeting planning business and get some experience for her resume. She persuaded a top events company to take her on by selling them on her good computer skills. Within three weeks, Allison got a job offer from another company after she followed up on a lead from someone in the office. When her internship boss was called for a reference, he offered Allison a paid position. Two years later, she's still there planning large-scale events.

6   Sometimes, locating a person's special talents takes a bit of digging. Take Sam, for example. He had chosen psychology for a major because it was easier for him than the business courses he'd started out in. He wanted to use **What are my special talents?** his degree and thought he might find a counseling job. The problem was Sam's verbal skills. They were pretty weak, and he recognized that. He was not good at talking to groups and had rather poor grammar skills. We did manage to uncover that Sam had excelled in his job as a pizza delivery man. He'd earned more tips than any driver they had ever hired. He was organized, courteous to customers and efficient. His productivity led to an assistant manager's job where he improved sales by suggesting optional items to customers and *ensuring* speedy delivery. He quit the job when he left college. I encouraged Sam to explore store management as a career. His organizational skills and ability to think like customers have served him well. He landed a job as a grocery distributor and went on to his second job as a deli manager for a large metropolitan store.

7   Peggy was in a different *predicament*. She went back to college after her kids started school and got a degree in sociology. She had never held a paid position. When I first **You don't always get a job in your major.** met with her she opened with "Will anybody hire me? I've got no work experience and I'm almost 40." She had discounted her skills that she acquired in school and through volunteer work, important skills that landed her a great job in fundraising.

8   Heather was a philosophy major and knew nothing about insurance, except that people sold it. Today, she has a good paying job as an underwriter for Prudential Insurance Company. Tanya became a legal assistant; Jason is a probation officer; Steve is a computer communications specialist; Stephanie works as a sales account executive. Eric went into customer service credit. All of these grads–as well as Dave, Allison, Sam, and Peggy–are real people. And, they're all liberal arts grads *delving* into new fields and new options. You can do it, too.

9   Where do you start? Start where the grads profiled here started: They evaluated past jobs, volunteer work, activities, and academic projects to identify the skills they had developed. They found that they had a lot of skills that matter to employers–and you will too. Start by completing the checklist provided to identify your skills.

Reprinted from Job Choices in Business: 1998 with permission of the National Association of Colleges and Employers, copyright holder.

Where Are the HOT Opportunities?

10 *Pursue* a field where you have a lot of interest—broadcasting, computers, fashion—and it can lead to greater lifetime satisfaction. If you have a practical way to mix interests with work, follow your dreams. Dave was discouraged that Nike didn't hire him, yet he now loves his job at the publishing company. The greatest number of opportunities lie within small companies, so look for small organizations—those employing fewer than 100 people. Typically, you'll find you have more responsibility in a small office than you would in a large one; that level of responsibility can propel your career along into future jobs. You'll find such employers in the yellow pages and in want ads and by asking family and friends for leads. Remember, too, that many good jobs are available with nonprofit organizations such as the American Lung Association, which has offices across the country and hires fundraisers, events planners, and communications people. And, consider state and local government jobs, not just those with the federal government.

> I can picture myself working for a small company.

11   The environmental, high-tech, service, telecommunications, and retail industries—as well as certain areas of healthcare—will remain strong. But racing after a job simply because it is in a hot field is like racing after a magnet company—your future job and happiness may not lie there. It's better to combine your interests and your abilities when you're looking for career satisfaction. Spend time investigating career options. Career centers and libraries have extensive resources available. The *Occupational Outlook Handbook* is a good place to start researching potential career areas.

Finding the Job

12 Job hunting is challenging, so learn the process. Visit your career center. Read books. Attend workshops and seminars on the job search, resume writing, and interviewing. Volunteering, doing internships, and working at temporary jobs can all give you valuable experience and often lead to that first paid position. Network—and start with your college's alumni. Many will be happy to clue you in on their job, field, and/or company.

13   Remember that careers are built one step at a time. The market is competitive, but *you are unique.* Always remember you have a lot to offer. Do what you like best, in organizations whose products and services you find interesting. You'll find more satisfaction and reward this way. Finding the right career opportunities becomes easier when you view this process as an exciting adventure and realize you can be anything you choose to be. So explore, and you'll discover opportunities you didn't know existed and talents you didn't know you had. Your future is what you make it.

Skills You've Acquired

(Check all that apply)

_Administering programs

_Advising people

_Analyzing data

_Budgeting

_Calculating numerical data

_Collecting money

_Compiling statistics

_Conducting experiments

_Coordinating events

_Dealing with customers

_Designing ads

_Drawing charts/graphs

_Editing

_Evaluating programs/
 products

_Fundraising

_Generating ideas

_Handling complaints

_Implementing ideas

_Inspecting physical objects

_Interpreting languages

_Interviewing people

_Investigating problems

_Making presentations

_Mediating between people

_Negotiating contracts

_Operating equipment

_Organizing people/
 projects/tasks

_Persuading others

_Planning programs/projects

_Problem solving

_Programming computers

_Promoting events

_Public speaking

_Recordkeeping

_Rehabilitating others

_Repairing mechanical devices

_Researching

_Running meetings

_Scheduling

_Selling products/services

_Supervising others

_Teaching others

_Updating files

Using a computer:

_IBM

_Macintosh

_Mainframe

_Other(s)

Using software:

_Word

_WordPerfect

_Windows

_Lotus

_Excel

_PageMaker

_QuarkXPress

_Other(s)

_Writing articles/reports

I never thought of *all* these skills.

After Reading

Word Connections

1. "Racing after a job simply because it is in a hot field is like racing after a magnet company—your future job and happiness may not lie there."

   Give a definition and example of a *magnet company* from the context of the reading.

   _____

   _____

   _____

2. Create a concept of definition map for *networking* as it relates to the job market.

Concept of Definition Map for Networking

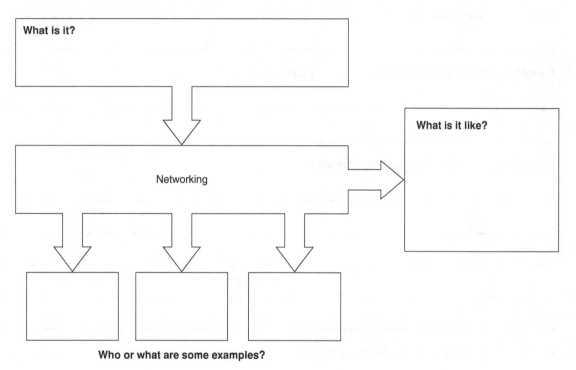

Who or what are some examples?

3. "Do you know what steps to take to *land* that job once you decide exactly what you want to do?" What does *land* in this sentence? What are some other meanings?

   _____

   _____

   _____

4. When looking for a job, it is good to have a *list of references* prepared ahead of time. A list of references is a record of

    a. the schools you attended.

    b. previous satisfied employers.

    c. all college courses.

    d. places you have lived.

5. A sorority is a social club for women most often found at a college. What is the male version called?

    _____

Connecting Meaning

1. What is the main idea of this selection?

    _____

    _____

2. Identify any common signals used in this selection.

    _____

    _____

3. Identify the major supporting details.

    _____

    _____

    _____

    _____

    _____

4. Determine the overall pattern of organization.

    _____

5. Give two examples of Liberal Arts majors who had difficulty finding a job after graduation. How did their skills relate to the position for which they were hired?

    _____

    _____

_____

_____

_____

Selection Two: **"Writing the Perfect Cover Letter"**

Michael Hattersley

Before Reading

Before you read "Writing the Perfect Cover Letter, " complete the following:

Predict the topic.

Skim the reading to see if you have correctly predicted the topic.

Think about your job hunting techniques. Do you have a plan or strategy to nail your dream job? Have you ever written cover letter for a job application? Do you think the cover letter is important or not?

Set your purpose for reading.

Words to Preview

crucial _(adj.)_ supreme importance; critical _(par.3)_
exhaustive _(adj.)_ comprehensive; thorough _(par.6)_
punchy _(adj.)_ forceful; spirited; vibrant _(par.9)_
analogy _(n.)_ relationship between things otherwise unlike _(par.14)_
query _(n.)_ question; inquire _(par.20)_
prominence _(n.)_ something that is widely known; noticeable _(par.21)_

During Reading

As you read "Writing the Perfect Cover Letter" continue to predict and visualize ideas, and monitor your comprehension. Look for signals for the chronological order or listing pattern. What does the author want you to know about writing a cover letter?

Writing the Perfect Cover Letter

Strategies for Nailing your Dream Job

1 It's a throwaway, right? The letter you attach to your resume saying you want that job interview. The resume will do the heavy lifting. The cover letter is just there because—well, because you need a cover letter.

2 But in business, every single piece of communication matters. Picture the average boss hunting for a new employee. She's got a pile of applications. She will go through the stack and rapidly narrow the candidates down to a few who fit the profile she's looking for.

3 Let's say half a dozen candidates survive, and the boss has time to interview three people. This is the point at which the cover letter becomes crucial. If it's done right, it can get you that interview.

Here are a few rules of thumb for winning cover letters:

4 **Open avenues of conversation.** Before writing your cover letter, get one of the standard guides on how to do a good job interview (referenced below). Emphasize aspects of your background that play into typical most asked questions.

5 **Make the hirer want to find out more about you.** Don't be so exhaustive in your cover letter that there's nothing left to discuss in an interview. Except in very special circumstances, your letter should fit on a page. Often half a page is enough.

6 **Show you're familiar with the organization you're applying to.** If you don't know the company, spend an hour in the library reading its latest annual report or search the Internet for information.

7 **Emphasize how your education and training especially qualify you.** For example, suggest tactfully that you're overqualified for your current position and it's time to move on.

8 **Be crisp and punchy.** By the time the boss gets to your letter, he may have read a hundred resumes. You want to grab attention while still maintaining a sense of style. Convey an energetic image through forceful writing. Use active rather than passive or intransitive verbs. Don't ramble. Make sure each paragraph has a clear thesis sentence and conveys a complete unit of thought.

9 **Don't make any mistakes.** Good writing matters; it can demonstrate to a prospective employer how well you can manage information. Proof carefully, and run the letter by a friend or colleague for suggestions.

10 **Make use of personal contacts.** If you know people who may have influence on the hiring decision, let them know you're interested either by personal contact or by copying them on the cover letter.

Writing the Perfect Cover letter.

Create an Argument That Fits the Purpose

11   Once past these general rules, however, the design of your cover letter depends on the type of job search. Are you highly qualified for the job, or are you taking a long shot? Is the organization seeking someone like you, or will you be appearing out of the blue? Consider the following guidelines:

- If you're highly qualified for the job, argue from experience: "I've had a terrific record as an assistant product manager at Company X, and I now feel ready to become product manager at Company Y." Highlight the experiences and any specific successes you have had that make you just right for the job.

- If, as in most cases, you have the right general background for the job but haven't been doing exactly the same thing at a lower level, argue from skills and analogy: "The training I've received as a production line manager gives me the background I need to become a quality control inspector." Show how your skills are clearly transferable to the new job.

- If you're not qualified for the job and you're not the type of person the organization would normally recruit, your only choice is to argue from interest: "Although I currently work on an oil rig, I've always wanted to be a fashion designer." It may sound absurd, but this approach works more often than you might expect. If you do have transferable skills, point them out.

Use a Structure That Fits the Argument

12   Good conventional cover letters adopt a **Me-You-We** model. Structure your letter using the standard logical formula established by Socrates: Given–Since–Therefore:

13   **Me** (first paragraph): I'm very interested in this job, and I have the following qualifications for it.

14   **You** (second paragraph): The following aspects of your organization challenge me and ensure I can make a contribution to it.

15   **We** (third paragraph): We will work well together, and you should give me the job. There's at least one exception to the Me-You-We structure, however: the broadcast letter. This is a case where you're casting a very wide net with the hope that you'll snag at least one or two expressions of interest. Say you're writing to every consulting firm listed in the library because you have a narrow but deep area of expertise. In this case, you have nothing to lose by being bold. In effect, you're trying to create a job opportunity, not applying for an existing position. Here you need to grab the reader's attention in a veryshort space. List your accomplishments vividly–"I've doubled my department's sales in two years" or "My job at Company X has allowed me to gain more knowledge of Y than anyone else in the country." Then close with a quick query about whether they might have a position that fits your background.

Writing the Perfect Cover letter.

But Enough About "I"

16   Avoid the worst fault of most cover letters, the "I" phenomenon. Overuse of "I" can make you sound grandiose or self-obsessed when you actually want to portray yourself as a team player. It's hard to sell yourself without using the word "I" a lot, but there are several alternatives to starting every sentence with it. Sometimes you can bury the "I" within the sentence: instead of "I was the best performer in the computer services department, "try "While working in the computer services department, I accomplished A and B and received the top ratings from my superiors among 20 colleagues." Don't have "I"s lead every paragraph, where they take on undue prominence and leap off the page. Even "my" or "me" makes a softer substitute.

17   Cover letters may be tossed aside, but often they're one of the last things the hirer will review before interviewing you. It's crucial that your writing makes a strong case to the prospective employer for taking the next step with your application.

MICHAEL E. HATTERSLEY

You've Got the Interview; What Do You Do Now?

The secret of successful interviewing is to focus on accomplishing two tasks: conveying something relevant to the interviewer about yourself, and creating a bond—the beginning of trust—between you and the interviewer. How do you manage those two objectives in what is admittedly a high-stress situation?

Have an Agenda

All too many interviewees see an interview as a largely passive activity, answering the questions that are asked. A successful applicant needs to have a prepared agenda that he will cover in the interview—no matter what questions are asked. The interview is a chance to bring your resume to life. What are your three key accomplishments that will help this prospective employer decide to hire you? What particular skills do you possess that will help you get this new job done? Develop a few well-stated, articulate mini-speeches that you can easily and tactfully slip in during the interview. Practice "bridging" from the question to your answer. You can tailor these prepared answers to specific job openings by doing a little research on the company before the interview and asking yourself, "What is the problem this company faces for which I am a solution?"

Mirror the Interviewer

Most interviewees are focused on their own nervousness. This heightened self-consciousness can lead to in advertent errors in what they say and do. Focus instead on making the interviewer's job easier. The interviewer is trying to determine whether or not you will make a good "fit" with the company. Many interviewees agree to anything in an effort to appear cooperative, while at the same time betraying their resistance with their body language. "Yes," they will say, "I'd be happy to move to Borneo," while crossing their arms defensively. The interviewer may notice this behavior consciously, or she may simply have a sense that the interviewee is not truly enthusiastic. The result is a lack of trust, and a mediocre interview.

Writing the Perfect Cover letter.

Instead, focus on making your body language congruent with the interviewer's while honestly voicing your concerns. In this way, you will create an atmosphere of candor with an underlying feeling of trust. If the interviewer leans forward, wait a second and then lean forward yourself. Sit when the interviewer sits (and invites you to do the same) and stand when the interviewer stands. The idea is not to mimic the other person exactly, but rather to adopt the same general physical posture. If you're interviewing with Bill Gates, and he starts rocking back and forth, you might not want to imitate that. Keep your mirroring within generally accepted norms of behavior.

Further Reading:

101 Best Cover Letters by Jay A.Block and Michael Betrus (1999, McGraw-Hill, 224 pp., $11.95, Tel.800-352-3566 or 212-512-4100)

Best Answers to the 201 Most Frequently Asked Interview Questions by Matthew J. DeLuca (1996, McGraw-Hill, 182 pp., $11.95, Tel.800-352-3566 or 212-512-4100)

Cover Letters for Dummies by Joyce Lain Kennedy (1996, IDG Books Worldwide, 264 pp., $12.99, Tel.800-762-2974)

Cover Letters That Will Get You the Job You Want by Stanley Wynett (1993, Betterway Publications, 168 pp., $12.99, available through local and online bookstores)

Web sites:

Career Builder's "How to" Guide: Cover Letters www.careerbuilder.com/gh_cl_htg.html Provides a discussion on the importance of writing an effective cover letter, plus tips on content and format.

"20 Cover Letter Blunders to Avoid" http://www.smartbiz.com/sbs/arts/cla2.htm Excerpted from The Adams Cover Letter Almanac.

After Reading

Word Connections

1. What does the phrase *rules of thumb* mean in the fourth paragraph?

_____

_____

_____

2. "Overuse of 'I' can make you sound *grandiose* or self-obsessed when you actually want to portray yourself as a team player." What does *grandiose* mean?

_____

_____

_____

Writing the Perfect Cover letter.

3. Create a meaning from context map for *strategies*.

Context: "Writing the Perfect Cover Letter" - *Strategies* for nailing your dream job.

Meaning from Context Map–Strategies

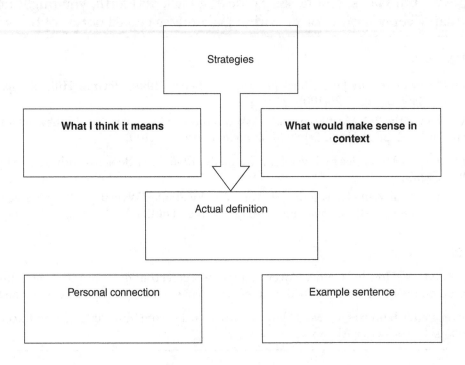

4. Define *interview* and *review* using your knowledge of word parts.

_____

_____

_____

5. In the selection, the phrase "It's a throwaway, right?" is used. What does it mean and in what other situations is the term used?

_____

_____

_____

_____

Connecting Meaning

1. What is the main idea of the selection?

   _____

   _____

   _____

   _____

2. Identify any common signals used in this selection.

   _____

   _____

3. Identify the major supporting details.

   _____

   _____

   _____

   _____

4. Determine the overall pattern of organization.

   _____

5. Describe the suggestions for a winning cover letter.

   _____

   _____

   _____

   _____

   _____

Portfolio Activities

Integrating Ideas

Use the checklist provided in the article "The Road to Career Success" to examine the skills you have acquired. Relate these skills to potential career opportunities in writing or in class discussion.

Extending Concepts

Write a cover letter for a job you would like to have in the future. Follow the suggestions given in the reading selection "Writing the Perfect Cover Letter."

Collaborative Activities

Design a job search plan. Consider how the Internet and e-mail may figure in a job search.

Additional Portfolio Suggestion

Explore the internship or cooperative education opportunities available on your campus or in your community.

Chapter Summary Graphic Organizer

Complete the graphic organizer by listing the signal words for chronological order and listing.

Pattern of Organization–Chronological & Listing

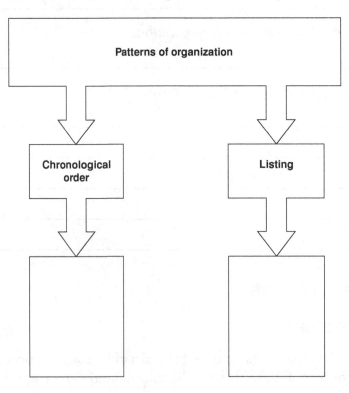

Chapter 9

Definition and Illustration/Example Patterns
Theme of Readings: Health Issues

"Learn from yesterday, live for today, hope for tomorrow."

ANONYMOUS

Health Issues

Open a magazine or newspaper, turn on the local or national news, or get together with friends and one issue–health–is frequently being discussed. In today's society, we are curious and concerned about all aspects of health. We want to know how to feel good and how to prevent or cure illness. Collectively the federal government, medical industry, and individual consumers spend billions of dollars on health-related issues.

With research being done in many areas, we face an avalanche of information. Cholesterol counts, weight reduction programs, the effects of second hand smoke and air pollution, herbal supplements, and gene therapy are just a few areas being studied and debated. In the past, mental health issues were generally less publicized than those relating to physical health. Today, information is readily available on depression, eating and anxiety disorders, and other mental health topics.

The readings for this chapter focus on the area of mental health. Being aware of these topics may help you or someone you know or may encourage you to read further in the important area of health.

Chapter Objectives

After completing this chapter, you will be able to:

1. Identify the signal words used for the definition and illustration/example patterns.

2. Distinguish between definition and illustration/example supporting details.

3. Identify the supporting details that determine the definition and illustration/example patterns.

Focus on Definition and Illustration/ Example Patterns

Definition Pattern

When authors want to give the precise meaning of something and convey its distinct characteristics or features, they use a definition pattern of writing. A definition pattern answers the question *what is it?* This pattern is often used in textbooks and academic journals, where understanding exact meanings of words and ideas is important to understanding a subject area. For instance, in an article about blood cholesterol an author may begin with a definition: "Cholesterol is a waxy substance made by the liver that is used to build cell membranes and brain and nerve tissues."

Common Signal   Signal words that may provide clues to the definition pattern are:

means   is   defines   consists of

Definitions may also be set apart by **punctuation** such as commas, parentheses, and dashes. For example, Prozac–a specific serotonin inhibitor–has become a widely used drug in the treatment of depression.

Read the paragraph below. Then read the guide questions and answers that follow. In the future, these guide questions will help you to analyze and determine the pattern of any paragraph or reading.

> Anorexia nervosa is a state of starvation and emaciation, brought about by severe dieting or by purging. People with anorexia nervosa become emaciated to the point of actual starvation, losing at least 15 percent to as much as 60 percent of normal body weight. Half of these patients, anorexic bulimic patients, maintain emaciation by purging. This behavior imposes additional stress on an undernourished body. Anorexia nervosa is a serious eating disorder which can be fatal.
>
> –adapted from www.noah.cuny.edu/wellconn/eatdisorders.html

What is the main idea?
The main idea is found in the first sentence. "Anorexia nervosa is a state of starvation and emaciation, brought about by severe dieting or by purging."

What are the common signals used in this paragraph?
Anorexia nervosa is being defined. The word *is* helps to indicate the pattern of definition.

What details support the main idea?
All of the sentences that follow the definition of anorexia nervosa continue to describe the illness. Patients lose 15 to 60 percent of normal body weight by starvation. Half of these patients maintain emaciation by purging. Purging imposes additional stress on an undernourished body. Anorexia nervosa can be fatal.

What is the pattern of organization?
This paragraph shows a pattern of definition because the term anorexia nervosa is defined. All other sentences expand the definition by providing the characteristics and features of this eating disorder.

Illustration/Example Pattern

Illustrations or examples are often given when an author wants to create a clearer picture of the main idea. These examples help to make difficult or confusing topics easier to understand. Relating the main idea to actual situations allows the reader to visualize the information. For example, in an article about cardiovascular disease an author may write: "To illustrate the blood flow of arteries blocked by cholesterol, visualize the movement of water through a clogged sink pipe."

Common Signals   Signal words that may provide clues to the illustration/example pattern are:

for example   for instance   to illustrate   including   such as

Examples may also be set apart by **punctuation** such as semicolons and commas.
Read the paragraph below. Then read the guide questions and answers that follow. In the future, these guide questions will help you to analyze and determine the pattern of any paragraph or reading.

> During the twentieth century, the medical milestones have been mind boggling. For example, antibiotics, a new class of medicines appropriately labeled miracle drugs, were created in the 1930s and 1940s. Imaging technology such as x-rays, ultrasound, CT skims, PET skims, and MRIs has provided an internal view of the body without actually invading it. Another example of medical milestones is organ transplants which became routine in the late 1970s due to the drug cyclosporine which suppresses the body's tendency to attack a new organ.
>
> —adapted from www.healthcentral.com/News

What is the main idea?
The main idea is found in the first sentence. "During the twentieth century, the medical milestones have been mind boggling."
What are the common signals used in this paragraph?
The words *for example, such as,* and *another example* indicate the pattern of example.
What details support the main idea?
The major supporting details are: antibiotics, imaging technology, and organ transplants are all medical milestones.
What is the pattern of organization?
This paragraph shows a pattern of illustration/example because of the illustrations given to clarify the main idea.

Determining the Pattern in Longer Selections

To find the definition or illustration/example patterns in longer selections, use the same guide questions that you used for single paragraphs. In longer selections, authors often combine the definition and illustration/example patterns by first defining a word or idea and then providing illustrations or examples for the reader. Look at the entire selection for the overall pattern.

Short Exercises: Definition and Illustration/Example Patterns

Directions: *Read each paragraph and complete the questions that follow.*

1. Prozac is an antidepressant medication which was introduced for use in the United States in December 1987. Since that time, Prozac has become the most widely pre-scribed antidepressant in America. Prozac is FDA approved for the treatment of depression and has been found useful in the treatment of obsessive compulsive disorder, bulimia, panic disorder, and other conditions.

   —from www. psych.helsinki.fi/~janne/mood/prozac

   What is the main idea of the paragraph?

   _____

   _____

   What are the common signals used in this paragraph?

   _____

   _____

   What details support the main idea?

   _____

   _____

   _____

   What is the pattern of organization?

   _____

2. You can take a huge step in reducing your fat intake at breakfast by making simple substitutions. For instance, replace pork bacon with turkey bacon, use one percent milk in your coffee instead of half and half, and try egg substitutes. Other breakfast

alternatives such as low fat spreads on toast in place of butter and fat free pound cake with fresh fruit rather than donuts and pastries can lessen your fat intake even more.

– adapted from "Ask Chef Ney" by Tom Ney, "Satisfying, Low-Fat Breakfasts,"
Prevention Home Page <http:healthyideas.com> [April 9, 1999]

What is the main idea of the paragraph?

_____

_____

What are the common signals used in this paragraph?

_____

_____

What details support the main idea?

_____

_____

_____

_____

What is the pattern of organization?

_____

3. Anorexia nervosa is an illness that mainly affects adolescent girls. The most common features are loss of weight and a change in behavior. The weight loss may become severe and life threatening. The personality changes will be those of increasing seriousness and introversion and an increasing tendency to become obsessional. She will usually begin to lose contact with her friends. She will regress and appear to lose confidence. She may become less assertive, less argumentative, and more dependant.

–from www.priority-hospital.co.uk/atm/anorex.htm

What is the main idea of the paragraph?

_____

_____

What are the common signals used in this paragraph?

_____

_____

What details support the main idea?

_____

_____

_____

_____

What is the pattern of organization?

_____

4. Bulimia is an eating disorder in which a person repeatedly binge eats, then uses self-induced vomiting, diuretics, laxatives, fasting, or excessive exercising to prevent weight gain. Symptoms of bulimia always include recurrent episodes of binge eating (defined as rapid consumption of a large amount of food in a brief period of time); a feeling of lack of control over eating during the binges; regular vomiting; use of laxatives or diuretics; strict dieting, fasting or vigorous exercise to prevent weight gain; a minimum of two binge eating episodes a week for at least three months; and a self-evaluation that is unduly influenced by body shape or weight.

   –from www.noah.cuny.edu/illness/mentalhealth/cornell/conditions/bulimia.html

What is the main idea of the paragraph?

_____

_____

What are the common signals used in this paragraph?

_____

_____

What details support the main idea?

_____

_____

_____

_____

What is the pattern of organization?

_____

5. Herbal remedies have become very popular over the last several years as an alternative to conventional prescription medications. For example, kava is used to reduce anxiety, ginkgo biloba has shown to provide cognitive benefits, valerian root is used to treat insomnia, and St. John's wort improves mild to moderate depression. For upset stomachs, indigestion, and nausea, some feel that herbs such as ginger and chamomile are known to be of help. Adapted from "A List of Common Herbal Medications," by K. B. Schomberg-Klaiss, D.O.

What is the main idea of the paragraph?

_____

_____

What are the common signals used in this paragraph?

_____

_____

What details support the main idea?

_____

_____

_____

_____

What is the pattern of organization?

_____

Reading Selections

Selection One: **"Forever Frazzled?"**

Maya Bolton

Before Reading

Before you read "Forever Frazzled?" complete the following:

Predict the topic.

Skim the reading to see if you have correctly predicted the topic.

Think about your attention span. Have you ever had problems paying attention for more than a few minutes? Do you know anyone who has been diagnosed with attention-deficit disorder? Relate what you know to the author's experiences with ADD.

Set your purpose for reading.

Words to Preview

lapse *(n.)* a failure; a slip *(par.3)*

pathological *(adj.)* relating to disease *(par.4)*

hypothesis *(n.)* uncertain explanation; a theory *(par.5)*

attest *(v.)* affirm to be true or correct *(par.5)*

predominantly *(adv.)* having greatest importance or influence *(par.6)*

skepticism *(n.)* a doubting state of mind *(par.8)*

du jour *(adj.)* of the day *(par.9)*

positron-emission tomography *(n.)* test that produces computer-generated images of activity within the body *(par.11)*

rigorous *(adj.)* very accurate; precise *(par.13)*

capper *(n.)* the finale *(par.18)*

pseudonym *(n.)* a fictitious name *(par.20)*

liberate *(v.)* to set free *(par.19)*

During Reading

As you read "Forever Frazzled?" continue to predict and visualize the information, and monitor your comprehension. Look for signals for the definition and illustration/example patterns. What does the author want you to know about attention–deficit disorder (ADD)?

Forever Frazzled

1   After years of feeling torn in a million directions, I finally got a diagnosis. And it wasn't stress.

2   Recently I had to cut short a telephone call to handle some urgent business. The distraction lasted only a few minutes, but by the time it was over I'd forgotten about the call. By chance something jogged my memory, and I called my friend back–but not until the following day.

© Health July/August 2008.

3   Unfortunately, that kind of disconnect is not unusual for me. Walking around my house in the morning, I find myself narrating reminders: "Turn off the iron," or, with a slap to my forehead as I'm heading out the door, "Keys!" Shortly after arriving at the office I often have to return home to retrieve a notebook or a file.

4   For years friends, family members, and colleagues kindly chalked up these *lapses* to my being a little "spacey." I have, they would tell me, plenty of charming qualities to compensate. But lately it seemed my absentmindedness had gone out of control.

> I think the author of this story wrote about me!

5   More and more people were getting insulted by those neglected phone calls. My tendency to procrastinate was reaching *pathological* proportions. And in the office, where I edit documents, my "eye" was becoming remarkably inconsistent. Even my boss had noticed. Eventually, at wit's end, I sought the advice of a psychologist.

6   After a lengthy conversation about my personal history, he offered a surprising *hypothesis:* Perhaps I had the adult version of attention-deficit disorder, or ADD. "But aren't people with ADD hyperactive?" I asked. The official name of the condition is, after all, attention-deficit/hyperactivity disorder, and as anyone who knows me will *attest,* I operate in anything but high gear. Even when the brain is working fast and furious, this body barely budges. That was even more true of me during childhood, when ADD is generally diagnosed.

7   It seems, however, that there are two distinct types of the condition: the more familiar one, called *predominantly* hyperactive, and the one that's gaining recognition, predominantly inattentive. People with the latter variety are notably absentminded, the day-dreamy types who quietly tune out at meetings or in class. Often they go undiagnosed because their symptoms are so subtle. The majority are female.

8   Perhaps, the psychologist suggested, I was suffering from ADD number two.

9   Over the next few weeks as I talked to people I knew about ADD, I heard *skepticism* and even contempt. "You can focus," one colleague told me. "ADD people can't focus." (She was wrong. ADDers can focus—just not consistently.)

> I thought only children had ADD.

10   "You've simply got too much on your plate," a friend said. (She had a point. I was working on many projects at once. Was I merely overextended?)

11   "Oh, ADD," moaned someone else. "Isn't that the disorder *du jour*?"

12   It seems that it is. Since 1990 diagnoses of ADD have more than doubled, and the curve seems to be getting steeper. Books on the topic are selling briskly. At conferences with themes like "Living the ADDventure," vendors hawk ADD-pride paraphernalia, special ADD date books, and coaching services for the terminally scattered. In some places high school and college students who have ADD can get extra time on standardized tests because of their disability.

© Health July/August 2008.

13   The boom in part reflects a rise in diagnoses among children. But a portion of the newly diagnosed are adults. In 1990 Alan Zametkin, a psychiatrist at the National Institutes of Health, published evidence from *positron-emission tomography* scans that ADD was associated with at least one physical marker in the brain: lower levels of activity in the prefrontal cortex, from which planning and self-control proceed. Other researchers have suggested the condition tends to run in families.

> I don't understand prefrontal cortex.

14   The findings haven't settled a raging debate about how common adult ADD really is. Some critics charge that psychologists are too quick to diagnose it without the proper testing. But even skeptics agree that at least some of the newly identified are the personality type described by the psychologist I saw and could benefit from treatment.

15   So I decided to go for the more *rigorous* evaluation. During the three-hour session, I took numerous tests of comprehension, memory, and problem-solving skills. The *capper* was a particularly frustrating one called the TOVA (Test of Variability of Attention), which consists of watching an orange square appear and disappear on a computer screen. When the square appears below the screen's center, you do nothing. When it appears above, you hit a button. Simple, right? Wrong. Despite humming and even biting my lip to stay focused, I ended up making an incredible number of errors.

16   It turns out my childhood history was also riddled with signs of the disorder. I recalled that often when I asked my mother a question, she'd first want to know precisely how long she had to answer. She knew at some point I would get that glazed look— distracted by other concerns, impatient to move on. At school I was a classic underachiever; lost in my thoughts, I had difficulty concentrating on the subject at hand.

> ADD must be hereditary.

17   Looking at the overwhelming evidence, both the doctor and I ended up convinced that mine was a classic case of attention-deficit/hyperactivity disorder, inattentive type. My reaction when she told me her opinion further convinced me: I cried, both fearful of the implications of the diagnosis and relieved to find an explanation for the problems that have plagued me all these years.

18   And what next? There are any number of behavioral approaches to treating ADD, such as workbooks and coaching programs designed to help people focus. But for the underlying attention problem, particularly for someone like me who does detail-oriented work, the doctor favored a low dose of Ritalin, the chief medication used to treat ADD.

19   Though I can't begin to address the controversy surrounding this drug, particularly about its use on children, I can testify that a minimal dose works wonders for me. It keeps my editorial eye focused for three to four hours at a stretch. I feel less scattered, and I've noticed a definite improvement in my moment-to-moment memory. (And all these benefits come to me without side effects.) When I went back to take the TOVA on medication, I got a perfect score.

> Wow, a perfect score!

© Health July/August 2008.

20   Still, even though my behavior has improved, I worry. If people, particularly coworkers, knew about my diagnosis, might they consider me one of the shirkers, someone who just wants an excuse for flaky behavior? That fear is why I've used a *pseudonym* for this story.

21   And I can't say ADD isn't a fad diagnosis. But to tell you the truth, in my case the treatment was so *liberating* that I don't really care.

After Reading

Word Connections

1. "By chance something jogged my memory. . ." Define *jogged* as used in this sentence.

_____

_____

2. "For years friends, family members, and colleagues kindly chalked up these lapses to my being a little "spacey." What does the phrase *chalked up* mean in this context?

_____

_____

_____

3. " The findings haven't settled a raging debate about how common adult ADD really is." What is a *raging debate*?

_____

_____

4. "And I can't say ADD isn't a *fad* diagnosis." What is a fad? Give some examples of a fad.

_____

_____

5. I was working on many projects at once Was I merely *overextended?* List five compound words that use *over-* (more than, to an excess).

_____

_____

_____

© Health July/August 2008.

Connecting Meaning

1. What is the main idea of this selection?

   _____

   _____

2. What are two types of attention-deficit disorder?

   _____

   _____

   _____

3. Give at least three examples of the author's behavior that provide evidence of ADD.

   _____

   _____

   _____

   _____

   _____

4. Why did the author choose to use a pseudonym for this story?

   _____

   _____

   _____

Selection Two: **"Understanding Obsessive-Compulsive Disorder"**

Catherine Weiskopf

Before Reading

Before you read "Understanding Obsessive-Compulsive Disorder," complete the following:

Predict the topic.

Skim the reading to see if you have correctly predicted the topic.

Think about obsessive-compulsive behavior (OCD). Have you ever been obsessed with anything or anyone? Do you have to repeat actions over and over without reason? As you read, relate what you know about everyday obsessions or compulsions to those seriously afflicted with OCD.

Set your purpose for reading.

Words to Preview

ritualistic *(adj.)* practicing a ritual or ceremonial act *(par.3)*
neurotransmitter *(n.)* a chemical substance that transmits nerve impulses *(par.11)*
serotonin *(n.)* a chemical that transmits nerve impulses *(par.11)*

During Reading

As you read "Understanding Obsessive-Compulsive Disorder," continue to predict and visualize the information, and monitor your comprehension. Look for signals for the definition and illustration/example patterns. What does the author want you to learn about OCD?

Understanding OCD

1 What's it like to have obsessive-compulsive disorder (OCD)? Stephanie, age eighteen, knows all about how OCD can turn a life upside down.

2 Stephanie had trouble with math when her OCD was in high gear. "If I got to number 17 on the math test, I would have to tap my pencil seventeen times."

3 Like any major illness, OCD affects everyone in the family. "My parents have gone through so much because of me," says Stephanie. It's often difficult for family members to accept that a person with OCD cannot stop his or her *ritualistic* behavior. This can cause anger and resentment. On the other hand, the family may end up assisting in the rituals to keep peace.

4 It can affect every aspect of life: school, family, and friends. Although Stephanie has lost some friends because of it, most people have been very supportive. "My friends have known me all my life, and OCD is just part of who I am," she says.

A Painful Disorder

5 Obsessive-compulsive disorder, as the name implies, consists of obsessions and/or compulsions. Have you ever spent hours daydreaming about a movie star? While we may call these thoughts obsessions, they are not OCD because they involve

pleasurable thoughts. Maybe you can't stop thinking about your math test next Friday, or you wonder if you remembered to shut your locker. If you have OCD, these thoughts could take over your day. OCD obsessions are unwanted, recurrent, and unpleasant thoughts that cause anxiety. A person with OCD may continue to worry about his or her locker, even after checking it ten times. People with OCD can become obsessed with anything, but some of the most common obsessions are about contamination, lucky and unlucky numbers, fear of intruders, and an intense need for order.

6 Compulsions, the second part of OCD, are repetitive ritualistic behaviors that the person feels driven to perform to relieve the anxiety caused by the obsessions. A person with OCD feels driven to perform these rituals according to some self-prescribed rules. For example, if a person with OCD is worried about safety, his or her compulsion may be to lock and relock each door fifteen times. Following such a routine may make the person feel less anxious, but the relief is often incomplete and short-lived. Although their behavior sounds "crazy," people with OCD are not crazy. They describe their actions as "silly" and "dumb" but still find they have little or no control over them.

7 We witnessed how difficult OCD is to live with when it hit the big screen recently with Jack Nicholson's Oscar-winning performance in *As Good As It Gets.* We watched him twist and turn to avoid cracks, scare customers away from his table, and go through multiple bars of soap washing his hands.

Good News and Bad News About Treatment

8 Living with OCD is difficult, but it is a treatable disease. The bad news, however, is that people often spend years suffering before they get help. Many factors stand in their way:

1. People with OCD know something is wrong, but they commonly don't know what it's called and that it's treatable. It took Marc Summers, an OCD sufferer and the host of "Double Dare," twenty-five years to learn that his symptoms had a name and could be treated.

2. People also often hide their symptoms because they are embarrassed by them. They know their compulsions appear "crazy," so they don't tell anyone and perform their rituals in secret.

3. When people with OCD finally do seek help, they are frequently misdiagnosed. People with OCD typically see three or four doctors before a correct diagnosis is made.

9 All these factors have led to inaccurate statistics about OCD. Researchers once thought OCD was rare, but now they think between 2 and 3 percent of the population will suffer from it during their lifetime.

10 The good news about treatment is that there have been major break-throughs over the last few years. The two main avenues of treatment are medication and behavioral therapy, which are often used in combination for the best results.

11 "Clinical trials in recent years have shown that drugs that affect the *neurotransmitter serotonin* can significantly decrease the symptoms of OCD," says the National Institute of Mental Health. These drugs are called serotonin reuptake inhibitors (SRIs) and also are used to treat depression and other anxiety disorders. Because OCD patients respond well to this treatment, scientists have abandoned the theory that OCD is caused by a parent's rigid rules. They now believe it's caused by abnormal chemical activity in the brain.

12 While traditional psychotherapy is generally not helpful in relieving OCD, behavioral therapy can be. Behavioral therapy involves exposing patients to whatever triggers their compulsive behavior. For example, a person who has a contamination obsession and a washing compulsion may be asked to remain in contact with a "germy" object and not be allowed to wash his or her hands for gradually lengthening time periods. Through this repetition, the person's anxiety about germs can be reduced.

13 But the advancements of recent years do no good if people don't ask for help. What should you do if you are suffering from OCD? Stephanie says: "Don't be ashamed of it. I was ashamed for many years. I tried to hide it and make up excuses. One day I didn't care anymore, and I became more open." Stephanie is a straight A student this year because of the person she has become and the help she has received.

After Reading

Word Connections

1. Create a concept of definition map for *rituals*.

Concept Map for Rituals

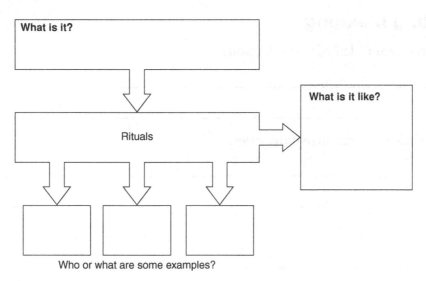

2. Distinguish between an *obsession* and a *compulsion*.

_____

_____

_____

3. "This can cause anger and *resentment*." What does *resentment* mean?

_____

_____

_____

4. A person with contamination obsession is afraid of

    a. locked doors.

    b. germs and diseases.

    c. people.

    d. heights.

5. One of the main avenues of treatment for OCD is behavioral therapy. Define *behavioral therapy*.

_____

_____

_____

Connecting Meaning

1. What is the main idea of this selection?

_____

_____

2. Define obsessive-compulsive disorder.

_____

_____

_____

_____

3. Give examples of obsessive and compulsive behaviors.

_____

_____

_____

_____

4. "People often spend years suffering before they get help." List three factors that stand in the way of treatment.

_____

_____

_____

_____

Selection Three: **"An Armful of Agony"**

Claudia Kalb

Before Reading

Before you read "An Armful of Agony," complete the following:

Predict the topic.

Skim the reading to see if you have correctly predicted the topic.

Think about painful experiences. Have you ever had a deep or bloody cut? What was your reaction? Read about people who cut themselves intentionally.

Set your purpose for reading.

Words to Preview

articulate *(v.)* to give words to *(par.1)*
incarnation *(n.)* bodily form *(par.2)*
unfathomable *(adj.)* incapable of being understood *(par.4)*

outed *(v.)* spoke out *(par.2)*

dissociate *(v.)* to separate *(par.3)*

imposed *(v.)* forced on another *(par.3)*

demeaned *(v.)* degraded or put down *(par.4)*

loathing *(v.)* disliking greatly *(par.4)*

quelled *(v.)* quieted *(par.4)*

dialectical *(adj.)* arriving at the truth by using conversation involving question and answer *(par.4)*

devise *(v.)* to form a plan *(par.4)*

During Reading

As you read "An Armful of Agony," continue to predict and visualize the information, and monitor your comprehension. Look for signals for the definition and illustration/example patterns. What does the author want you to know about self-mutilation?

Armful of Agony

1   STACY is a churchgoing midwesterner, a twenty-five-year-old secretary who wears cardigan sweaters and wire-rimmed glasses. She's the blond, blue-eyed girl next door—seemingly about as wholesome as they come. But for more than ten years, Stacy secretly indulged in a passion fit for B-grade horror movies: She scratched at her skin, burned it with hot knives, and sliced it repeatedly with razor blades and shards of glass. Today Stacy's arms are a jumbled mess of thin white lines from elbow to wrist. They are not just physical wounds, but emotional battle scars. The cutting wasn't gruesome or even painful, Stacy says. It was soothing, a release for inner turmoil she could not *articulate.* "Once I did it," she says, "I felt better."

2   Self-mutilation—also called self-injury and, in its most basic *incarnation,* cutting—is alarming and *unfathomable* even to many therapists. For decades, patients like Stacy have been mental health's untouchables, bounced from emergency rooms to institutions. "They've been ignored, they've been shunned," says Dr. Armando Favazza, a psychiatrist at the University of Missouri-Columbia Medical School, who has written extensively on self-mutilation. But three years ago, Princess Diana *outed* cutting on a global scale when she admitted in a television interview that she had intentionally injured her arms and legs. "You have so much pain inside yourself that you try to hurt yourself on the outside because you want help," she said. There are two new books on the topic, *Bodily Harm* and *A Bright Red Scream.* And though research is still in its infancy, therapists say there are now promising treatments—from medications to intensive psychotherapy—for the estimated 2 million self-mutilators in this country.

3   The vast majority are women who started cutting as teenagers. Stacy recalls picking up a piece of broken glass in a parking lot when she was thirteen, but she

can't remember why or how she decided to slash herself. Some self-mutilators are suicidal as well, although most cut themselves not to die, but to cope with the pressures of staying alive. Experts say that at least half were sexually abused as children. Many learned to shield themselves from horror in their lives by *dissociating* from their emotions. They say cutting snaps them back into consciousness. "It proves 'I'm alive, I'm human, I have blood coursing through my veins,'" says Marilee Strong, author of *A Bright Red Scream*. Others, many of whom also suffer from anorexia or bulimia, self-mutilate to gain control over their bodies or to express their feelings about being abused. "They're wearing a visible symbol of the violation *imposed* on them," says Dr. Joseph Shrand, director of the Child and Adolescent Outpatient Clinic at McLean Hospital in Belmont, Mass.

4   Cutters come from less tormented backgrounds, too. As children, some endured their parents' bitter divorces or may have been verbally abused–*demeaned* as too fat or lazy. Others were told never to cry. Whatever the trauma, experts say almost all grew up in homes with poor communication between parent and child. They suffer not just low self-esteem, but absolute self-*loathing*. "Cutting is literally like letting out bad blood," says Strong. Many are high achievers, even perfectionists, but they are failures when it comes to emotions. "They have no language for their own feelings," says Steven Levenkron, a psychotherapist and author of the book *Cutting* . . . "Cutting is the replacement for the absent language." Experts say they can help. Self-mutilators often suffer from related conditions like depression, anxiety, eating disorders, and posttraumatic stress syndrome. Treatment varies accordingly. Some patients benefit from antidepressants. In certain cases, the cutting impulse can be *quelled* by the drug Naltrexone, commonly used to treat heroin addicts. Medication alone, though, is unlikely to be enough. Cutters are often unreceptive to traditional talk therapy, but some psychologists are finding success with *dialectical* behavior therapy, *devised* in the 1980s by University of Washington psychologist Marsha Linehan. The treatment teaches patients skills for tolerating distress and controlling behavior.

5   Intensive inpatient therapy can work, too. Karen Conterio and Wendy Lader, authors of *Bodily Harm*, run a thirty-day clinic for self-mutilators outside Chicago. Stacy is one of their successes. A year after entering the program, she's stopped cutting. "It just seems so absurd," she says. Experts hope that through compassionate counseling, other cutters will one day be able to say the very same thing.

After Reading

Word Connections

1. In the reading, find the synonym for *self-mutilation*.

_____

_____

2. Define the word *shunned* as given in the context of the story.

_____

_____

3. Define *demean* in your own words.

_____

_____

4. A year after entering the program, she's stopped cutting. "It just seems so absurd," she says. Experts hope that through *compassionate* counseling, other cutters will one day be able to say the very same thing."

Meaning From Context Map Compassionate

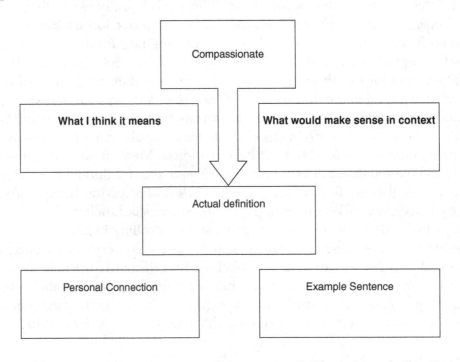

5. Using your knowledge of word parts, define *untouchable* and *psychotherapy*.

_____

_____

_____

Connecting Meaning

1. What is the main idea of this selection?

_____

_____

_____

2. Give an example of the behavior of a self-mutilator.

_____

_____

_____

3. What are some of the causes of self-mutilation?

_____

_____

_____

_____

Portfolio Activities

Integrating Ideas

Each of the readings deals with a health issue. What other health issue interests you? Is your interest based on personal experience? What sources can you use to increase your knowledge about the subject? Reflect on these ideas in writing or in class discussion.

Extending Concepts

Every decade the younger generation seems to engage in activities that meet with the disapproval of older generations. Today tattooing and body piercings are in vogue. Why do you think some people object to these activities? Is there a point where you find these activities excessive or unacceptable? Write about your opinion and/or experience with tattooing and body piercing.

Collaborative Activity

As a group, research an area related to health. Give a short oral presentation to the class. It should include definitions, causes, treatments, and other interesting facts.

Additional Portfolio Suggestion

Health products are advertised in a variety of ways. Find two full page print advertisements. For each, define the product being advertised. Give examples of its claims. Do you think these claims are true? What documentation does the product give for its claims? Would you use this product?

Chapter Summary Graphic Organizer

Complete the graphic organizer by listing the signal words for definition and illustration/example.

Definition/Illustration/Example

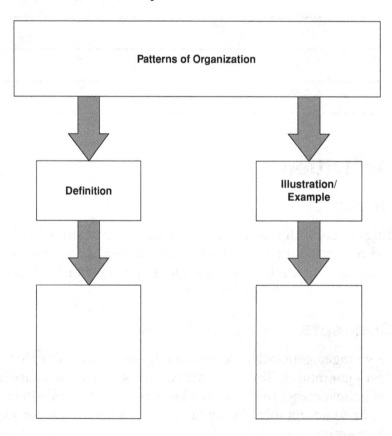

Chapter 10

Comparison and Contrast Patterns

Theme of Readings: Censorship

"*The worst thing about censorship is* [deleted by the censorship bureau]."

ANONYMOUS

Censorship

"Congress shall make no law respecting an establishment of religion, or prohibiting the free exercise thereof; or abridging the freedom of speech or of the press, or the right of the people peaceably to assemble, and to petition the government for a redress of grievances." The first amendment to the Constitution of the United States was written to ensure that Americans would enjoy a free exchange of ideas. While essential in a democratic society, this right is not absolute. From the start of this nation, Americans have struggled to find a balance between the freedom and the limits of expression.

When the Bill of Rights was written in 1791, people did not have as much access to mass media as they do today. Now newspapers, magazines, books, radio, television, movies, music, and the Internet are all avenues of expression. With the increase in mass communication has come an increase in questions about censorship: What constitutes obscenity? What secrets can a government hide in the interest of national security? What books are suitable for children to read? What words are offensive to others? How can the right to free speech be balanced with the right for freedom from discrimination? Do any ideas undermine democracy? Should television, movies, or song lyrics be censored? How would you feel if you went to the store and were unable to purchase your favorite CD because it had obscene lyrics? Who should set guidelines for what is acceptable or not acceptable to the general public?

The debate over these questions and over what is acceptable will always be complex and ongoing. The right to debate these issues is in itself an expression of the freedom of speech.

Chapter Objectives

After completing this chapter, you will be able to:

1. Identify the signal words used for the comparison and contrast patterns.

2. Distinguish between comparison and contrasting supporting details.

3. Identify the supporting details that determine the comparison and contrast patterns.

Focus on Comparison and Contrast Patterns

Comparison Pattern

Authors use a comparison pattern when they want to stress similarities between two or more people, places, things, or ideas. The comparison pattern gives readers information and shows connections and likenesses. For example, someone comparing two newspapers could discuss similarities in the feature stories, editorials, and level of vocabulary. A reviewer writing about a movie and its sequel could comment on the sameness of the plots, characters, and special effects in each. This pattern may also be used to clarify a difficult concept by comparing it to something familiar to the reader. A chemistry teacher may explain the chemist's unit of amount, a mole, as being like a dozen or a gross, common units of amount.

Common Signals   **Signal words** that may provide clues to the comparison pattern are:

like	likewise	just like	just as	both
similarly	same	alike	same as	in the same way
in comparison		similarities	resembles	compare

Read the paragraph below. Then read the guide questions and answers that follow. In the future, these guide questions will help to analyze and determine the pattern of any paragraph or reading.

Some parents find that two best selling books by Judy Blume are not appropriate for children for similar reasons. *Are You There God? It's Me Margaret* and *Superfudge* both contain profane language. In addition, the books are alike in their use of offensive and immoral material. In *Superfudge*, references to bodily functions and toilet humor were found to be offensive. In *Are You There God?* the idea that Margaret is without religious background and yet speaks to God about non-religious, adolescent issues is objectionable to some.

What is the main idea?
The main idea is found in the first sentence. Some parents think the two Judy Blume books are inappropriate for children.

What are the common signals used in this paragraph?
The words similar, both, and alike indicate a comparison pattern.

What details support the main idea?
The books are inappropriate for profane, offensive and immoral material. Examples of offensive material are given.

What is the pattern of organization?
This paragraph shows a pattern of comparison because it shows similar reasons why two books were found to be inappropriate for children.

Contrast Pattern

Authors use the contrast pattern to describe differences between two or more people, places, things, or ideas. This pattern helps readers evaluate and organize information and see the differences. For example, a writer may contrast a politician's view on a subject expressed several years ago and in the present.

Common Signals   **Signal words** that may provide clues to the contrast pattern are:

in contrast	but	yet	although
while	instead	on the other hand	rather
however	than	on the contrary	differs from
unlike	nevertheless	different in spite of	as opposed to

Read the paragraph below. Then read the guide questions and answers that follow. In the future, these guide questions will help to analyze and determine the pattern of any paragraph or reading.

In 1998, the United States Supreme Court decision in *National Endowment for the Arts versus Finley* stated government officials who administer the National Endowment for the Arts (NEA) can be required to take common standards of decency, respect for the diversity and American values into account when they award grants to artists and organizations. In the opinion of the NEA chairman, this ruling would not affect the day-to-day operations of the organization. Many artists and art supporters hold a contrasting opinion. Unlike the chairman, artists feel NEA choices for funding will be affected because the standards of decency are vague and leave no artistic avenue for controversial protest or political art.

What is the main idea of this paragraph?
Government officials and artists hold contrasting opinions about the *NEA v. Finley* decision.

What are the common signals used in this paragraph?
The words *in contrast* and *unlike* indicate a contrast pattern.

What details support the main idea?
The chairman feels operation of the NEA will not be affected while artists and art supporters feel funding will be affected.

What is the pattern of organization?
This paragraph shows a contrast pattern because it described differences between two opinions.

Comparison/Contrast

An author will often combine the comparison and contrast patterns and state both similarities and differences. The signal words will help to identify whether two or more people, places, things, or ideas are being compared and/or contrasted.

Short Exercises: Comparison and Contrast Patterns

Directions: *Read each of the following paragraphs and complete the questions that follow.*

1. The freedom of speech that was possible on the Internet could now be subjected to governmental approvals. For example, China is attempting to restrict political expression, in the name of security and social stability. It requires users of the Internet and electronic mail (e-mail) to register, so that it may monitor their activities. Similarly, in the United Kingdom freedom of speech on the Internet is restricted as state secrets and personal attacks are off limits. Laws are strict and the government is extremely interested in regulating the Internet with respect to these issues.

Craig Atkinson

What is the main idea of this paragraph?

_____

_____

What are the common signals used in this paragraph?

_____

_____

What details support the main idea?

_____

_____

_____

_____

Determine the pattern of organization.

_____

_____

2. The books *Flowers in the Attic, Garden of Shadows, Petals in the Wind*, and *Seeds of Yesterday* were written by V. C. Andrews. Besides the author, these titles have other similarities. Each book was removed from the Oconee County, Georgia school libraries in 1994. The reason stated for their removal was also the same, "due to the filthiness of the material."

Banned Books 1999 Resource Guide

What is the main idea of this paragraph?

_____

_____

What are the common signals used in this paragraph?

_____

_____

What details support the main idea?

_____

_____

_____

_____

Determine the pattern of organization.

_____

3. Television censorship of musicians has a long history. However, the reasons behind the censorship differ. In the 1950s, Elvis Presley was shown only from the waist up. His gyrating hips were too sexually suggestive to be shown on television. In the 1960s, the Beatles' views on religion were not aired as they might offend mainstream beliefs. In the 1990s, MTV censored a KISS video featuring a fire-breathing scene because of the fear it would be imitated by children.

Adapted from "MTV Censors KISS Video"

What is the main idea of this paragraph?

_____

_____

What are the common signals used in this paragraph?

_____

_____

What details support the main idea?

_____

_____

_____

_____

Determine the pattern of organization

_____

4. Stealth censorship, the unofficial censoring of a book collection, cannot be compared to the outright banning of books. Yet the results are the same, fewer books are available for the public to read. Instead of a formal removal of a book, a book may quietly disappear from a library shelf after a parent complains. With ever tightening budgets, both librarians and school administers are cautious about their purchases. Publishers, with economic pressures, reject many manuscripts that contain problematic language or stories on tough subjects like sexual abuse. These quiet book bannings affect the book world just as the officially banned books do.

Adapted from "What Johnny Can't Read"–Censorship in American Libraries

What is the main idea of this paragraph?

_____

_____

What are the common signals used in this paragraph?

_____

_____

What details support the main idea?

_____

_____

_____

_____

Determine the pattern of organization.

_____

5. Almost six score years ago, a poor white boy known as Huckleberry Finn rafted
down the Mississippi River and into the American imagination. For the better part of
the following century his story, as told by Mr. Mark Twain, has been regarded as a
classic work of American fiction. Poet T. S. Eliot is said to have read the book at least
once each year throughout his life, and novelist Ernest Hemingway declared, "All
American literature comes from one book by Mark Twain called _Huckleberry Finn_. ...
It's the best book we've had."

During the same century, _Huckleberry Finn_ has repeatedly been banned from
library shelves, removed from classrooms, and challenged by censorious voices
for promoting improper or indecent conduct and for being insensitive to matters
of race. As early as 1885, the book was banned in Concord, Massachusetts, as
"trash and suitable only for the slums." In 1905 the book was taken from the
Children's Room of the Brooklyn Public Library because "Huck not only itches
but scratches"; and in 1969 it was deleted from the required reading list at
Miami-Dade Junior College, Florida, because it "inhibits learning" by black
students.

Frances Leonard

What is the main idea of this paragraph?

_____

_____

What are the common signals used in this paragraph?

_____

_____

What details support the main idea?

_____

_____

_____

Determine the pattern of organization.

_____

Reading Selections

Selection One: **"Free Speech: Lyrics, Liberty and License"**

Sam Brownback

Before Reading

Before you read "Free Speech," complete the following:

Predict the topic.

Skim the reading to see if you have correctly predicted the topic.

Think about free speech and music lyrics. Have you ever found music lyrics to be offensive? Do you think they should be censored? Relate your knowledge and opinion about music censorship to the author's view of the subject.

Set your purpose for reading.

Words to Preview

civility *(n.)* politeness *(par.4)*

discourse *(n.)* speech; conversation *(par.9)*

pervasive *(adj.)* having the tendency to spread throughout *(par.9)*

debase *(v.)* to lower in value; to degrade *(par.10)*

perverse *(adj.)* directed away from what is right and good *(par.11)*

bigotry *(n.)* intolerance of those who differ *(par.13)*

latitude *(n.)* a range of values or conditions *(par.14)*

immunity *(adj.)* not subject to an obligation *(par.15)*

predisposition *(n.)* tendency *(par.15)*

bulwark *(n.)* defense *(par.15)*

discern *(v.)* to recognize or comprehend mentally *(par.15)*

edify *(v.)* to instruct especially so as to encourage intellectual, moral or spiritual improvement *(par.15)*

refute *(v.)* to prove false *(par.15)*

During Reading

As you read "Free Speech," continue to predict and visualize the ideas, and monitor your comprehension. Look for signals for the comparison and contrast patterns. What does the author want you to understand about censorship of music lyrics?

The following is an excerpt from a speech given by Sam Brownback, United States Senator from Kansas, on March 23, 1998.

Free Speech: Lyrics, Liberty and License

by Sam Brownback

1   I want to talk with you today about music and freedom about lyrics, liberty, and license. This is an issue that is important to me–as it is, I suspect, important to you. I can't think of a more fitting place for this discussion than here, at a forum dedicated to upholding the principle of free speech, in Cleveland, the home of the Rock and Roll Hall of Fame.

2   As many of you know, I recently held a Senate hearing on the impact of violent music lyrics on young people. During this hearing, we heard a variety of witnesses testify on the effects of music lyrics that glorified rape, sexual torture, violence, and murder. Some of these lyrics are almost unbelievably awful, but they are backed by huge, powerful, prestigious corporations. I have grown more and more concerned about the content and the impact of these lyrics. And I have publicly criticized the entertainment executives who produce, promote, and profit from such music.

> Should the government regulate music lyrics?

3   I am also the only Senator on the Commerce Committee to vote against a very popular bill that would coerce TV stations into labeling their programs. I publicly opposed V-chip legislation. I have consistently voted against any sort of government involvement in regulating or rating music or television. Some people don't think the two go together. They think that if you talk about some music lyrics being degrading and violent, then you must be in favor of censorship. Others think that if you vote against various government restrictions on television programs, or music content, you must approve of those programs and songs. Both views are mistaken.

4   And today, I'd like to talk about legislating in a way to maximize freedom, and agitating for *civility* and decency, and why the two not only can go together, but should–and indeed, if we are to preserve freedom, they must.

5   Most of you here have strong ideas about music. As indeed, you should. Music is powerful. It changes our mood, shapes our experience, affects our thoughts, alters our pulse, touches our lives. The rhythm, the beat, and the lyrics all impress us with their message. Thousands of years ago, the great philosopher Plato stated, "Musical training is a more

> Music is very powerful.

Excerpted from "Free Speech: Lyrics, Liberty and License" by Senator Sam Brownnback.

potent instrument than any other, because rhythm and harmony find their way into the inward places of the soul, on which they mightily fasten."

6   As such, music lyrics have profound public consequences. In many ways, the music industry is more influential than anything that happens in Washington. After all, most people spend a lot more time listening to music than watching C-Span or reading the newspaper. They're more likely to recognize musicians than Supreme Court justices. Most of us spend more time thinking about music than laws, bills, and policies. And that's probably a good thing.

7   And as many of you know, no one spends more time listening to music than young people. In fact, one recent study conducted by the Carnegie Foundation concluded that the average teenager listens to music around four hours a day. In contrast, less than an hour is spent on homework or reading, less than 20 minutes a day is spent talking with Mom, and less than five minutes is spent talking with Dad. If this is true, there are a lot of people who spend more time listening to shock-rock artist Marilyn Manson or Snoop Doggy Dogg than Mom or Dad. In fact, Marilyn Manson himself said: "Music is such a powerful medium now. The kids don't even know who the President is, but they know what's on MTV. I think if anyone like Hitler or Mussolini were alive now, they [*sid*] would have to be rock stars."

What is the Carnegie Foundation?

8   In short, because of the power of music, the time we spend listening to it, and the potency of its messages, music has a powerful public impact. It affects us, not only privately, but publicly. It helps shape our attitudes and assumptions, and thus, our decisions and behavior—all of which has [*sid*] a public dimension, and merits public debate.

9   Frankly, I believe there needs to be more public *discourse* over music. It is too important to ignore. Its influence reaches around the world. American rock and rap are popular exports. They are listened to by billions, in virtually every nation on earth. And for good or bad, our music shapes the way in which many people around the world view the United States—American music is the most *pervasive* (and loudest) ambassador we have. Unfortunately, its message is too often a destructive one.

10   Many of you may already know the kind of lyrics I am talking about. If not, it is useful to read some of them—they won't be hard to find; they are quite popular. Then ask yourself: What are the real-world effects of these lyrics? What do these lyrics celebrate, and what do they ridicule or denounce? What are the consequences of glorifying violence and glamorizing rape? Have record companies behaved responsibly when they produce music that *debases* women? You and your friends may come up with different answers. But they are good questions to think about. And I hope recording industry executives think about them as well.

If the government tells us what to listen to, what will be next?

Excerpted from "Free Speech: Lyrics, Liberty and License" by Senator Sam Brownnback.

11   There are no easy answers to those questions. It is impossible to quantify the ways in which such lyrics affect us. But it is equally impossible to believe they have no effect at all. Of course, most rock and rap do not have hyperviolent or *perverse* lyrics. In the grand scale of things, it is a small number of songs from an even smaller number of bands that produces these sorts of lyrics. They are the exception, not the rule.

12   It is also true that people will disagree over which music is offensive. Some people thought the Beach Boys were a problem, and some think the Spice Girls are. I do not happen to be one of them. There will always be songs about which reasonable people with good judgement will disagree.

13   But there should also be some things that we can all agree on. And one of those things is that music that glorifies rape, violence, and *bigotry* is wrong. It may be constitutionally protected. The huge entertainment corporations that produce, promote, and profit from this sort of record may have a right to do so. But it is not the right thing to do.

14   For free societies to endure, there must be a distinction between what is allowed and what is honored. I believe that the First Amendment assures the widest possible *latitude* in allowing various forms of speech–including offensive, obnoxious speech. But the fact that certain forms of speech should be allowed does not mean that they should be honored, or given respectability. There are many forms of speech that should be thoroughly criticized, even as they are protected. Freedom of expression is not *immunity* from criticism.

15   The proper response to offensive speech is criticism–not censorship, and not apathy. Vigorous criticism of the perverse, hateful, and violent reflects a willingness on the part of citizens to take ideas seriously, evaluate them accordingly, and engage them directly. A cultural *predisposition* to care about ideas and to judge between them–while protecting the liberty of others, is the best *bulwark* of a free society. A citizenry that evaluates ideas, that *discerns* the true from the false, that values reason over reaction, that affirms that which is *edifying,* and that *refutes* that which is wrong– is exactly the society most likely to value, to have, and to keep free speech.

After Reading

Word Connections

1. From the context of the second paragraph, define *prestigious*.

_____

2. "Most rock and rap do not have hyperviolent or perverse lyrics." What do you think *hyperviolent* means?

_____

_____

Excerpted from "Free Speech: Lyrics, Liberty and License" by Senator Sam Brownnback.

3. Give at least two examples of *apathy*.

_____

_____

_____

4. "I am also the only Senator on the Commerce Committee to vote against a very popular bill that would *coerce* TV stations into labeling their programs.

_____

Meaning from Context Map–Coerce

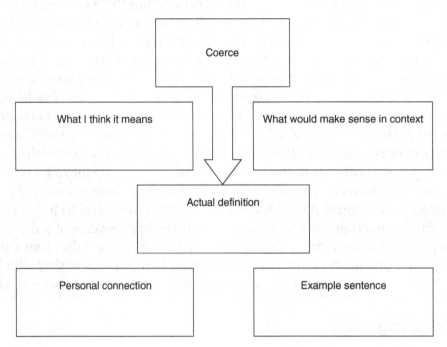

5. An obnoxious person is likely to

   a. agree with everything you say.

   b. be a good friend.

   c. disagree with everything you say.

   d. be interested in what you have to say.

Connecting Meaning

1. What is the main idea of this selection?

   _____

   _____

   _____

2. More time is spent listening to music than a variety of other activities, for example, listening to music rather than watching C-Span or reading the newspaper. What other activities listed in the reading contrast to the listening of music?

   _____

   _____

   _____

   _____

3. Senator Brownback described two kinds of responses to offensive lyrics or speech. What are these two responses? Which does the senator feel is most effective?

   _____

   _____

   _____

4. Do you think music lyrics should be censored? If so, by whom and for what reasons? If not, give reasons to support your opinion.

   _____

   _____

   _____

   _____

Selection Two: **ACLU Files Two Free-Speech Lawsuits Against Police For Arresting People Who Used "Naughty Language"**

American Civil Liberties Union

Before Reading

Before you read "ACLU Files Two Free-Speech Lawsuits Against Police for Arresting People Who Used 'Naughty Language'" complete the following:

Predict the topic.

Skim the reading to see if you have correctly predicted the topic.

Think about free-speech. Do you think everyone has the right to say whatever they want? How would you feel if you were arrested for the language you use? Relate your knowledge and opinion about free-speech to the author's view.

Set your purpose for reading.

Words to Preview

subsequently *(adv.)* following in time or order; succeeding *(par. 3)*
contravention *(n.)* violation *(par. 7)*
statute *(n.)* an established law or rule *(par. 9)*

During Reading

As you read "ACLU Files Two Free-Speech Lawsuits," continue to predict and visualize the information and monitor your comprehension. Look for signals of the comparison and contrast patterns. What does the author want you to understand about free speech?

ACLU Files Two Free-Speech Lawsuits Against Police For Arresting People Who Used "Naughty Language"

American Civil Liberties Union

1 PITTSBURGH–In two federal civil rights lawsuits filed today, the American Civil Liberties Union of Greater Pittsburgh said that police violated the rights of a retired Army officer and two college students who were arrested for using profanity in public.

2   "The ACLU intends to use these lawsuits, and others that are likely to follow, to teach Western Pennsylvania police officers that they are not Miss Manners and they cannot send people to jail simply for using naughty language," said Witold Walczak, Executive Director of the Pittsburgh ACLU. "Understandably, many people don't like to hear profanity, but under our Constitution it is not, and cannot be, a crime."

3   The first case involves East Hills resident Erica Upshaw, 28, a mother of three who was honorably discharged from the United States Army. At the time of the incident, Upshaw was a school-bus driver and church-school counselor. On July 15, 2000, North Braddock police pulled Ms. Upshaw over for allegedly running a stop sign. After a lengthy detention, the police advised Ms. Upshaw that her car was being towed because of a suspended license, something that later was shown not to be true. When Ms. Upshaw responded, "Boy am I having a bull__ day," she was arrested for disorderly conduct. A judge *subsequently* dismissed all charges.

4   The second case involves Amy Johnston, 27, a Chatham University undergraduate student and part-time children's nanny, and Gregory Lagrosa, 29, a library assistant with the Carnegie Library and part-time graduate student at the University of Pittsburgh. On November 26, 2000, the couple was existing the Homestead Giant Eagle grocery store when a police car nearly ran them over in the crosswalk. When Amy yelled, "It's a crosswalk, ass__," the officer chased them down and made enraged comments about being called an "ass__." He then arrested both of them. A judge subsequently dismissed all charges.

5   Not one of these three people did anything illegal," said Bruce Boni, a volunteer ACLU lawyer handling the Upshaw case. "The police officers were offended by profanity, so they abused their authority and misused the public trust by arresting upstanding, law-abiding citizens."

6   Several witness to the Johnston/Lagrosa arrest protested to the arresting officer that Johnston and Lagrosa had done nothing wrong and that he was not hired to arrest people because he doesn't like their language.

7   Scott Hare, a volunteer ACLU lawyer representing Johnston and Lagrosa, agreed. "The police are hired to protect the public from criminal conduct, not coarse language. Unfortunately, this officer used the authority of his badge and the Pennsylvania criminal code, in *contravention* of the First Amendment to the United States Constitution, to enforce his personal dislike of certain protected speech," he said. "I hate to imagine what would have happened if a real crime were taking place a block away while this officer was spending time arresting two law-abiding citizens for calling him a name."

8   A review of the police blotter for the days surrounding the Johnston/Lagrosa arrest indicates the Homestead police responded to a robbery, a burglary, two missing persons reports, and numerous drug offenses, domestic disputes, traffic accidents and DUI's.

9   Walczak said that the ACLU gets several similar complaints every year about police officers who arrest people either for swearing or making offensive gestures. Police routinely misinterpret Pennsylvania's disorderly conduct *statute*, which makes it a crime to use "obscene language." But while the courts have been nearly

unanimous that this provision applies only to *sexually* obscene speech, and that police cannot arrest people for swearing, far too many police departments allow their officers to punish people for simple profanity, he said.

10   Walczak said that today's lawsuits were intended to serve notice on other police departments that they should train their officers better about how the disorderly conduct statute should be applied and that it cannot be used to punish people simply for swearing.

11   The two cases, filed separately today in the U.S. District Court in Pittsburgh, are *Upshaw v. North Braddock Police Dept., et al.,* CA-02-1171, and *Johnston and Lagrosa v. Homestead Boro, et al.,* CA-02-1170. The complaints are online at http://www.aclu.org/court/johnston.pdf and http://www.aclu.org/court/upshaw.pdf

After Reading

Word Connections

1. How would you define profanity?

   _____

   _____

2. What does the phrase, "upstanding, law-abiding citizens" mean?

   _____

   _____

   _____

   _____

3. The *alleged* murderer was already convicted of the crime.

   a. True

   b. False

Connecting Meaning

1. What is the main idea of the selection?

   _____

   _____

   _____

2. Is it a crime to use obscene language in Pennsylvania? Explain.

_____

_____

_____

3. What does the ACLU see as the problem with these three arrests?

_____

_____

_____

_____

4. How does the police officers' opinion about offensive language contrast with the judges' opinion about the language?

_____

_____

_____

Selection Three: **The Schools Are Destroying Freedom of Speech**

John W. Whitehead

Before Reading

Before you read "The Schools Are Destroying Freedom of Speech" complete the following:

Predict the topic.

Skim the reading to see if you have correctly predicted the topic.

Think about your public school experience. Was your right to free expression ever silenced? Relate your knowledge and opinion about censorship to the author's view.

Set your purpose for reading.

Words to Preview

Self incrimination *(n.)* to cause yourself to be appear guilty of crime *(par. 3)*

implementing *(v.)* putting into effect *(par. 4)*

proselytizing *(v.)* to cause someone to join one's faith or beliefs *(par. 9)*

condoned *(v.)* disregarded without protest *(par. 11)*

skewed *(adj.)* distorted or biased in meaning *(par. 13)*

eradicate *(v.)* to get rid of completely *(par. 13)*

ramifications *(n.)* consequences *(par. 13)*

authoritarian *(adj.)* favoring absolute obedience to authority, against individual freedom *(par. 13)*

civil libertarian *(n.)* one actively concerned with protecting individual rights guaranteed by law *(par1. 14)*

totalitarian *(adj.)* a form of government in which political authority has absolute and centralized control over all aspects of life. *(par. 15)*

During Reading

As you read "The Schools Are Destroying Freedom of Speech," continue to predict and visualize the information and monitor your comprehension. Look for signals of the comparison and contrast patterns. What does the author want you to understand about free speech?

The Schools Are Destroying Freedom of Speech

John W. Whitehead

"The Constitution makes clear there can be no religious test for holding office, and it is just as clear there can be no religious test for individual expression of free speech—or censorship thereof, including at a high school graduation."

–Nat Hentoff, author and journalist

1   Looking at America's public schools, it is difficult to imagine that they were once considered the hope of freedom and democracy.

2   That dream is no longer true. The majority of students today have little knowledge of the freedoms they possess in the Constitution and, specifically, in the Bill of Rights.

3   For example, a national survey of high school students reveals that only 2% can identify the Chief Justice of the Supreme Court; 35% know the first three words of the U.S. Constitution; 1.8% know that James Madison is considered the father of the U.S. Constitution; and 25% know that the Fifth Amendment protects against double

---

John W. Whitehead, "The Schools Are Destroying Freedom of Speech," *Right Side News*, March 25, 2009. Reprinted by permission of the author. Constitutional attorney and author John W. Whitehead is founder and president of The Rutherford Institute.

jeopardy and self incrimination, among other legal rights. Clearly, high school civics classes are failing to teach the importance of our constitutional liberties.

4 Public educators do not fare much better in understanding and implementing the Constitution in the classroom. A study conducted by the University of Connecticut found that while public educators seem to support First Amendment rights in principle, they are reluctant to apply such rights in the schools. Consequently, the few students who do know and exercise their rights are forced to deal with school officials who, more often than not, fail to respect those rights.

5 Unfortunately, instead of being the guardians of freedom, the courts increasingly are upholding acts of censorship by government officials. As a result, the horrific lesson being taught to our young people is that the government has absolute power over its citizens and young people have very little freedom. Two incidents come to mind to illustrate this sad state of affairs, both having to do with school officials heavy-handedly silencing student expression at high school graduation ceremonies.

6 The first incident involves Nicholas Noel, the senior class president of his graduating class at Grand Rapids Union High School in Michigan. With more than 1,000 people in the audience listening to Noel deliver his commencement address, school officials turned off the microphone when he strayed from his approved speech and referred to the high school as a "prison." Noel said he described the school as a "prison" because it stressed conformity and students were "expected to act alike." His message was that high school paints an incomplete picture of life for students. "The colors of life are yet to come," Noel said. "It was really nice, nothing in bad taste. I tried to be different, and I was punished." Adding insult to injury, school officials even initially refused to award him his diploma.

7 The second incident, strikingly similar to Noel's, also involves a student whose microphone was cut off during her graduation speech simply because she voiced her personal convictions. Brittany McComb, the graduating valedictorian at Foothill High School in Nevada, was instructed by school officials to reflect over past experiences and lessons learned, say things that came from her heart and inject hope into her speech. Brittany adhered to the school's guidelines and wrote about the true meaning of success in her life—her religious beliefs. However, when she submitted her speech in advance to school administrators, they censored it, deleting several Bible verses and references to "the Lord" and one mention of "Christ."

8 Believing that the district's censorship amounted to a violation of her right to free speech, McComb attempted to deliver the original version of her speech at graduation. The moment school officials realized that she was straying from the approved text, they *unplugged* her microphone. The move drew extended jeers from the audience, with some people screaming, "Let her speak!"

9 School officials justified their actions by claiming that McComb's speech amounted to proselytizing. McComb disagrees. "I was telling my story," she said. "And if what I said was proselytizing, it was no more so than every other speaker who espoused his or her personal moral viewpoint about success. We're talking

John W. Whitehead, "The Schools Are Destroying Freedom of Speech," *Right Side News*, March 25, 2009. Reprinted by permission of the author. Constitutional attorney and author John W. Whitehead is founder and president of The Rutherford Institute.

about life here: opinions about the means of success in life, from whatever source, are indeed forms of individual religious expression. It's also hard for me to believe that anyone at graduation could think I or any other speaker was speaking on behalf of the school system."

10   McComb filed a First Amendment lawsuit in federal court. But on March 19, 2009, a federal appeals court held that school officials did not violate her First Amendment rights by censoring her speech and unplugging the microphone. McComb, who is majoring in journalism at Biola University, plans to appeal to the U.S. Supreme Court.

11   She should not expect much help from the ACLU. Despite being a longtime champion of student expression, the ACLU actually condoned the school's act of censorship. As ACLU lawyer Allen Lichtenstein remarked about the case, "It's important for people to understand that a student was given a school-sponsored forum by a school and therefore, in essence, it was a school-sponsored speech."

12   Frankly, if the ACLU applied this logic consistently, then nowhere in the schools would students have the right to say anything that wasn't approved by their teachers or high-level school officials since every area in a public school is controlled and sponsored by the school.

13   Unfortunately, the trend in the federal courts is to agree with this type of skewed reasoning. However, this type of logic will only succeed in eradicating free expression by students in schools, and the ramifications are far-reaching. Eventually, it will mean that government officials can pull the plug on microphones when they disagree with whatever any citizen has to say. Yet the lessons of history are clear: every authoritarian regime from Hitler to Saddam Hussein has not only unplugged citizens' microphones but stopped those with whom the government disapproved from speaking.

14   Civil libertarians and the courts have long held that the First Amendment right to free speech applies to everyone, whatever their beliefs. This includes what many people consider offensive or deplorable speech. It also includes speech that persuades, as well as religious speech, non-religious speech or pointedly atheistic speech. Thus, unless we want free speech to end up in a totalitarian graveyard, no one, no matter their viewpoint or ideology, should be censored in any state institution.

After Reading

Word Connections

1. How would you describe "heavy-handed silencing"? *(par. 5)*

_____

_____

John W. Whitehead, "The Schools Are Destroying Freedom of Speech," *Right Side News*, March 25, 2009. Reprinted by permission of the author. Constitutional attorney and author John W. Whitehead is founder and president of The Rutherford Institute.

2. Define and give an example of *conformity*.

_____

_____

_____

_____

3. What are some characteristics of a democracy?

_____

_____

_____

_____

Connecting Meaning

1. What is the main idea of the selection?

_____

_____

_____

_____

2. What does the First Amendment of the U.S. Bill of Rights guarantee?

_____

_____

_____

_____

3. What did Nicholas Noel do and what was the school's response?

_____

_____

_____

_____

_____

4. What are the author's and the ACLU's contrasting positions on the McComb Case?

_____

_____

_____

_____

5. According to the author, federal courts tend to agree that schools can limit free speech. How does the opinion of civil libertarians contrast with this opinion?

_____

_____

_____

_____

6. What lesson does the writer believe public schools are teaching young people? Do you agree? Why?

_____

_____

_____

_____

Portfolio Activities

Integrating Ideas

Do you think censorship is necessary for any facet of the media or for a particular age group? Who should set censorship guidelines? Does your view of censorship differ for obscenity, national security, racism, or sexism? Reflect on these ideas in writing or in class discussion.

Extending Concepts

Write an evaluation of the rating given to a movie of your choice. State whether or not you agree with the rating. Support your opinion with specific examples from the movie.

Collaborative Activity

Choose a fairy tale and rewrite it to avoid any elements that might be inappropriate for children by today's standards. You may also want to use politically correct terminology. Compare your version to the original story. Is it as captivating and powerful?

Additional Portfolio Suggestion

Read a book that has been challenged or banned in the United States within the last ten years. The American Library Association provides lists of these books. Ask your local librarian for information. After reading the book, do you feel it should be banned from library shelves?

Chapter Summary Graphic Organizer

Complete the graphic organizer by listing the signal words for comparison and contrast.

Compare/Contrast

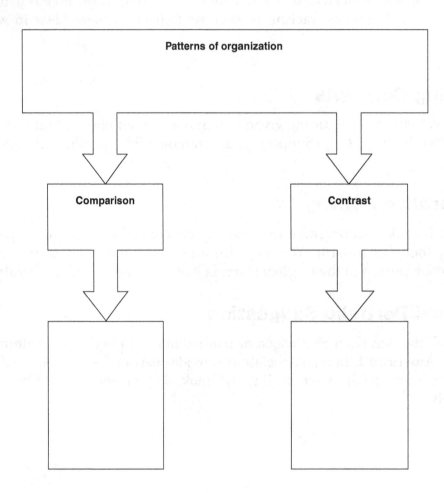

Chapter 11

Cause and Effect Pattern

Theme of Readings: Violence in America

"You cannot shake hands with a clenched fist."

INDIRA GANDHI

Violence

The news media reports on shootings, bombings, hijackings, crimes and acts of war on a daily basis. Do we notice these violent images and stories? Are we shocked by them? To some degree, we have become desensitized. Violence tends to become real only when we are somehow directly involved—as victims or witnesses. The tragedy of 9/11 affected us as a nation.

Even our everyday lives have been affected by violence. Children are taught to be wary of strangers. Schools have programs to help children guard their personal safety and learn conflict resolution techniques. Many young men and women attend self-defense classes. Homeowners purchase burglar alarms, heavy duty locks, and even, in some cases, guns to protect themselves and their families. Business owners purchase alarms, surveillance equipment, and guard dogs. Through these means, people hope to prevent violence and crime from intruding into their daily existence.

What causes violent behavior? No one knows for sure. Research has suggested that contributing factors may be drug use, physical abuse, easy access to guns, and perhaps even the high number of violent scenes shown in popular media. The causes are complex and debatable, but the effects are undeniable. The question remains—when, if ever, will the violence stop?

Chapter Objectives

After completing this chapter, you will be able to:

1. Identify the signal words used for the cause and effect pattern.

2. Distinguish between cause and effect supporting details.

3. Identify the supporting details that determine the cause and effect pattern.

Focus on Cause and Effect Pattern

Cause and Effect Pattern

Authors use a cause and effect pattern to discuss the reasons why something has happened or will happen in the future. This pattern answers the questions *why?* (to establish a cause) and *what resulted?* (to establish the effect or effects). An author may use this pattern to explain, for example, how Mrs. Rosa Park's non-violent action in 1955 (her refusal to give her bus seat to a white male passenger) resulted in her arrest, which resulted in the boycott of the bus company, and eventually an end to "Jim Crow" laws.

Common Signals   Signal words that may provide clues to the cause and effect pattern are:

because	because of	caused by	since
reason	leads to	effects	as a result
if ... then	therefore	consequences	due to
outcomes	thus	results	results in

These words may indicate either cause or effect so it is important to look for answers to the questions of *why?* (cause) and *what resulted?* (effect).

Read the paragraph below. Then read the guide questions and answers that follow. In the future, these guide questions will help you to analyze and determine the pattern of any paragraph or reading.

Family violence can have serious long term effects on children who live in the home. Difficulties in school such as poor grades or discipline problems are often a result of living in violent homes. Living with family violence may also cause low self-esteem. In addition, it may result in children imitating the violent behavior they have seen.

What is the main idea of this paragraph?
The main idea is found in the first sentence. Family violence can have serious long term effects on children who live in the home.

What are the common signals used in this paragraph?
The words *effects, result of, cause,* and *result in* indicate the cause and effect pattern.

What details support the main idea?
The major supporting details are difficulties in school, low self-esteem, and imitation of violent behavior.

What is the pattern of organization?
This paragraph shows a cause and effect pattern because it states the effects caused by family violence in the home.

Determining the Cause and Effect Pattern in Longer Selections

In longer selections, authors rarely use the cause and effect pattern to describe one cause and one effect. There may be several causes for one effect, several effects for one cause, or a chain of events, one event being caused by the previous one. For example, in an article about the effects of a gun control law, an author may discuss the impact on crime rates, the impact on the legal system, and the impact on the illegal sale of firearms.

Short Exercises: Cause and Effect Pattern

Directions: *Read each paragraph and complete the questions that follow.*

The paragraphs were chosen from "The Man Who Counts the Killings" by Scott Stossel.

1. In 1977 Ronny Zamora, a fifteen-year-old, shot and killed the eighty-two-year-old woman who lived next door to him in Florida. Not guilty, pleaded his lawyer, Ellis Rubin, by reason of the boy's having watched too much television. From watching television Ronny had become dangerously accustomed to violence. Suffering from what Rubin called "television intoxication," he could no longer tell right from wrong. "If you judge Ronny Zamora guilty," Rubin argued, "television will be an accessory." The jury disagreed: Ronny was convicted of first-degree murder.

   What is the main idea of the paragraph?

   _____

   _____

   What are the common signals used in this paragraph?

   _____

   _____

   What details support the main idea?

   _____

   _____

   _____

   _____

2. A 1956 study investigated a cause of violent behavior in children by comparing the behavior of twelve four-year-olds who watched a Woody Woodpecker cartoon containing many violent episodes with that of twelve other four-year-olds who

watched "The Little Red Hen," a nonviolent cartoon. Due to the watching of violent cartoons, the Woody Woodpecker watchers were much more likely than the Red Hen watchers to hit other children, break toys, and be generally destructive during play time.

What is the main idea of this paragraph?

_____

_____

What are the common signals used in this paragraph?

_____

_____

What details support the main idea?

_____

_____

_____

_____

3. In 1960 Leonard Eron, a professor of psychology at the University of Michigan's Institute for Social Research, studied third-graders in Colombia County in semi-rural New York. He observed that the more violent television these eight-year-olds watched at home, the more aggressive they were in school. Eron returned to Colombia County in 1971, when the children from his sample were nineteen. He found that the boys who had watched a lot of violent television when they were eight were more likely to get in trouble with the law when older. Eron returned to Colombia County a third time in 1982, when his subjects were thirty. He discovered that those who had watched the most television violence at age eight inflicted more violent punishments on their children, were convicted of more serious crimes, and were reported more aggressive by their spouses than those who had watched less violent television.

What is the main idea of this paragraph?

_____

_____

What are the common signals used in this paragraph?

_____

_____

What details support the main idea?

_____

_____

_____

_____

4. The latest burst of activity around the issue of television violence, ending in the legislating of the V-chip, can trace its initial cause to a night in the mid-1980s when a weary
Senator Paul Simon, of Illinois, lying in his motel bed, flipped on the television and
saw, in graphic detail, a man being sliced in half with a chain saw–a victim, Simon's
staff later figured, of Colombian drug dealers in the movie, _Scarface._ Upset that there
was nothing to prevent a child from witnessing such grisliness, Simon urged the pas-
sage of a law reducing gore on television. The result, the 1990 Television Violence Act,
was a compromise between the broadcasting industry and those who, like Simon,
wanted somehow to reduce the violence on shows that children might be watching.

What is the main idea of this paragraph?

_____

_____

What are the common signals used in this paragraph?

_____

_____

What details support the main idea?

_____

_____

_____

_____

_____

5. There are several reasons for the prevalence of violence on television news. Watch
your local newscast tonight: it is not unlikely that the majority of news stories will be
about crime or disaster–and it may well be that all six stories will be outside your
state, especially if you live far from any major metropolis. Fires and shootings are
much cheaper and easier to cover than politics or community events. Violent news

also generates higher ratings, and since the standards for television news are set by market researchers, what we get is lots of conformity, lots of violence.

What is the main idea of this paragraph?

_____

_____

What are the common signals used in this paragraph?

_____

_____

What details support the main idea?

_____

_____

_____

_____

Reading Selections

Selection One: "Bullying at School Among Older Adolescents"

Sandra Harris

Before Reading

Before you read "Bullying at School among Older Adolescents," complete the following:

Predict the topic.

Skim the reading to see if you have correctly predicted the topic.

Think about bullying at school. Have you ever been the victim of bullying? Have you ever been the bully? What do you think can be done about bullying at school?

Set your purpose for reading.

Words to Preview

escalating *(v.)* to increase in amount and intensity *(par.2)*
alienation *(n.)* separation of a person's affection from object or position *(par.2)*
provocation *(n.)* something that causes anger or resentment *(par.3)*
precursor *(n.)* one that comes before and indicates approach of another *(par.15)*

During Reading

As you read "Bullying at School Among Older Adolescents," continue to predict and visualize the ideas and monitor your comprehension. Look for signals for cause and effect pattern. What does the author want you to know about bullying in schools?

Bullying at School Among Older Adolescents

1 The Justice Department's Bureau of Justice Statistics and the Department of Education's National Center for Education Statistics (2001) reported that overall juvenile crime rates have dropped since 1992 from 48 crimes per 1,000 students ages 12 through 18 to 33 per 1,000 students. At the same time, data indicated that students who said they were victims of any crime of violence or theft at school decreased from 10% to 8%. However, before the 2003–04 school year had even completed the first quarter, there had been school shootings in and around Chicago and Minnesota, gang feuds in Arizona, stabbings in Texas and Florida, apparent murder-suicides in California and Kentucky; and armed students in standoffs in Washington and California (Toppo, 2003).

2 Many argue that school violence is a product of a sense of escalating alienation and rage that seems to exist in many of today's young people. The fuel for this violence is often considered to be school bullying. In fact, a 2002 report by the Families and Work Institute interviewed 2,000 students and found that small things, such as teasing, often trigger serious episodes of violence. On school campuses, studies have found anywhere from 20% to 30% of students are frequently involved in bullying incidents either as the victim or the bully (Juvonen, Graham, & Schuster, 2003). Consequently, high school students report that bullying has seriously affected their physical, social, and academic well-being.

3 Bullying is intentionally harmful, aggressive behavior of a more powerful person or group of people directed repeatedly toward a less powerful person, usually without provocation. The most common form of bullying among adolescents is verbal– name calling and hurtful teasing. Bullying also includes threatening gestures, hitting, stealing, spreading rumors, intentionally excluding others, and using weapons to threaten or harm. Sexual harassment is another harmful form of bullying that increases in adolescence. In fact, Stein (1995) has noted that even as early as kindergarten there appears to be bullying conduct with sexual overtones.

Bullying at school among older adolescents.

4   High school bullies tend to pick on students who don't fit in. Boys tend to select victims who are physically weak, who are short tempered, based on who their friends are, or by their clothing. Girls, on the other hand, choose victims based on looks, emotionalism, being overweight, or who get good grades.

5   Being a victim of school bullying causes students to feel less connected with the high school, which often leads to poor physical health, lowered participation in extra-curricular events, violence, substance use, and suicide (Resnick et al., 1997). The ability to form natural relationships is often impaired and this rejection by peers often leads to emotional disturbances in adulthood (Ross, 1996). In high school, victims of bullying are more anxious than their high school peers, are likely to be targeted for racism or actions that cross traditionally accepted gender behaviors (such as sexual orientation), and have poorer relationships with classmates and feel lonelier than bullies, especially boys (Nansel et al., 2001).

High school students are more likely to bully with ridicule, rejection, and other forms of emotional abuse, rather than using physical bullying.

6   While bullies demonstrate some of the same characteristics as their victims, they are more likely to be depressed than their victims; hold higher social status than victims; use alcohol and smoke; have poorer academic achievement and perceive a poorer school climate. They are more likely to manifest defiant behavior (Nansel et al., 2001) and are more likely to have racist attitudes (Ross, 1996). The students that seem to be the most seriously affected by bullying are the bully victims. Bully victims are more likely to smoke, drink and have poorer academic achievement than victims; and have poorer relationships with classmates and are lonelier than bullies (Nansel et al., 2001). They also need to retaliate following acts of aggression against them (Glover et al., 2000).

Table 1   What Kind of Bullying Do Students Observe at School?

	Never	**Sometimes**	**Often**
Being Called Names	485 (26%)	880 (47%)	503 (27%)
Being Left out of Activities	607 (33%)	792 (43%)	441 (24%)
Teasing	697 (37%)	846 (45%)	320 (17%)
Hit/Kicked	999 (53%)	665 (35%)	211 (11%)
Threatened	1,082 (58%)	619 (33%)	178 (9%)

Note.n= 1,893
Because stealing and sexual harassment were not included in earlier surveys, those categories are not reported here.

Study Design

7 It has only been within the last few years that bully studies have been done in the United States and many of these studies have concentrated on children and young

---

Bullying at school among older adolescents.

adolescents. Since 2000, my colleagues and I have conducted several studies on bullying. For this article, I used data from students in grades 8–12 to gain an understanding of bullying among older adolescents.

8   Participants in the study included 1,893 students in grades 8–12. Ethnic breakdown of participating students was 11% African American, 22% Hispanic, and 77% Anglo. Fifty-one percent were boys and 49% girls. Twenty-two percent of the participants were in the 8th grade, 53% were in the 9th grade, 14% were in the 10th grade, 8% were in the 11th grade, and 3% were in the 12th grade.

9   A diverse group of schools were represented. They were located in rural and suburban areas in Texas, Georgia, and Nebraska, and sizes varied from a small school of 250 students to a large high school of 1,500 students. Schools were selected based on convenience to the researchers and willingness of administrators to permit the studies. None of the school leaders thought that they had a problem with bullying.

10   The survey sought to gather data regarding the types of bullying that occurred, where bullying took place, how safe students felt at school, how bullying made them feel, who they told when they were bullied, and how interested they felt their teachers and administrators were in stopping bullying. Surveys were administered in English classes or in physical education classes by the regular classroom teacher from 1999–2004. Since the survey was revised several times during this time frame, only selected questions on each survey were used. The survey has a reliability alpha of. 69, which is appropriate.

Findings

11   *What kind of bullying do students observe at school?* As can be seen from Table 1, the most common form of bullying at school was being called names, followed by being left out of activities and teasing. Other studies have reported similar findings, noting that high school students are more likely to bully with ridicule, rejection, and other forms of emotional abuse, rather than using physical bullying (Juvonen etal., 2003).

Table 2   Where Do Students Observe Bullying at School?

	Never	**Sometimes**	**Often**
Classroom	315 (17%)	1,162 (62%)	398 (21%)
Lunchroom	473 (25%)	1,051 (56%)	348 (19%)
At Break	556 (32%)	879 (50%)	319 (18%)
Extracurricular Events	676 (36%)	977 (52%)	215 (12%)
Initiations of Clubs/Athletic	924 (50%)	786 (42%)	147 (8%)
On the Way Home from School	1,137 (61%)	602 (32%)	123 (7%)
On the Way to School	1,279 (70%)	465 (25%)	83 (5%)

Note.n = 1,893
Because students frequently wrote in "restrooms" and "hallways" these locations were added to later surveys, but those categories are not reported here.

———————

Bullying at school among older adolescents.

12   *Where do students observe bullying at school?* When students were asked how often they observed bullying in certain school locations, surprisingly, 83% identified the classroom as a place where bullying occurred at least sometimes. Seventy-four percent of the students reported that the lunchroom was a place where bullying occurred at least sometimes. (See Table 2).

13   *Student Experiences Being Bullied.* While 60% of students indicated that they were never bullied at school, an alarming 16% reported that they were bullied at least once a week, while 24% reported being bullied less than once a week. When students were asked how it made them feel when they were bullied at school, 15% admitted that it made them feel angry, and 16% said they felt sad and miserable. Thirty-four percent of students indicted that it did not bother them when they were bullied.

14   We asked students who they would tell if they were bullied or if they became aware of someone being bullied. Forty-six percent said they would tell a friend, 27% would tell their mother, and 14% would tell their father. However, only 13% of students would tell a teacher or an administrator.

15   Only half of the students responded to the next question which asked if students had told someone about being bullied and, if so, what happened. Nearly 37% reported that when they told, things got better. However, 17% said they never told anyone that they had been bullied, 37% reported that nothing changed even though they told, and 9% admitted that when they told the bullying only became worse.

A critical element in reducing bullying is the leadership of adults.

16   *How safe do students feel at school?* Despite the high reported occurrences of bullying, 39% of students reported that they always felt safe at school, and 45% indicated that they usually felt safe. However, 16% of students admitted that they did not feel very safe when they were at school. Consequently, 9% of students reported that they had even stayed home from school at least once because of bullying and 14% said they had considered staying home.

17   *How interested is the faculty?* When asked if administrators were interested in stopping bullying at school, 24% of students did not think that they were; while 34% admitted that they were not sure how administrators felt about this. Only 42% of students believed that administrators were interested in stopping bullying. Students felt nearly the same way about their teachers, with 22% admitting that they did not think teachers were interested in stopping bullying and 33% were not sure how their teachers felt. Only 45% felt that teachers were interested in stopping bullying.

The Dismal Conclusions

This study looked at 1,893 self-reports of older adolescents about bullying and findings suggested the following conclusions:
  • Three out of four students are aware of name-calling, students being left out of activities, and teasing at least sometimes at school.

Bullying at school among older adolescents.

- Bullying happens at many places on the campus, even locations where there is teacher supervision, such as the classroom.

Bullying at School Among Older Adolescents

- Nearly one-third of students admit that being bullied causes them to feel sad and miserable, or angry.
- A small percentage of students tell school faculty about being bullied; and when they do tell, for more than one third, nothing changes, and for a small but significant number of students, things get worse.
- Over one-half of students are not convinced that administrators or teachers are interested in stopping bullying.

What Can We Do About Bullying at School?

A critical element in reducing bullying is the leadership of adults. Lazarus (1996) identified the importance of adults in helping young people cope with stressful situations. Likewise in the early 1970s, Daniel Olweus led Sweden and Norway to implement an anti-bullying campaign characterized by adult involvement as a critical component. Two years later, incidents of bullying had been reduced by 50% (Olweus, 1993). Yet, too often, teachers cannot identify bullies or victims at school (Leff, Kupersmidt, Patterson & Power, 1999). Due in part to a lack of trust in adults, students very rarely break the "code of silence" to "rat" on bullies. Furthermore, studies indicate that adults are not viewed by students as being committed to reducing bullying at school (Rigby, 1996). In fact, teachers are not even sure if other teachers are committed to reducing bullying, nor, they admit, do they know how to help when they do become aware of bullying (Harris & Willoughby, 2003).

Building on the importance of adult involvement, the following model for reducing bullying at school is recommended (Harris & Willoughby, 2003).

- **Be Aware.** Adults must first recognize bullying as harmful and a precursor to more severe forms of school violence.
- *Strategies:* Participate in training to recognize bullies and victims; survey students, teachers, and parents regularly to identify kinds of bullying and locations on campus that are high risk; increase supervision; and develop school policies that define bullying.
- **Build Trusting Relationships.** Adults must develop a culture of trust and respect on the campus.
- *Strategies:* Talk with students in class discussions about bullying; encourage students to share how bullying makes them feel; be responsive to bullies' needs, as well as victims' needs; and show students that adults care about student achievement and about personal achievements.
- **Accept the Challenge to Provide Support.** Adults must be willing to accept the challenge to provide support for all students.

Bullying at school among older adolescents.

- *Strategies:* Accept the responsibility to advocate for students in need; present a united front that establishes behavior guidelines that emphasize bullying is not acceptable behavior; encourage students to tell when bullying occurs; involve parents; and be encouraged to support one another in preventing and intervening in bully situations.
- **Know How to Help.** Adults must have the skills to be able to respond appropriately to bullying situations.
- *Strategies:* Work collaboratively with school and community personnel to adopt school policies with antibully guidelines; create policies that address appropriate consequences that include counseling for the bully, as well as the victim; participate in training that provides strategies for supporting students.

Conclusion

Bullying breeds violence. It teases, torments, and taunts. While many young people ignore bullying or overcome it, some succumb to the pain it inflicts. Most suffer in silence, but a few turn to horrible acts of school violence, such as 15 year old Charles "Andy" Williams. He brought a revolver to school, fired 30 bullets, and killed two schoolmates and wounded 13 others. His father later said, "[they] accused him of being gay ... they made fun of him for being a country boy, for his big ears. It didn't matter what he did, they made fun of him" (Booth & Snyder, 2001, A1, A6). When adults are aware, when they build trusting relationships, when they accept the challenge to provide support, and when they have the skills to know how to help hurting students, schools will be safer for everyone.

References

Booth, W., & Snyder, D. (2001). No remorse, no motive from shooting suspect. *San Antonio Express-News*, March 7, A1, A6.

Bureau of Justice Statistics and DOE National Center for Education Statistics. (2001). *Indicators of School Crime and Safety.* Washington, D.C.: Author.

Glover, D., Gough, G., Johnson, M., & Cartwight, N. (2000). Bullying in 25 secondary schools: Incidence, impact and intervention. *Educational Research, 42*, 141–156.

Harris, S., & Petrie, G. (2002). *Bullying: The Bullies, the Victims, the Bystanders.* Lanham, MD.: The Scarecrow Press, Inc.

Harris, S., & Willoughby, W. (2003). Teacher perceptions of student bullying behaviors. *ERS Spectrum, 21(3)*, 11–18.

Juvonen, J., Graham, S., & Schuster, M. (2003). Bullying among young adolescents: The strong, the weak, and the troubled. *Pediatrics, 112(6)*, 1,231–1,237.

Lazarus, R. (1966). *Psychological Stress and the Coping Process.* New York: McGraw-Hill.

Leff, S., Kupersmidt, J., Patterson, C., & Power, T. (1991). Factors influencing teacher identification of peer bullies and victims. *The School Psychology Review, 28(3)*, 505–517.

From The Prevention Researcher, Vol. 11, No. 3, September 2004, pp. 12–14. Copyright © 2004 by Integrated Research Services, Inc. Reprinted by permission.

Nansel, T., Overpeck, M., Pilla, R., Ruan, W., Simons-Morton, B., & Scheidt, P. (2001). Bullying behaviors among U.S. youth: Prevalence and association with psychosocial adjustment. *Journal of American Medical Association, 285*(16), 2,094–2,100.

Olweus, D. (1993). *Bullying at School.* Cambridge, MA: Blackwell Publishers, Inc.

Resnick, M., Bearman, P., Blum, R., Bauman, K., Harris, K., Jones, J. et al. (1997). Protecting adolescents from harm: Findings from the National Longitudinal Study on Adolescent Health. *Journal of the American Medical Association, 278,* 823–832.

Rigby, K. (1996). *Bullying in Schools: And What To Do About It.* London: Jessica Kingsley Publishers.

Ross, D. (1996). *Childhood Bullying and Teasing: What School Personnel, Other Professionals, and Parents Can Do.* Alexandria, VA.: American Counseling Association.

Stein, N. (1995). Sexual harassment in school: The public performance of gender violence. *Harvard Educational Review,* 65, 145–162.

Toppo, G. (2003, October 21). Troubling days at U.S. schools. *USA Today,* 1A, 2A.

Sandra Harris received her PhD, in Educational Leadership from the University of Texas, Austin. She has more than 30 years of experience as a teacher and administrator and is currently an associate professor of educational leadership at Lamar University in Beaumont, Texas. She is the co-author of the book: Bullying: The Bullies, the Victims, the Bystanders (Scarecrow Press, 2003).

After Reading

Word Connections

1. While many young people ignore or overcome bullying, some *succumb* to the pain it inflicts. Define *succumb.*

_____

_____

2. Define *advocate.* Give an example of an advocate.

_____

_____

3. "Due in part to a lack of trust of adults, students very rarely break the "code of silence" to "rat" on bullies." What is a code of silence? What does "rat" mean in this sentence?

_____

_____

_____

_____

4. Define bullying according to this article.

_____

_____

_____

_____

Connecting Meaning

1. What is the main idea of this selection?

_____

_____

_____

_____

2. What is considered to be the cause(s) of violence at schools?

_____

_____

_____

_____

3. What was the result of adult involvement in the anti-bullying campaign in Sweden and Norway?

_____

_____

_____

_____

4. What are your ideas on how to eliminate bullying at schools today?

_____

_____

_____

_____

Selection Two: "'Roofies': Horror Drug of the '90s"

Judy Monroe

Before Reading

Before you read, "Roofies: Horror Drug of the '90s," complete the following:

Predict the topic.

Skim the reading to see if you have correctly predicted the topic.

Think about the drug rohypnol. What do you know about the drug? Do you know anyone who was a victim of this drug? Relate your knowledge about rohypnol to the author's information.

Set your purpose for reading.

Words to Preview

rohypnol *(n.)* a tasteless, odorless and colorless sedative that can be easily added to a beverage *(par. 8)*

anonymity *(n.)* one who is unknown *(footnote)*

During Reading

As you read "Roofies: Horror Drug of the '90s" continue to predict and visualize the ideas, and monitor your comprehension. Look for signals for the cause and effect pattern. What does the author want you to know about the drug rohypnol?

ROOFIES

1   "Thanks for offering to drive me home".

2   Barney grinned. "No prob-lem-o. I'll get us a drink to go."

3   Amy smiled as she thought about her luck in meeting Barney at her first party in college. He was funny and cute and interested in her!

4   When Barney returned, he handed her a plastic cup filled with beer, and the two pushed their way through the crowd. They talked as Barney drove Amy home.

5   Barney refused to drink while he drove, and Amy mentally added another point to his appeal rating. About fifteen minutes later, Barney pulled up to Amy's house. She complained she was sleepy and dropped her house key several times. Barney opened the front door, guided Amy inside, then told her he'd put her to bed since her roommates weren't home. Amy remembered nothing after that.

---

6   Early the next morning Amy woke feeling shaky and sore. Stumbling out of bed, she saw that she was half naked and bruised. She had been raped. Crying, she phoned the number Barney had given her.

7   The sleepy voice at the other end said no Barney lived there. Amy realized she didn't even know Barney's last name.

8   Across the United States, sexual assaults like Amy's are being connected to Rohypnol, a sedative drug often called the "date-rape drug." That's what happened to Amy. Barney had slipped Rohypnol, a white pill that quickly dissolves, into Amy's beer. It left no odor, color, or taste. The powerful drug made Amy sleepy and wiped out her memory for six to eight hours.

9   It's hard to catch people who use drugs such as Rohypnol to commit crimes, particularly in rape cases. That's because, when someone slips Rohypnol into a drink, the victim seldom remembers any details of the rape. About ten to twenty minutes after ingesting the drug, many victims feel dizzy and disoriented, hot or cold, and nauseated. Some have trouble speaking and moving. Most pass out and have no memory of what happened while under the drug's influence.

An Illegal Depressant

10 Rohypnol ranks as the most widely prescribed sedative or sleeping pill in Europe, but it is not approved for sale in the United States. Most Rohypnol in the United States is imported from Mexico and South America, where it is sold legally.

11   Rohypnol often is sold in the manufacturer's bubble packaging, which looks like a package for cold pills. The tablets are white and are single- or cross-scored on one side with "ROCHE" and "1" or "2" encircled on the other. It is cheap-users can get it for as little as $1 to $1.50 per tablet. Some users believe it is a "safe" drug because it looks legal. However, Rohypnol is illegal in the United States-and it is not safe.

12   On October 13, 1996, President Bill Clinton signed into law the "Drug-Induced Rape Prevention and Punishment Act of 1996." This law makes it a felony to distribute Rohypnol or similar substances to someone without that person's knowledge and with the intent to commit violence against that person, including rape. If Barney were tried and convicted for raping Amy, he could be sentenced to 20 years in prison.

13   Rohypnol is a central-nervous-system depressant like Valium, but it is ten times stronger. Larger than aspirin but smaller than an antacid tablet, the pills are taken by mouth or crushed and inhaled through the nose.

14   The drug's effects begin within thirty minutes, peak within two hours, and may persist for up to eight hours or more. When used illegally, adverse effects include decreased blood pressure, memory impairment, drowsiness, vision problems, dizziness, confusion, nausea, and inability to urinate. Repeated Rohypnol use can lead to dependence. If a user tries to stop taking the drug, withdrawal symptoms result, including headache, muscle pain, extreme anxiety, tension, restlessness, confusion, and irritability. Numbness, tingling, convulsions, shock, and collapse also may occur.

Horror Stories

15 In the 1970s, Rohypnol was introduced in Europe and South America. Beginning in the '80s, drug users in Europe started using it to come down from a cocaine or methamphetamine (speed) high. Americans discovered the drug in the '90s.

16   Although small in size, these pills have powerful effects. Early in 1994, the late grunge rock star Kurt Cobain fell into a coma after taking Rohypnol and drinking champagne while on tour in Italy. After his stomach was pumped, he revived, only to commit suicide under the influence of drugs shortly afterward. Like Cobain, some teens take Rohypnol with alcohol. The combination greatly impairs a person's motor ability and memory and can be deadly.

17   Sometimes Rohypnol causes aggression, rage, or hallucinations. More often it causes short-term amnesia for six to eight hours. It also reduces inhibitions and makes users feel fearless. In 1995, Rob, age 19, lived in Houston, Texas, and often used Rohypnol. He explained, "You take it-you black out. The next day people tell you what you did, and you're like, 'Wha-a-a-t?'"

18   In 1995, Annette*, age 16, was buying Rohypnol regularly in Austin, Texas. Less than a year later she entered Odyssey House, a teen treatment facility in Houston. "I'm the kind of person who wouldn't take one or two. I would take three or four and drink at the same time. We used to call them 'run-trip-and-falls.' ... I would black out for days."

19   Tim's* story is another common one. A couple of years ago, while on a business trip in Florida, he stopped at a bar for a drink. After twenty minutes or so, he felt sleepy and had trouble sitting upright. Hours later, he woke up in an alley, bleeding and bruised with torn clothing. His wallet was gone, and he had no memory of what had happened. When Tim told his story to the police, they said that someone had probably slipped Rohypnol in his drink, and when he blacked out, he was taken outside, beaten, and robbed.

Be Aware

20 To protect yourself from drugs like Rohypnol, watch what you drink at parties or when you're out on dates. Do not take any drinks (soda, coffee, as well as alcohol) from someone you do not know well and trust. Refuse open container drinks. If you think you were drugged, call 911 right away or get to an emergency room. If possible, try to keep a sample of the beverage.

After Reading

Word Connections

1. "When used illegally, adverse effects include decreased blood pressure, memory impairment, drowsiness, vision problems, confusion, nausea, and iability to urinate." Define *adverse* from context.

---

2. "It also reduces inhibitions and makes users feel fearless." What does *inhibition* mean?

_____

3. Annette's called her combination of drugs and alcohol "run-trip-and-falls." What do you think this phrase means?

_____

_____

_____

4. Create a word map for the prefix *dis-*.

Word Map for dis-

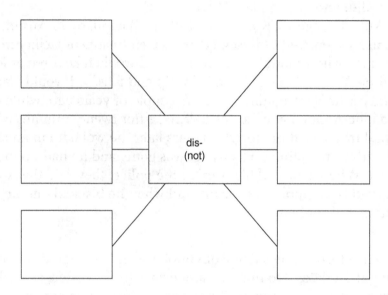

5. Amy's date had an illegal *intent* to drug her with Rohypnol. Someone with an *intent* has

  a. an illegal substance.

  b. a purpose or plan.

  c. a bad attitude.

  d. a personal aide.

Connecting Meaning

1. What is the main idea of this selection?

_____

_____

_____

2. What crimes are committed with the help of rohypnol?

_____

_____

_____

3. When used illegally, what are some of the adverse effects of rohynpol?

_____

_____

_____

4. Why is it difficult to prosecute a crime in which rohynpnol was used?

_____

_____

_____

Selection Three: **Firearms, Violence, and the Potential Impact of Firearms Control**

Franklin E. Zimring

Before Reading

Before you read "Firearms, Violence and the Potential Impact of Firearms Control" complete the following:

Predict the topic.

Skim the reading to see if you have correctly predicted the topic.

Think about gun use. How do you feel about gun ownership? Relate your knowledge and opinion about firearms control to the author's view.

Set your purpose for reading.

Words to Preview

potential *(adj.)* existing possibility *(par. 1)*

lethality *(n.)* death *(par. 5)*

differential *(adj.)* relating to or constituting a difference *(heading)*

deterrence *(n.)* act of preventing, checking or restraining *(par. 6)*

instrumentality *(n.)* something by which an end is achieved; means; *(par. 7)*

assertion *(n.)* the act of declaring positively and often forcefully *(par. 8)*

ambiguously *(adv.)* understood in two or more possible ways *(par. 9)*

contingency *(n.)* something liable to happen as a result of something else *(par. 17)*

corollary *(n.)* something that naturally follows; result *(par. 18)*

sanguine *(adj.)* optimistic *(par. 18)*

plausible *(adj.)* appearing worthy of belief *(par. 18)*

propensity *(n.)* often intense natural inclination or preference *(par. 19)*

econometric *(adj.)* relating to the study of economic data and problems *(par. 21)*

regression *(n.)* the act of going back to previous place or state; return *(par. 21)*

fallacy *(n.)* false or mistaken idea *(par. 26)*

aggregation *(n.)* a group or mass composed of many distinct parts or individuals *(par. 26)*

During Reading

As you read "Firearms, Violence, and the Potential Impact of Firearms Control" continue to predict and visualize the information and monitor your comprehension. Look for signals of the cause and effect patterns. What does the author want you to understand about firearms control?

Firearms, Violence, and the Potential Impact of Firearms Control

Franklin E. Zimring

1 This paper organizes the question of gun controls as violence policy under two quite different headings. The first issue to be discussed is the relationship between gun use and the death rate from violent crime. The second question is whether and how firearms control strategies might reduce the death rate from violence. When we review the evidence on the relationship between guns and violence, it seems clear that gun use, usually handgun use, increases the death rate from violence by a factor of three to five. Nobody in mainstream social science or criminology argues against such weapon effects these days, although some are more skeptical of the magnitude estimated than others (one example is Lance Stell).[1] Thus the problem is both genuine and important. When we review the extent to which particular approaches to controlling firearms might reduce the death rate from violence, the evidence for

modern attempts at gun control saving lives is much weaker than the evidence that gun use causes death. So gun control is a potential life-saving tool but only if the use of guns in attack can be reduced, and achieving that in our city streets will neither be easy or cheap.

Gun Use and Violence

2 It is not true that guns are used in most criminal events, nor can we say that guns are employed in most violent crimes. . . .

3   Guns are only used in 4% of all crimes, and only 20% of all violent crimes, but about 70% of all criminal killings. This tells us immediately what the special problem of gun use is in violent crime—an increase in the death rate per 100 violent attacks. If the problem you worry about is crime, guns are involved in 4% of the acts. If the problem is lethal violence, the market share for firearms is 70%. Guns alone account for twice as many criminal deaths as all other means of killing combined. Why is that?

4   Most criminal homicides result from violent assaults without any other criminal motive such as robbery or rape. Gun assaults are seven times as likely to kill as all other kinds of criminal assault,[2] and about five times as likely to kill as are knives, the next most deadly weapon that is frequently used in criminal attacks. Firearms robbery is about four times as likely to produce a victim death as a non-firearms robbery.

5   In this section, I discuss what elements of gun use might increase the lethality of gun assaults and then briefly discuss the situation with gun versus non-gun robbery.

The Causes of Differential Lethality

6 Guns may cause increases in the death rate from assault in a variety of different ways. The use of guns as opposed to other weapons in assault may be associated with both mechanical and social changes in violent assault that can increase its death rate. Among the mechanical or instrumentality aspects of gun use that can increase death rates are: the greater injurious impact of bullets; the longer range of firearms; and the greater capacity of firearms for executing multiple attacks. Among the features in social setting related to gun use are: the need to use more lethal instruments of assault in situations where an attacker fears that his adversary may have a gun, the need to sustain or intensify a deadly assault because an opponent possesses or is using firearms, and the increased willingness to use guns and other lethal weapons in personal conflict because such weapons are used generally. All of these aspects may increase the lethality of assaults committed with guns, but by no means to the same degree. There are also two social impacts of gun possession and use that can lower death rates: the deterrence of assaults because of fear of gun-owning victims and the prevention of attempted assaults by an armed victim.

From *Journal of Law, Medicine and Ethics*, vol. 32, issue 1, Spring 2004, pp. 34–37. Copyright © 2004 by American Society of Law, Medicine & Ethics. Reprinted by permission.

7   In this paper, I will stress the most important of the mechanisms that increase death rates when guns are used, so-called instrumentality effects. For a summary of all these other potential causes and their assessment, see Zimring and Hawkins.[3]

Instrumentality Effects

8 Of all the possible ways that gun use increases the deadliness of attacks, the theory that gunshot wounds inflict more damage than other methods of personal attacks is considered the most important and has been the subject of the most research. The early debate about the dangerousness of guns on deaths from assault involved different theories of the types of intention that produced assaults that lead to death. Marvin Wolfgang in his study of homicide doubted that the weapon used in an attack made much difference in the chance that a death would result since so many different weapons could produce death if an attacker tried hard enough.[4] I responded to this assertion with a study of knife and gun assaults in Chicago.[5]

9   My data suggested that many homicides were the result of attacks apparently conducted with less than a single-minded intent to kill. Unlike the Wolfgang study where only fatal attacks were examined, the Zimring studies compared fatal and nonfatal gun and knife assaults in Chicago over four police periods in 1968 and gun assaults in 1972. The studies found that 70 percent of all gun killings in Chicago were the result of attacks that resulted in only one wound to the victim,[6] and that most attacks with guns or knives that killed a victim looked quite similar to the knife and gun attacks that did not kill.[7] From this data, I argued that most homicides were the result of ambiguously motivated assaults, so that the offender would risk his victim's death, but usually did not press on until death was assured.

10   Under such circumstances, the capacity of a weapon to inflict lifethreatening injury would have an important influence on the death rate from assault. The 1908 Chicago study found that gun attacks were about five times as likely to kill as knife attacks, and this ratio held when the comparison was controlled for the number of wounds inflicted and the specific location of the most serious wound.[8] Since knives were the next most deadly frequently used method of inflicting injury in attacks, the large difference in death rate suggested that substituting knives or other less dangerous instruments for guns would reduce the death rate from assault.

11   This weapon dangerousness comparison was first reported for Chicago in 1908 and has been replicated in other sites.[9] The follow-up study demonstrated that a difference in weapon as subtle as firearm caliber can double the death rate from gun assaults.[10] The summary conclusion from this line of research can be simply stated: the objective dangerousness of a weapon used in violent assaults appears to be a major influence on the number of victims who will die from attacks. This "instrumentality effect" is the major documented influence of guns on death rate.[11]

12   The use of guns in robbery is different from their use in woundings since the weapon is not necessarily used to inflict harm. Because robberies with guns frighten

their victims into complying with the robbers' demands more often than other robberies, a smaller number of gun robberies result in woundings than personal force robberies and robberies with knives. Still, the greater dangerousness of guns when they are fired more than compensates for the lower number of wounds. For street robberies and those that take place in commercial establishments, the death rate for every 1,000 gun robberies is about three times that generated by robberies at knife point, and about ten times the death rate from robberies involving personal force.[12]

Firearms as a Contributing Cause of Lethal Violence

13 The use of firearms in assault and robbery is the single environmental feature of American society that is most clearly linked to the extraordinary death rate from interpersonal violence in the United States. But the strength of this relationship does not mean that firearms ownership and use has a simple, invariable, or independent influence on homicide rates. In this section, I consider the question of the causal connection between gun use and lethality. I do this not only because it is an important issue in relation to firearms and lethal violence, but also because reflecting on the questions of causation that arise in connection with firearms teaches us an important lesson about the role of many other environmental influences on the incidence of lethal violence.

14   The American debate about guns has produced one of the few causal critiques ever to appear on a bumper sticker: the famous slogan "Guns don't kill people, people kill people." Behind the strong sentiment that inspired this and a multitude of related appeals lies an important logical point. Firearms ownership and use is neither a necessary nor a sufficient cause of violent death in the United States. Firearms are not a necessary cause of killings because of the wide army of alternative methods of killing that are available ranging from the strangler's hands to car bombs. Even in the United States at the turn of the 21st century, nearly 30 percent of all killings did not involve guns. Moreover, the widespread availability of firearms is not a sufficient condition for intentional homicide by a wide margin. Almost one-half of all American households own some kind of guns and it is estimated that one-quarter of all households own a handgun—the weapon used in more than three-quarters of all gun homicides. Yet only a small fraction of all gun owners become gun attackers. The logical point here is that guns do not become dangerous instruments of attack if they are not used in an attack.

15   If gun use is neither a necessary nor a sufficient cause of violent death, what is the proper descriptive label for the role gun use plays in deaths due to intentional injury? The most accurate label for the role of firearms in those cases of death and injury from intentional attacks in which they are used is contributing cause. Even where

the availability of a gun plays no important role in the decision to commit an assault, the use of a gun can be an important contributing cause in the death and injury that results for gun attacks. When guns are used in a high proportion of such attacks, the death rate from violent attack will be high. Current evidence suggests that a combination of the ready availability of guns and the willingness to use maximum force in interpersonal conflict is the most important single contribution to the high U.S. death rate from violence. Our rate of assault is not exceptional; our death rate from assault is exceptional.[13]

16   The role of gun use as a contributing cause means that the net effect of firearms on violence will depend on the interaction of gun availability with other factors which influence the rate of violent assaults in a society and the willingness of people to use guns in such assaults. So the precise contribution of firearms to the death toll from violence is contingent on many other factors that may influence the number and character of violent attacks.

17   Some implications of this contingency deserve emphasis. Introducing 10,000 loaded handguns into a social environment where violent assault is a rare occurrence will not produce a large number of additional homicide deaths unless it also increases the rate of assault. The percentage increase in homicide might be considerable if guns become substitutes for less lethal weapons. But the additional number of killings would be small because of the low rate of attack. Introducing 10,000 handguns into an environment where rates of attack and willingness to use handguns in attack are both high is a change that would produce many more additional deaths. The net effect of guns depends on how they are likely to be used.

18   One corollary of viewing guns as an interactive and contributing cause to intentional homicide is that societies with low rates of violent assault will pay a lower price if they allow guns to be widely available than will societies with higher rates of violence. The sanguine sound bite encountered in American debates about guns is: "An armed society is a polite society."[14] As stated on the bumper sticker, this does not seem particularly plausible, but it does seem likely that only a very polite society can be heavily armed without paying a high price.

19   The United States of 2004 is far from that polite society, although things are better now than they were as recently as 1994. Our considerable propensity for violent conflict would be a serious societal problem even if gun availability and use were low. But the very fact that the United States is a high-violence environment makes the contribution of gun use to the death toll from violence very much greater. When viewed in the light of the concept of contributing causation, the United States has both a violence problem and a gun problem, and each makes the other more deadly.

From *Journal of Law, Medicine and Ethics*, vol. 32, issue 1, Spring 2004, pp. 34–37. Copyright © 2004 by American Society of Law, Medicine & Ethics. Reprinted by permission.

Varieties of Firearms Control

20 The objective of almost all forms of firearms control is to reduce the use of loaded guns in attacks and robberies and thus to reduce the death rate from crime. There turns out to be several different strategies of control, many different intensities of gun regulation, and many different contexts in which controls can be attempted. One common strategy is to prohibit dangerous uses of guns—so that hundreds if not thousands of statutes prohibit concealed handguns from being carried at all, and from being taken into airports, churches, schools, and courthouses. Other "time, place and manner laws" prohibit shooting in city streets. The idea is that some settings are so dangerous that otherwise allowable weapons and uses should be prohibited.

21 One dispute about a "time, place and manner" regulation generated its own considerable literature in the late 1990s. John Lott provided an econometric study which argued that expanding the criteria for concealed weapons permits was associated with lower crime rates.[15] Several published criticisms have undermined Lott's findings either by criticizing the quality of his multi-variate regression evidence[16] or by counter-demonstrations using similar methodology.[17] Because the impact of such laws on citizen gun carrying behavior and the use of guns in self defense has not been measured, the evidence that "shall issue" permit-to-carry laws has impact on crime rates is thin.

22 A second class of controls attempt to restrict dangerous users from obtaining and using guns. In federal law, convicted felons, youth, and certain diagnosed and previously institutionalized persons with emotional illnesses are excluded from being eligible to obtain weapons. This is the primary type of firearms control strategy in federal law and in most states.

23 A third approach is to try to exclude from general ownership particular types of guns that are too easily misused. Federal law has all but banned automatic weapons and sawed-off shotguns since 1934, and the Federal Gun Control Act of 1908 added "destructive devices" such as bazookas and hand grenades to the list of classes of weapon thought too dangerous for general ownership.[18] In the late 1980s, a controversy arose over semi-automatic weapons with large ammunition magazines—so-called assault weapons—which have been restricted in a variety of ways under different laws with different definitions.[19] And special restrictions also exist in a few states and cities for handguns.

24 A "dangerous uses" approach tries to govern the use of guns without reference to the people who can possess them or the kind of guns that can be owned. A "dangerous user" strategy tries to segregate higher risk users without making any guns unavailable for the rest of the population. A "dangerous guns" strategy tries to restrict the general availability of certain types of guns. Every state and city has a mix of different laws—there are no examples in the United States of jurisdictions that rely on only one general approach and not any I know of with only one set of regulations.

Can Gun Control Work?

25 The answer to this general question is a highly qualified "yes, but." If and to the extent that regulation reduces the use of loaded guns in crimes it will save American lives. But reducing the share of violence with guns is not an easy task to achieve in urban environments with large inventories of available handguns. Most gun control efforts do not make measurable impacts on gun use, particularly low budget symbolic legislation. If Congress when creating what it called a "gun-free school zone" by legislation did reduce firearms violence, the result would be on a par with that of the miracle of loaves and the fishes. But New York City's effort to tightly enforce one of the nation's most restrictive handgun laws did apparently have a substantial payoff in reduced shootings that saved many lives.[20]

26   What I would emphasize here is the fallacy of categorical generalizations. We have no business asking whether broad classes of laws—criminal prohibitions, anti-theft statutes or gun control strategies—work or don't. That is an aggregation error as long as guns are a contributing cause to the death rate from violent crime in the United States. The serious work is in identifying the specific strategies and contexts in which regulation can reduce the use of firearms in violent assault and attempting to achieve these results at tolerable public and personal cost.

References

1. J. B. Jacobs, Can Gun Control Work? (New York: Oxford University Press, 2002).

2. F. E. Zimring and G. Hawkins, Crime Is Not the Problem: Lethal Violence in America (New York: Oxford University Press, 1997): at 108.

3. See Zimring and Hawkins, supra note 2: 113–122.

4. M. Wolfgang, Patterns in Criminal Homicide (Philadelphia: University of Pennsylvania Press, 1958).

5. F. E. Zimring, "Is Gun Control Likely to Reduce Violent Killings?" University of Chicago Law Review 35 (1968):721–737.

6. F. E. Zimring, "The Medium is the Message: Firearms Caliber as a Determinant of the Death Rate from Assault," Journal of Legal Studies 1 (1972): 97–123.

7. See Zimring, supra note 5.

8. Zimring, supra note 5.

9. T. Vinson, "Gun and Knife Attacks," *Australian Journal of Forensic Sciences* 7 (1974): 76; R. Sarvesvaran and C.H.S. Jayewarclene, "The Role of the Weapon in the Homicide Drama," *Medicine and Law* 4 (1985): 315–326.

10. Zimring, supra note 6.

11. P. J. Cook, "The Technology of Personal Violence," in M. Tonry, ed., *Crime and Justice: A Review of Research* (Chicago: Chicago University Press, 1991).

12. F. E. Zimring and J. Zuehl, "Victim Injury and Death in Urban Robbery: A Chicago Study," *Journal of Legal Studies* 15 (1986):1–40; Cook supra note 11: 17.

13. Zimring and Hawkins, supra note 2: 34–50.

14. Handgun Control Inc., *Carrying Concealed Weapons: Questions and Answers* (Washington, D.C.: Handgun Control Inc., 1995).

15. J. R. Lott, *More Guns, Less Crime* (second edition) (Chicago: University of Chicago Press, 2000).

16. D. Black and D. Nagin, "Do 'Right-to-Carry' Laws Deter Violent Crime?" *Journal of Legal Studies* 27 (1998): 209–219; F. E. Zimring and G. Hawkins, "Concealed Handguns: The Counterfeit Deterrent," *The Responsive Community* 1 (1997): 46–60.

17. J. Donohue and I. Ayers, "Shooting Down the More Guns, Less Crime Hypothesis," National Bureau of Economic Research (working paper no. w9336, 2002); J. Donohue and I. Ayers, "The Latest Misfires in Support of the More Guns, Less Crime Hypothesis," *Stanford Law Review* 55 (2003): 1371–1398.

18. F. E. Zimring, "Firearms and Federal Law: The Gun Control Act of 1968," *Journal of Legal Studies* 4 (1975): 133–198.

19. F. E. Zimring, "The Problem of Assault Firearms," *Crime and Delinquency* 35 (1989): 538–545.

20. J. Fagan, F. E. Zimring, and J. Kim, "Declining Homicide in New York City: A Tale of Two Trends," *Journal of Criminal Law and Criminology* 88 (1998): 1277–1323.

After Reading

Word Connections

1. In paragraph 6, part of the sentence is "where an attacker fears that his adversary may have a gun", re-read the entire sentence, then define the word, adversary.

_____

_____

_____

_____

2. Define the word *replicated* as used in paragraph 11.

_____

_____

_____

_____

3. Several times in the article the phrase "polite society" is used. What is your definition of a "polite society."

_____

_____

_____

_____

_____

4. In this article firearms are referred to as a "contributing cause of lethal violence." What is meant by contributing cause?

_____

_____

_____

_____

_____

_____

5. Choose two words from the Words to Preview list and use each in sentence.

_____

_____

_____

_____

_____

Connecting Meaning

1. What is the main idea of this selection?

_____

_____

_____

_____

_____

_____

2. What does current evidence suggest is the most important cause of the high rate of U.S. death rate from violence?

_____

_____

_____

_____

_____

_____

3. Explain the bumper sticker, "Guns don't kill people, people kill people."

_____

_____

_____

_____

_____

_____

4. State the three different strategies of firearms control presented in this article.

_____

_____

_____

_____

_____

_____

_____

_____

_____

5. At the end of this selection the author poses the question, "Can gun control work?" What is the author's answer to this question? What is your answer to this question?

_____

_____

_____

_____

_____

_____

_____

_____

_____

_____

Portfolio Suggestions

Integrating Ideas

What do you think causes violent behavior? Has violence in society increased or decreased? How do you think violence has affected you personally? Reflect on these ideas in writing or in class discussion.

Extending Concepts

Make a guess as to how many times physical violence occurs on television each hour in the evening. Then actually count the number of violent acts you see. Write about your observations and opinion.

Collaborative Activity

Examine violence in the newspapers. Bring several newspapers to class. Note photographs, words, and articles that show or describe violence. Discuss with the group the impact of the photos and print on the reader.

Additional Portfolio Suggestion

Investigate one recent law either federal or state that has been passed to curb violence, such as the Brady Bill or Megan's Law. Discuss the pros and cons of the bill.

Chapter Summary Graphic Organizer

Complete the graphic organizer by listing the signal words for cause and effect.

Graphic Organizer for Cause/Effect

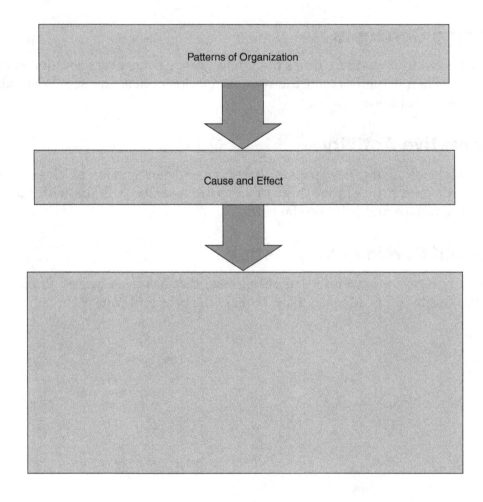

Patterns of Organization

Cause and Effect

Patterns of Organization

In this unit, you examined several patterns of organization used by authors and the signals associated with them. In each pattern, the main idea is supported by major and minor supporting details. These patterns of organization helped you to make sense of the readings. Authors may choose one pattern or a combination of patterns to explain the main idea.

Chronological Order and Listing

- Chronological order organizes information according to the time order in which it occurs.

- Listing is used by authors to list details that support the main idea.

Definition and Illustration/Example

- A definition pattern answers the question *what is it?* by giving the precise meaning of words and ideas.

- Illustrations or examples are often given when an author wants to create a clearer picture of the main idea.

Comparison and Contrast

- The comparison pattern connects two or more people, places, things, or ideas by describing how they are alike.

- The contrast pattern examines two or more people, places, things, or ideas by describing the differences between them.

Cause and Effect

- The cause and effect pattern is used by authors to discuss the reasons why something has happened or will happen in the future.

Unit Review Graphic Organizer

Complete the graphic organizer by identifying the types of patterns of organization covered by the unit.

Patterns of Organization

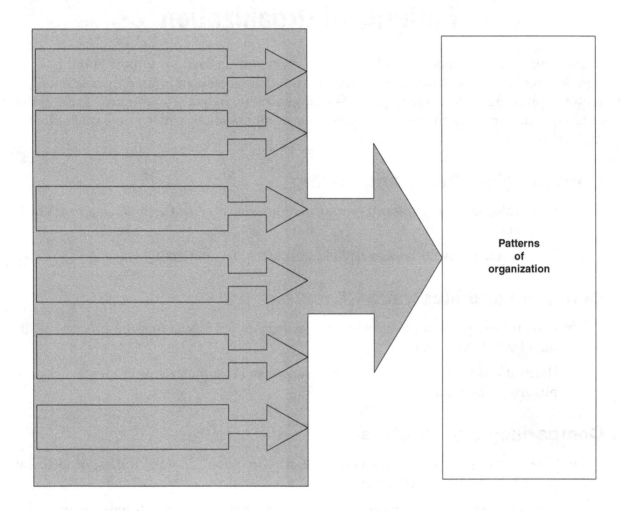

Patterns
of
organization

Portfolio Vocabulary Suggestion

List the words that signal each pattern of organization.

Chrono-loigcal	Listing	Definition	Example	Compare	Contrast	Cause	Effect

Portfolio Suggestion

In your outside reading, find one example of each pattern of organization presented in Unit IV.

Want to Know More?

If you are interested in knowing more about social issues, the following books and websites further explore this theme. You can find these books at your local library to read more about these topics or use the Internet to investigate the websites.

Books

Censorship Opposing Viewpoints, Bender, David and Bruno Leone, Series Editors. San Diego, CA: Greenhaven Press, Inc., 1997. Opposing Viewpoints is an informative series of books that presents both sides of an issue. In this case, censorship is examined from both perspectives. The series presents over 90 issues.

A Bright Red Scream: Self-Mutilation and the Language of Pain, Strong, Marilee. New York: Penguin Books, 1999. Marilee Strong is an award-winning journalist who interviewed more than fifty self-injurers while researching this disturbing topic. This book is a chilling yet compassionate look into self-mutilation.

Knock 'em Dead Resumes: Standout Advice from America's Leading Job Search Authority (Resumes That Knock 'em Dead), 9th ed. Martin Yate, Adams MediaInc, 2010. Continue your quest to right the perfect resume by exploring the suggestions in this current text. Its companion text *Knock 'em Dead Cover Letters* provides additional information for your job search.

Websites

www.bls.gov/oco/ On this website, you will find the Occupational Outlook Handbook. It is a nationally recognized source of career information, designed to provide valuable assistance to individuals making decisions about their future careers.

www.ncadv.org The National Coalition Against Domestic Violence (NCADV) is dedicated to the empowerment of battered women and their children and is committed to the elimination of violence in the lives of these women and their children. The site gives information on how to get help and many other resources.

www.ocfoundation.org The Obsessive-Compulsive Foundation (OCF) was founded by a group of individuals with OCD to educate the public and professional communities, to provide assistance and to support research about OCD and related disorders. The site provides information and many resources.

Chapter 12

Introduction to Inference

Theme of Readings: Advertising

"Advertising is the 'wonder' in Wonder Bread."

JEF I. RICHARDS

Advertising

Just as an author communicates to the reader through writing, a business communicates to the consumer through advertising. Consumers are exposed to hundreds of ads each day through television, radio, newspapers, magazines, and the Internet. It is estimated that the average consumer will spend a year and a half of his or her lifetime watching television commercials alone. Entertaining, slick, and persuasive, advertising continues to be somewhat of a mystery because many consumers believe it does not work on them. Yet businesses continue to use advertising, and it has been proven that ads do have an effect on people's buying patterns.

In order to gain the attention of the consumer, advertising provides general information given through words, pictures, people, and graphics. Often only minimal information is given. The consumer must therefore use clues to infer a complete message. He or she takes in the information and message and decides if that particular product or service is something to buy or not. Personal knowledge, experience, need, and the possession of enough money also influence the decision, of course.

Because of the prevalence of advertising, it impacts almost every aspect of our social, political, and economic life. It is important for us, as consumers, to be able to make valid inferences and judge advertisements and the information in them as sound or misleading.

Chapter Objective

After completing this chapter you will be able to use facts, details, and opinions given to make an inference.

Focus on Introduction to Inference

Writers do not always place everything they want you to know on the printed page. Often writers will give you information so that you can "read between the lines" and interpret or infer what they are telling you. Inferences are educated guesses, conclusions, or judgments that you make when you read. These guesses are not made randomly. You must carefully examine the facts, details, and opinions given.

A fact is a statement that can be proven as true by observation or written records. Direct observation may provide evidence of truth. "The sky looks blue today," is an example of an observable fact. A writer may present statements as fact but these claims may not be true. It is up to the reader to decide if the facts presented can be verified. Facts may be verified through written records such as dictionaries or reference books. They are often reported using dates, numbers, statistics, and measurements. Reading critically does not mean that you must necessarily prove every fact that you read. It is enough to keep a critical eye open and question whether or not the statement can be determined to be true or false. A factual statement does not reflect the author's personal feelings or attitudes. In addition, it is important to note the author's qualifications on the subject area. In contrast to a fact, an opinion cannot be proven as true or false. An opinion states a writer's personal feelings, attitudes, or beliefs about a subject. Words used when stating opinions mean different things to different people.

You also need to use your own knowledge and experience to form judgments about the information. You may not be sure that your inference is correct. However, if you use information, knowledge, and experience, you will be able to support your inference.

No where is the use of inference so evident as in advertising. Advertisements use words, pictures, or symbols to create a message for the viewer. For example, an advertisement, sponsored by a food company, shows a person smiling as they take a bite of food. The smile in the ad indicates that the person enjoys the activity. Your experience shows that to enjoy eating, the food must be tasty. You infer or conclude that the food is tasty.

As you infer, you must remember not to go beyond the evidence or clues given. Inferences must be based on information, not wild guesses. For example, from the advertisement previously described, you could not infer that the person is smiling while eating because the food reminds that person of home cooking. No clues were given in the ad to infer this information.

Critical readers make inferences as they interpret the author's message. Just as with advertisements, the reader bases conclusions on information provided as well as experience and knowledge to form valid and supported inferences about all types of readings.

Short Exercises: Introduction to Inference

Directions: *Examine each advertisement carefully and answer the questions that follow.*

"Don't Ambulate": Ad For The American Heritage Dictionary (2001)

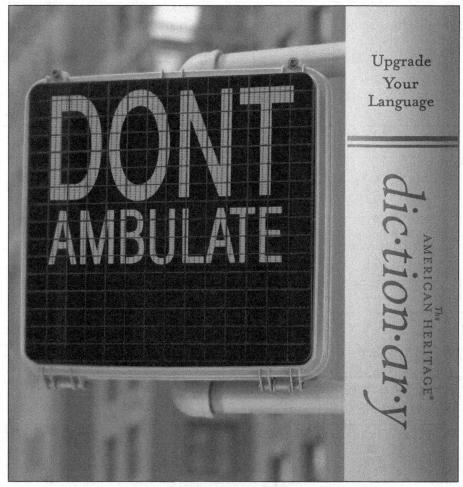

All images © 2001 Dan Nourie photography. Used with permission of Mullen (Wenham, MA) and Dan Nourie.

1. What audience does this ad appear to have in mind? How do you know?

_____

_____

2. What would you infer from the photo and text of this ad?

_____

_____

_____

Don't Ambulate, American Heritage Dictionary.

_____

_____

3. What would the ad like the audience to do or think?

_____

_____

_____

_____

4. Do you think the ad is effective? Explain why or why not.

_____

_____

_____

_____

_____

"Marry Rich": Ad for ABC Daytime Television (2001)

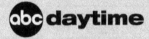

Marry rich.
Kill husband. Repeat.
abc daytime

Reprinted courtesy of TBWA\Chiat\Day

_____

Marry Rich ABC.

1. This ad was originally created as a billboard. What audience does it appear to have in mind? How do you know?

   _____

   _____

   _____

   _____

2. What message can you infer from this advertisement?

   _____

   _____

   _____

   _____

3. Do you think the advertisement is effective? Explain your opinion.

   _____

   _____

   _____

4. Why might someone voice an objection to this ad?

   _____

   _____

   _____

   _____

Marry Rich ABC.

"See. You do have an Opinion.": Public Service Announcement by the League of Women Voters of Minneapolis (2000)

1. This advertisement was originally created as a poster. What audience does it appear to have in mind? How do you know?

_____

_____

See. You do have an opinion. League of Women Voters.

_____

_____

2. What message can you infer from this advertisement?

_____

_____

_____

_____

3. What is the key comparison being made in this ad?

_____

_____

_____

_____

4. Do you think the advertisement is effective? Explain your opinion.

_____

_____

_____

_____

5. Do you consider voting a right, a duty, a privilege, a chore, an irrelevancy, or some combination of those things? How do you think your prior attitude affects the way you "read" this ad?

_____

_____

_____

_____

_____

_____

See. You do have an opinion. League of Women Voters.

"For the Safety of Womanhood": World War I Poster Promoting the Sale of War Bonds, Originally Published in *The Delineator* (April, 1918)

Library of Congress Prints and Photographs Division: LC-USZC4-8020

1. Who was the sponsor of this advertisement? What do you infer as the message of this advertisement?

_____

_____

_____

For the Safety of Womanhood, Liberty Loan Committee.

_____

_____

_____

2. What do you think of the various reasons for war presented in this poster? Do they still apply today? Do they carry the same emotional force?

_____

_____

_____

_____

_____

3. Explain the phrase "Help 'Till It Hurts"? What attitude toward participation in the war effort does this phrase imply? How does this compare to today's attitudes? Explain your opinion.

_____

_____

_____

_____

_____

4. Do contemporary appeals for support of the armed forces use strategies similar to those used in this poster? Think in particular about the appeals to patriotism in the wake of the September 11, 2001 attacks.

_____

_____

_____

_____

_____

For the Safety of Womanhood, Liberty Loan Committee.

"In the Fight to Save Endangered Species . . .": Public Service ad Sponsored by EarthJustice (2002)

IN THE FIGHT TO SAVE ENDANGERED SPECIES WE THOUGHT WE'D BETTER INCLUDE OUR OWN.

EARTHJUSTICE
Because the earth needs a good lawyer

Sure, there are laws on the books designed to protect our children and communities from pollution. But those laws are useless if they are not enforced.

That's where Earthjustice comes in. We're a nonprofit law firm dedicated to upholding the laws that safeguard our environment, wildlife, and public health. Since 1971, Earthjustice has protected millions of acres of land, hundreds of different species, and dozens of communities. All without charge.

Visit our website and see what we're doing to keep our environment safe for all types of wild creatures. Including the screaming, tag-playing ones in your own backyard.

©2002 EarthJustice

1. Who is the sponsor of this advertisement?

_____

_____

In the Fight to Save Endangered Species, EarthJustice.

2. What audience does this public service ad appear to have in mind? How do you know?

_____

_____

_____

_____

3. What do you infer is the message of this advertisement?

_____

_____

_____

_____

_____

4. Do you think this advertisement is effective? Explain why or why not.

_____

_____

_____

_____

5. Can you think of a reason why anyone might object to this ad or find it offensive?

_____

_____

_____

_____

6. Why do you think the organization uses the tag line: "Because the earth needs a good lawyer"?

_____

_____

_____

_____

_____

In the Fight to Save Endangered Species, EarthJustice.

"Sex. Math. Violence.": Public Service ad Sponsored by the American School Counselor Association and Created by Jill Applebaum, Young and Rubicam, New York (2002)

© 2002 The American School Counselor Association

1. Who is the sponsor of this advertisement?

_____

_____

2. What message do you infer from this advertisement?

_____

_____

_____

_____

3. Do you think this advertisement is effective? Explain your opinion.

_____

_____

_____

_____

4. List some reasons why someone might object to this ad.

_____

_____

_____

_____

Reading Selection

How Alcohol Ads Target Teens

Nina Riccio

Before Reading

Before you read "How Alcohol Ads Target Teens," complete the following:

Predict the topic.

Skim the story to see if your prediction is correct.

Think about alcohol advertisements. Do you think these ads target teenagers?

Sex. Math. Violence. American School Counselor Association.

Set your purpose for reading.

Words to Preview

insignias *(n.)* distinguishing mark or sign *(par.4)*
admonishing *(v.)* to express warning or disapproval in earnest manner *(par.6)*

During Reading

As you read "How Alcohol Ads Target Teens," continue to predict and visualize the ideas and monitor your comprehension. What does the author want you to know about alcohol advertisements?

How Alcohol Ads Target Teens

Nina Riccio

1 They're cute. They're funny. But did you ever think that those funny, sometimes annoying frogs croaking the name of a beer could be dangerous to you?

2   Jesse, age 20, has been sober for about four years. But when he was drinking heavily, his choice of booze depended on image. "It couldn't be just any brand. Bud was OK—it has a cool image. There's another brand that's a lot cheaper, but no one would ever bring that to a party. It tastes all right, but the can just looks stupid."

3   The makers of Budweiser have spent millions of dollars making sure Jesse and others like him think Bud has a "cool" image. In 2000, for example, brewers spent $770 million on TV ads and another $15 million on radio commercials. Add a few hundred million more for promotions and sponsorships.

4   Besides the Budweiser frogs, you're probably familiar with a spotted dog named Spuds, lizards, and canines from outer space. The packaging on many of these products is humorous, goofy, and even cartoonish. Some feature college kids on spring break. Most of these manufacturers have their own Web sites, where viewers can log on and play games or enter contests to win prizes with insignias on them. Clearly, they're aimed at you, not your parents.

5   Jesse now understands that he played right into the hands of alcohol manufacturers. "Bud seems particularly shameful because they really play up to kids," he says. But they're certainly not the only ones. "Alcopops, like the hard lemonades, are aimed at people who don't like the taste of alcohol. They're like soda pop."

Who's in Charge Here?

6 The makers of beer, wine coolers, and alcopops deny that they market to teens. In fact, they point out, they spend millions of dollars on public service announcements telling underage kids not to drink. They put up billboards telling drinkers to "drink

How Alcohol Ads Target Teens.

responsibly," or others admonishing them not to drink and drive. They contribute to community groups and give grocers cards with tips on how to spot fake IDs. But the money they spend on these programs is just a small fraction of what's spent on overall advertising. In fact, it's estimated that for each public service message a kid hears about drinking responsibly, he or she is likely to see 25 to 50 ads promoting beer or wine.

7   The bottom line in business is that the more you advertise, the higher your sales. And studies show that the more they're exposed to beer ads, the more likely teens are to have positive feelings about drinking, and the more likely they will be to drink as adults.

8   Whether liquor manufacturers are intentionally pitching their ads to teens is not important. The fact is, teenagers are watching and absorbing the message that drinking is a fun, cool, and popular thing to do. "You don't have to be a rocket scientist to understand that the intended—or unintended—consequences of these youthful liquor ads is that young people are going to drink more," says Dr. Edward Jacobs, a Seattle pediatrician and a member of the American Academy of Pediatrics' Committee on Substance Abuse. A company might say that they're just trying to get viewers to remember the product's name. But if that's the case, it seems unnecessary to spend millions per ad on directors, animation, and actors. "Why not simply put the name on a billboard?" asks Dr. Jacobs.

What's the Big Deal?

9 So why is it such a problem if a teen starts drinking before age 21? Besides the fact that it's against the law, studies show that teens who begin drinking are four times as likely to become alcoholics as those who don't begin drinking until age 21. Alcohol is the drug most used and abused by adolescents—more than marijuana, heroin, cocaine, and pills combined. Students with grades below C are three times as likely to be drinkers as those with A's. Alcohol is usually a factor in the three leading causes of death among youth: accidents, suicide, and homicide. Needless to say, drinking encourages reckless behavior.

10   "The major problem of drinking is not addiction," sums up Dr. Jacobs. "It's the consequence of use—the auto crashes, the lousy grades, the family problems, and the sexual risk behaviors. Many times, these are the statistics that don't show up anywhere."

11   "I wouldn't say that kids would never drink if there were no ads," says 14-year-old Justin, a freshman at a suburban high school in Connecticut. "But the ads sure give kids a sense that drinking is just something you do—that it's part of normal life. What's mainstreamed is what we see on TV."

12   Dr. Jacobs agrees. "The ads send a uniform message: You can't get maximum pleasure from an activity without alcohol." It's easy to understand why a somewhat awkward teen who's trying to fit in would believe that alcohol would make him feel less clumsy.

How Alcohol Ads Target Teens.

13   To their credit, the major television stations have voluntarily banned ads for hard liquor (rum, vodka, scotch, etc.) for years. Earlier this year, NBC announced that it would end its ban and allow ads for hard liquor. Months of criticism from legislators, the public, and advocacy groups forced the station to change that decision. Some say that TV stations should ban ads for beer and wine coolers, or at least monitor them to be sure they're not so youth-oriented. It's not as far-fetched as it seems. Sweden and Norway prohibit all advertising to children under 12. In Greece, commercials for toys can run only at certain hours, and Belgium forbids the running of commercials during children's programs and for five minutes before and after. Lawmakers in these countries understand that the very young are not yet mature enough to make critical choices when it comes to what they see advertised.

14   "Ads make it seem as if drinking is a very casual thing," says Justin. "Obviously, beer ads show people enjoying themselves. They don't show the negative consequences, like drunk driving or date rape. But sometimes, you know, it seems as if half my high school is in rehab."

You Be the Judge

15   "Most of the ads for wine coolers and alcopops don't state or even imply that they have alcohol in them," says Dr. Jacobs. He's right. Media messages are created by people whose job it is to come up with interesting images, songs, or graphics that will make you want to buy their product. They do that by creating an image of the product or of the people who use it—often not telling the whole truth. The next time you see an ad on TV, on the Web, or in print, take a moment to think about it.
    Then answer the following questions:
- Is this ad telling the whole story? If not, what important information about the product is left out?
- What image do the producers of this ad want me to have of this product?
- If I use product, will it make me look and act like the people in the ad?
- If I were to write my own ad, what would I do differently?

The Alcohol Risk Factor

16   Teens who use and abuse alcohol are more likely to engage in other risky behavior that can be fatal. Check out these findings:

Drinking and Driving

17   Auto crashes are the No.1 killer of teens. In one survey, 20 percent of the nearly 8,000 drivers ages 15 to 20 who were killed in auto crashes had been drinking.

Suicide

18   A correlation exists between alcohol use among teens and planning, attempting, or completing suicide. In one recent study, 37 percent of eighth grade girls who drank heavily reported attempting suicide.

How Alcohol Ads Target Teens.

Sexual Behavior

19 Twenty-nine percent of sexually active teens ages 15 to 17 reported in a survey that alcohol influenced their decision to have sex. And 26 percent of teens ages 15 to 17 said they worried about STDs or pregnancy because of becoming sexually active while drinking or using drugs.

Violence

20 Teens who drink are much more likely to engage in violence against others. One national survey found that of the teens who reported drinking regularly, 50 percent had been in a physical fight in the past year and 16 percent had carried a weapon to school in the past month. Other studies have found that alcohol plays a key role in violent crimes committed by teens, including murder, assault, and rape.

After Reading

Directions: *Look at some advertisements for alcohol products on television, on the internet or in print. Then answer the following questions. If you are having difficulty finding a television ad, try searching for SuperBowl TV ads.*

1. Is this ad telling the whole story? If not, what important information about the product is left out?

_____

_____

_____

_____

_____

2 What image do the producers of this ad want you to have of this product?

_____

_____

_____

3. If you use this product, what will change about how you look and act according to the ad?

_____

_____

_____

_____

How Alcohol Ads Target Teens.

4. If you were to write your own advertisement, what would you do differently?

_____

_____

_____

5. Do you think that television stations should be allowed to advertise hard liquor on their stations or not?

_____

_____

_____

Portfolio Activities

Integrating Ideas

Do you think advertisements influence your purchasing of a product or service? What should you be aware of when reading advertisements? How does an understanding of inferences help you with reading both advertisements and other selections? Reflect on these ideas in writing or class discussion.

Extending Concepts

Using an advertisement from a magazine or newspaper, write the facts, details, and opinions given that provide clues to the inferred message of the ad.

Collaborative Activity

Create your own advertisement for a product or service that is either real or imaginary. Use the medium of your choice: print, tape, video, or live demonstration.

Additional Portfolio Activity

A parody uses comedy or ridicule to imitate an artistic work such as a piece of writing, a song, or an advertisement. You can often find examples of parodies of advertisements on the Internet or on television. Choose an advertisement and create your own parody of it.

Chapter Summary Graphic Organizer

Complete the following equation.

Prior Knowledge + Experience + Visuals + Opinions + Facts = _____

Appendix A

Parts of Speech

Adjective

Abbreviation: *adj.*
An adjective describes a noun. For example, I have *four red* cats.

Adverb

Abbreviation: *adv.*
An adverb describes a verb. For example, John swam *slowly* around the lake.

Conjunction

Abbreviation: *conj.*
A conjunction is a word used to join words or groups of words.
For example, Money *and* power are often seen as markers of success.

Interjection

Abbreviation: *interj.*
An interjection is a word or phrase that expresses strong feelings.
For example, *Wow!* That's great.

Noun

Abbreviation: *n.*
A noun is a person, place, or thing.
For example, *Mary* has a *friend* who lives in *New York City*.

Preposition

Abbreviation: *prep.*
A preposition is a word that combines with a noun or pronoun to form a phrase.
For example: The student placed his money *into* a savings account.

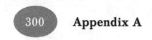

Pronoun

Abbreviation: *pron.*
A pronoun is a word used in place of a noun.
For example: *She* is coming home tomorrow.

Verb

Abbreviation: *v.*
A verb is a word or group of words that express action or state of being.
For example: Yesterday it *rained* all day.

Appendix B

Literacy Autobiography

These questions have been developed to help you in writing your literacy autobiography. Please understand that this is a list of questions to stimulate your thinking about your own literacy development. You do not have to respond to each question and restrict your thinking. Be creative as you record your literacy experiences.

- What are your earliest recollections of reading and writing?
- Were you read to as a child?
- Before you were able to read, did you pretend to read books? Can you remember the first time you read a book?
- Can you recall your early writing attempts (scribbling, labeling drawings, etc.)
- Was a newspaper delivered to your home? Do you recall seeing others read the newspaper? Did you read the newspaper?
- Did you subscribe to children's magazines? Did your parents or siblings have magazine subscriptions?
- Can you remember any indications that reading and writing were valued in the environment in which you grew up?
- Can you detail your first memories of reading and writing instruction?
- Can you recall reading for pleasure in elementary school?
- Did you ever use a public library? For what reason?
- Do you feel that you've ever read a book that has made a difference in your life?
- Were you a reader in your intermediate, junior high and /or high school years? Did you read because it was required and/or for your own pleasure?
- What is your all-time favorite children's book? Novel? Nonfiction work?
- What contributions have your reading and writing abilities made to your life?
- What are you currently reading? Writing?

Adapted from: M. McLaughlin and M. Vogt, <u>Portfolios in Teacher Education</u>.

Appendix C

Reader Response Journal

Responding to literature in a variety of ways helps you to think critically about what you read, to construct meaning from literature, and to connect writing and reading. A reader response journal is an important way of evaluating your understanding of what you read and gives you an opportunity to respond to literature.

In your journal, you are encouraged to go beyond just writing a simple summary of what you have read. Some possible responses are to:

> make comparisons and predictions,
> give opinions about the literature and the author,
> discuss an author's writing style,
> generate new interpretations or points of view,
> answer open-ended questions,
> or explain how you can relate to the characters through experiences or other readings.

You may ask yourself questions such as:

> What was worth remembering?
> What was disappointing or confusing?
> What did was interesting or thought provoking?
> What did you object to, if anything?

You may include any other thoughts about your reading.

For each entry include: your name, title and author of the reading, and the pages of the reading that are covered by this entry.

Appendix D

Concept of Definition Map Format*

What is it?

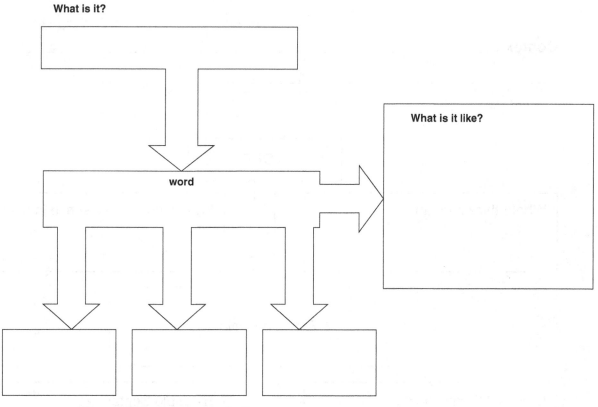

Who or what are some examples?

*Source: Schwartz, Robert and Taffy Raphael. "Concept of Definition: A Key To Improving Student's Vocabulary" *The Reading Teacher.* 39 November 1985.

Meaning From Context Map Format*

Context: _____

_____

```
                    ┌──────────────┐
                    │     WORD     │
                    └──────┬───────┘
┌───────────────────────┐ │ ┌───────────────────────────────┐
│ What I think it means  │ │ │ What would make sense in context │
│                        │ │ │                                 │
└───────────────────────┘ │ └───────────────────────────────┘
                          ▼
              ┌─────────────────────────┐
              │    Actual definition     │
              │                          │
              └─────────────────────────┘
┌───────────────────────┐   ┌───────────────────────────────┐
│ Personal Connection    │   │ Example Sentence                │
│                        │   │                                 │
└───────────────────────┘   └───────────────────────────────┘
```

*Adapted from Context-Content-Experience graphic, *Words, Words, Words, Janet Allen* 1999.

Appendix F

Word Parts

Common Prefixes

Prefix	Meaning	Example
a	on, toward	aboard
ab	away, from	abduct
ante	before	antedate
anti	against	anti-aircraft
bi	two	bicycle
circum	around, about	circumscribe
com/col/con	together, with, joint	committee/collect/contact
contra	against, opposite	contraband
counter	contrary	counterclockwise
de	reverse, remove	dethrone
dis	reversal	disapprove
equi	equal	equilateral
ex	out of, former	exit/ ex-wife
extra	outside, beyond	extraordinary
hyper	over, above, beyond	hyperventilate
in/il/ir/im	not	inactive/illegal irresponsible/immature
inter	between, among	interoffice
intra	within	intramural
intro	in, inward, inside	introvert
mal	bad, wrongly	malformed

micro	small	microsurgery
mis	wrongly	misconduct
mono	one, single	monorail
multi	many	multilevel
non	not	nonfat
post	after	postoperative
pre	before	prerequisite
re	again, back	recall
retro	backward	retrorocket
semi	half	semisweet
sub	under	subfreezing
super	above, over	superimpose
trans	across, on the other side	transportation
tri	three	tricycle
un	not	uncommon

Source: The Complete Word Book by Mary A. DeVries

Common Roots

Root	Meaning	Example
aud	hear	auditory
bene	good, well	beneficial
bibl	book	bibliography
bio	life	biology
cap	take, seize	capacity
capit	head	capital
cede	to go	precede
chron(o)	time	chronometer
cred	believe	credible
cur	run	concurrent
dict	tell, say	contradict

duc/duct	lead	conduct
equi	equal	equivalent
fact/fac	make, do	factory
fid	trust	confide
geo	earth	geography
graph	write	autograph
hetero	different	heterosexual
log/logo/logy	study, thought	sociology
mit/miss	send	dismiss, submit
mort	death	mortal
neuro	nerve	neurotic
path	feeling	apathy
poli	city	cosmopolitan
port	carry	portable
pos	place, put	dispose
reg	rule	regal
rupt	break	erupt
scop	see	telescope
scrib/script	write	prescription
sect	cut	intersection
sen/sent	feel	sensitive, resentment
spec/spic/spect	look	spectator, specimen
stru	build	structure
tele	far	television
tend/tens	stretch	attend
ten/tent	hold	tenant, detention
terr/terre	land, earth	terrain
tort	twist	distort
tract	draw, drag	attraction
vac	empty	vacant
ven/vent	come	invention
vert/vers	turn	revert

| vis/vid | see | vision, evident |
| voc/vok | call | advocate, evoke |

Source: *Word Mastery Made Simple* by A. Waldhorn and A. Zeiger *College Vocabulary Skills* by J. Shepherd

Common Suffixes

Suffix	Meaning	Example	Part of Speech
able	capable of	manageable	adjective
an	belonging to	American	noun
ance	state of, action	resistance	noun
ant	causing, being	participant	noun
ation	state, condition of	information	noun
eer	one concerned with	auctioneer	noun
ence	state of	independence	noun
ent	state of	resident	noun
er	performer of action	teacher	noun
fy	form, make	magnify	verb
hood	condition	brotherhood	noun
ible	capable of	divisible	adjective
ic	pertaining to	heroic	adjective
ion	act, process	union	noun
ism	system	symbolism	noun
ist	agent, doer	chemist	noun
ity	condition, degree	community	noun
ive	tending toward	active	adjective
ize	cause to be	maximize	verb
ly	like	friendly	adverb
ment	act, process	government	noun
ness	state, quality	neatness	noun
or	performer of action	instructor	noun
ous	characterized by	joyous	adjective

ship	condition, state	friendship	noun
tion	act, process	irritation	noun
ty	state of, condition	loyalty	noun
ward	direction	homeward	adjective/ adverb
y	full of	foamy	adjective

Source: The Complete Word Book by Mary A. DeVries

Appendix G

Reading Log

A reading log is an excellent place to collect information so that you can learn more about your attitude, habits, and preferences in reading. Keep track of your reading for the period of time specified by your instructor. (See chart) When you have completed your chart, think about yourself as a reader. Use the following questions to guide you. Write about what you learned about yourself.

1. When you look over your reading log, what do you notice about yourself as a reader? What do you like to read? How much do you read? Where do you read?

2. Overall, how would you rate the books you have been reading? Are they easy, medium, or difficult for you? Explain why.

3. What is your favorite genre? Favorite book?

4. Do you have a favorite author? Why?

5. Think about yourself as a reader. How would you describe yourself as a reader?

6. What would make you a better reader?

Adapted from *Literacy Portfolios In Action* by Sheila W. Valencia

Reading Log

Date

Title

Author

Pages

Comments

Date

Title

Author

Pages

Comments

Date

Title

Author

Pages

Comments

Date

Title

Author

Pages

Comments

Date

Title

Author

Pages

Comments

Date

Title

Author

Pages

Comments

Date

Title

Author

Pages

Comments

Date

Title

Author

Pages

Comments

Date

Title

Author

Pages

Comments

Date

Title

Author

Pages

Comments

Date

Title

Author

Pages

Comments

Date

Title

Author

Pages

Comments